Communist China:

The Early Years, 1949–55

Communist China:
The Early Years
1949–55

A. DOAK BARNETT

FREDERICK A. PRAEGER, *Publishers*
New York • Washington • London

FREDERICK A. PRAEGER, *Publishers*
111 Fourth Avenue, New York, N.Y. 10003, U.S.A.
5, Cromwell Place, London S.W.7, England

Published in the United States of America in 1964
by Frederick A. Praeger, Inc., Publishers

Fourth printing, 1968

© 1964 by Frederick A. Praeger, Inc.

Library of Congress Catalog Card Number: 64–22487

Printed in the United States of America

Dedicated to

Arnold Wolfers

PREFACE

The Chinese Communists won their struggle for power on the China mainland in 1949. But, as they themselves asserted at the time, they had barely begun their revolution. The task of consolidating power and reorganizing Chinese society lay before them.

In mid-1949, Mao Tse-tung made it amply clear that military victory marked the beginning rather than the end of the Communist-engineered revolution in China. Writing on the twenty-eighth anniversary of the founding of his Party, he declared: "Twenty-eight years make a long period," but "our Party has achieved one thing only, namely basic victory in the revolutionary war. . . . Our past work is only the first step in a long march of 10,000 li."

Thus the Communists did not attempt to freeze the *status quo* or to stabilize the existing situation in China. Instead, since 1949, they have tried to promote continuous revolution. Their aim has been to push forward, step by step and stage by stage, toward the ultimate goals of a Communist society as they envision them.

As a result, the past fifteen years have been a period of continuing struggle, tension, motion, and change in China, as the most populous nation on earth has undergone the most tremendous revolutionary upheaval in its history. The course of this revolutionary process has not been smooth. In the Chinese Communists' view, historical development requires constant struggle and a dialectical clash of contending social forces. History, as they see it, moves forward in a series of struggles, in stages—zigzagging two steps forward and one step back, or fluctuating in a "wavelike" pattern.

The analysis of these stages of development is extremely important in the Chinese Communists' own thinking. They place great emphasis on the need to determine correctly—in their own Marxist-Leninist terms—the essential characteristics of society at any particular time, identifying the key "contradictions" and major "enemies," and defining priority revolutionary goals and policies to achieve them.

As they themselves view the decade and a half since 1949, Communist China's leaders divide the revolution in China into several distinct major stages. The years 1949–52 are labeled the period of "reconstruction," when prime emphasis was placed on the task of rehabilitating the existing economy. A new stage was begun in 1953, when the Communists initiated China's First Five-Year Plan and announced their "general line of the state for a period of transition to socialism"; the emphasis then shifted to socialization and rapid industrial development. The year 1958 marked the start of a second Plan, but, even more important, it dramatically ushered in another revolutionary stage, a three-year period of radical new policies, symbolized by the so-called "three red banners"—the "Great Leap Forward," the communes, and a new "general line for socialist construction"—which called for accelerated economic development primarily through massive mobilization of organized manpower and intensified ideological fervor. Since the end of 1960, however, it has not been entirely clear, either to the Chinese Communists themselves or to outside observers, how best to characterize the current stage of the revolution. For over three years, Communist China has been undergoing a period of retreat and "adjustment," and its leaders have been attempting to recover from some of the mistakes made during the Great Leap, to cope with basic economic problems that persistently plague the regime, and to formulate new goals and new policies for the future.

In terms of the above periodization of the Chinese Revolution, this book, covering the years from late 1949 until early 1955, encompasses the period of "reconstruction" and about half of the first Plan and the initial period of "transition to socialism."

The simple slogans used by the Chinese Communists to label these years fall far short, however, of revealing the varied characteristics of the revolutionary process in China and give little idea of the dimensions of the political, social, and economic changes in the early years of Communist rule or the enormous impact of Communist political power on the Chinese nation in that period.

In non-Communist terms, the first five years of Chinese Communist rule can perhaps best be described as: (1) a period of rapid political consolidation, in which centralized control was effectively established over all of mainland China and new forms of totalitarian mass political organization were imposed in an unprecedented fashion on the entire country down to the grass-roots level; (2) a period of intense social revolution, in which the Communists, through a series of emotional mass campaigns, worked steadily to break down the fabric of traditional Chinese society in order to lay the foundations for socialization (the big push toward collectivization in China began in the second half of 1955); and (3) a period of successful economic rehabilitation, completed for the most part by the end of 1952, followed by fairly impressive initial efforts, starting in 1953, to promote rapid economic development. (It took the Chinese Communists some time after launching their First Five-Year Plan at the beginning of 1953, however, to draw up a definite over-all Plan; the Plan was not published, in fact, until mid-1955.) It should not be necessary to stress that many subsequent developments in Communist China cannot be fully understood without some knowledge of this 1949–55 period, when the regime was first established and some of its most basic policies first took shape.

This book focuses on a number of the most important and distinctive aspects of the revolutionary process in China from 1949 to 1955. It is not a general history or over-all analysis of events in those years, but it does attempt to probe some of the major developments of the period: the Communists' successful application of mass totalitarian forms of organization to the Chinese scene; the evolution and impact of unique Chinese Communist forms of propaganda and group indoctrination, through which the regime initiated its extraordinary program to "remold" an entire nation ideologically; the Chinese Communists' conscious and shrewd manipulation of social tensions in a series of intense and dramatic mass campaigns—directed against landlords, counterrevolutionaries, intellectuals, businessmen, and others—which shook Chinese society to its foundations; the evolution of a distinctive Chinese approach to collectivization and socialization based on the Soviet model but calling for a unique step-by-step process of social change; the start of Communist China's ambitious program of industrialization and general economic development; and the gradual building of a strong totalitarian state apparatus in China.

During almost the entire period covered by this volume, I was fortunate in being able to observe and report on the unfolding events in Communist China from a close vantage point. I was on the China mainland when the Communists took over in 1949, and I spent over six months under their rule.* During the latter part of 1949, in 1951–52, and in 1954–55, I lived in Hong Kong. During these years, first as a Fellow of the Institute of Current World Affairs and correspondent of the *Chicago Daily News* Foreign Serv-

---

* For my account of the takeover period, see A. Doak Barnett, *China on the Eve of Communist Takeover* (New York: Frederick A. Praeger, 1963).

ice, then as a Public Affairs Officer of the American Consulate-General in Hong Kong, and finally as an Associate of the American Universities Field Staff, I attempted to analyze and write about developments in Communist China.

All the reports that make up this volume were written during 1949–55. (The dateline appearing at the beginning of each chapter indicates when it was written.) They were based not only upon analysis of contemporaneous Chinese Communist written materials but also, in the case of the first few reports, on direct observation of developments on the China mainland in the months immediately after Communist takeover, and, in the case of the later reports, on extensive interviews in Hong Kong with travelers and refugees coming from the mainland.

Chapter 1, a general analysis of the situation in China at the time of establishment of the Communist regime, was written in late 1949 and early 1950 and published under the title "Profile of Red China" in the February 15, 1950, issue of *Foreign Policy Reports*. In large part, however, this "Profile" was itself a summarization and condensation of eleven reports written for the Institute of Current World Affairs in August and September, 1949, immediately after I arrived in Hong Kong from the mainland. Chapters 2 and 3—based not only on observations I had made in China, but also on research in Hong Kong utilizing Chinese Communist publications and on interviews with refugees—appeared as articles in scholarly journals: Chapter 2, under the title "Mass Political Organizations in Communist China," appeared in the September, 1951, issue of *The Annals of the American Academy of Political and Social Science*; Chapter 3, under the title "Social Controls in Communist China," appeared in the April 22, 1953, issue of *Far Eastern Survey*. Chapters 4 through 20 were all reports written in Hong Kong between 1952 and 1955 for either the Institute of Current World Affairs or the American Universities Field Staff. The following is a list of the numerical designations and titles under which they were originally distributed by these organizations:

Chapter 4: "Chinese Communist Party—A Period of Consolidation" (AUFS Report-ADB-2-1953).

Chapter 5: "Forced Labor in Communist China" (AUFS Report-ADB-1-1955).

Chapter 6: "Propaganda Methods" (INCWA Newsletter-ADB-11-1952; also AUFS distribution).

Hong Kong was clearly the best observation point in the early 1950's for persons unable to obtain direct access to Communist China, because it was possible to interview a wide variety of persons coming from the China mainland. My reports included in this volume relied heavily on information obtained through such interviews.

In putting these reports together for publication in a single volume, I have rearranged them by major subject categories, rather than organizing them solely on the basis of chronology. In all essentials, the reports are presented as originally written; cutting and editing have been kept to a minimum. Romanization of Chinese personal names follows a modified Wade-Giles system, without diacritical marks.

I am extremely grateful to the American Universities Field Staff and the Institute of Current World Affairs for permission to publish the reports and newsletters that make up the bulk of this volume. I should also like to express my appreciation to the Foreign Policy Association, the American Academy of Political and Social Science, and the former Secretary-General of the Institute of Pacific Relations for permission to use the three articles (noted above) originally published by them.

I am also indebted to Arnold Dolin for his editing, and to Mrs. Mary Schoch for her typing, of the manuscript.

My greatest debt, as always, is to my wife, Jeanne.

—A. D. B.

August, 1964

CONTENTS

Contents

PART I

ESTABLISHMENT OF THE
NEW REGIME

NEW DEMOCRACY AND PEOPLE'S DEMOCRATIC DICTATORSHIP

December, 1949–February, 1950

The Chinese Communists have not yet completed their revolution. They have just begun it; and no one knows what will happen in the long run to China under Communism or to Communism in China.

The complexity of the situation in China raises many questions about what forms Chinese Communism may take and whether or not Communist power will last indefinitely. However, the most important single aspect of the situation in China today is the fact that the Communists have won their struggle for power. They have become the rulers of a nation that for many years has been politically bankrupt, economically disrupted, and ideologically confused. They are virtually the only dynamic force in China today, and at present they face no significant organized opposition. The remaining Nationalist centers of anti-Communist resistance are localized and provide no over-all focus for resistance on a national scale.

This radical shift of power in China was symbolized by the establishment of a Central People's Government in Peking on October 1, 1949. The creation of this Communist regime alters the entire political scene in the Far East.

The reasons for Communist success in China must be sought in the basic social and political forces that have been at work in the country. During recent years, two major political trends have developed simultaneously. One has been the rise and organizational growth of the dynamic, revolutionary Communist Party. The other has been the demoralization of the Kuomintang. The former cannot be explained without reference to the latter. Communist opposition and subversion have been among the causes of the Kuomintang's defeat, but not the only causes. The Kuomintang failed to maintain its power because, confronted with a Communist threat, it gradually lost vitality and became an ineffective political organization, unable to meet the urgent needs of Chinese society.

The relative ease with which Communist military forces won control of China during 1949 was a reflection of the accelerating pace of Nationalist disintegration. The Kuomintang was split by hopelessly complicated internal schisms and weakened by inefficiency and corruption. The Nationalists' leadership—old, tired, and unimaginative—remained static. An infusion of new blood and leadership, which might have revitalized the government, failed to take place. The Kuomintang lost its own self-confidence and fervor as well as public support. Its bureaucracy lost touch with the people, and the Party's organizational roots withered and died. Over a period of time, the Nationalist Government alienated almost every major group in the population, including the urban mercantile, industrial, and middle classes, on which its support once rested. The morale of the government's mismanaged troops hit rock bottom; whole divisions were sacrificed as a result of ill-conceived military strategy, while others deserted or fell apart under attack.

Moreover, the Nationalist regime was unable to solve the urgent economic, political, and social problems confronting the country. Order, unity, and peace were prerequisites for an improvement of living conditions, but the Nationalists could not achieve stability of any sort, even in territory they controlled. A major reason for this was the economic burden and disruption caused by civil war, but however illogical it may seem, it was the Nationalists rather than the Communists who received most of the blame for the chaos in China. Conditions became progressively worse until the prevailing sentiment in the country favored change of any kind and peace at any price. The Nationalists' response to this alienation of popular support was an increasing use of measures of repression whenever and wherever the situation approached calamity, and such measures merely hastened the process of disintegration and defeat.

There have been many fundamental pressures for change underlying the course of recent events in China. Probably the two strongest have been those giving rise to insistent demands for agrarian reform and for the development of a strong, united, modernized China.

The agrarian crisis is one that has become more and more critical as increases in China's population have outdistanced increases in food supplies. This demographic trend and the progressive concentration of land ownership have produced dissatisfaction, unrest, and scattered rebellion among China's predominantly rural population. A fundamental solution of this agrarian crisis can be achieved only by raising the per capita productivity of China's peasants, but in China public attention has been focused on reform of the antiquated land-tenure system as a palliative measure.

The Kuomintang—partly because the social and economic base of its political power came to rest heavily on agricultural vested interests—never attempted to attack the agrarian problem energetically. The Communists, on the other hand, effectively exploited 'peasant unrest. In north China, where they built up their power, they used first a program of rent reduction and then one of land redistribution to gain political support as well as to alleviate the plight of land-poor peasants. On the basis of these programs, they recruited a powerful peasant army which had a vested interest in Communist success because of tangible rewards that the Communists offered in the form of land.

The insistent demand in China for creation of a strong, united, modernized country is an expression of growing nationalism, which is most prevalent in urban areas where Western influence has been the strongest. In concrete political form, it has been directed mainly against foreign influence in China. The Kuomintang, because of its increasing dependence on foreign support, became extremely vulnerable to charges of serving the interests of "foreign imperialism." These charges were made by non-Communists as well as Communists, but Communists exploited the theme with great effectiveness. Although their movement is based on an imported ideology and they owe a much stronger allegiance to a foreign power than the Kuomintang ever did, the Communists gathered strength in remote rural areas far from the main centers of visible foreign influence in coastal China, and consequently they have been able to channel Chinese resentment against "foreign imperialism" toward the Western powers.

To these factors must be added a steady drift toward the Left among Chinese intellectuals. Private capitalism has been discredited by the growth in China of semiofficial monopoly enterprises, controlled by a few individuals associated with the Nationalist regime, which have stifled the growth of independent, private capitalists in modern industry. The prevailing opinion among almost all politically conscious people in China has favored some sort of socialism adapted to Chinese needs. Even the Kuomintang has espoused a kind of state socialism. Consequently, there has been little ideological resistance to Marxism, and no important group has effectively sponsored a nonsocialist state.

This background helps to explain why it has been possible for the Communists to rise to power on the basis of a revolutionary program of rooting out "feudalism, foreign imperialism, and bureaucratic capitalism." They have gained control of China because there has been no effective opposition. In a sense, they have merely filled a vacuum created by the disintegration of the old regime. The most important reasons for Communist victory are to be found in these indigenous factors in the Chinese situation. U.S. support and aid delayed the Kuomintang's decline, and Soviet inspiration and assistance helped the Communists' development, but neither the United States nor the Soviet Union determined the course of events in China.

In addition to all other factors, one fundamental explanation for the Chinese Communists' rise to power is to be found in the vigor and dynamism of their movement and the fact that they have been able to create the most efficient political and military machine in modern Chinese history.

As a result of Soviet influence in the 1920's, both the Kuomintang and the Communists attempted to become revolutionary parties with an organized mass membership under strict discipline and control. In its early years, the Kuomintang made some progress toward achieving this objective, but it subsequently failed. The Communists, however, have had outstanding success in building a vigorous party machine, and "iron discipline" is one of their main sources of strength.

The leaders of the Chinese Communist Party (CCP) form a tightly knit brotherhood of experienced, competent, devoted, tough revolutionaries. At the top are the members of the Central Committee, who hold key posts in the government and army, as well as in the Party itself, throughout the country. They decide policy and supervise its execution. The fate of China, for the foreseeable future, is largely in their hands.

As a group, the Central Committee is held together by personal as well as professional ties. Most are old-time Party members, and "old school ties" of a unique sort are of considerable importance. Participation in the founding of the Party in Shanghai or of its branches abroad, in the Nanchang or "Autumn Harvest" uprisings, in the Kiangsi Soviet, and in the "Long March" are marks of distinction. There are few newcomers in the top ranks who did not take part in at least one of these important phases of early Party history.

The predominance of Chinese from central and south China in the Central Committee is striking. Roughly a quarter of the regular members are natives of Mao Tse-tung's own province of Hunan. Almost one-half of the regular members come from the three provinces of Hunan, Hupeh, and Szechwan. A very large majority come from the region south of the Yangtze River. These men, however, have built their army and Party machine largely in north China.

A majority of the members of the current Central Committee have studied abroad—the largest number in the Soviet Union, but many in France and Germany. Mao Tse-tung, until his recent trip to Moscow, was one of a minority in the Central Committee who had never been outside China's borders.

The class origin of the Central Committee members is varied. Both peasantry and gentry are represented. However, the Chinese Communist Party has a larger proportion of top leaders recruited from the lower classes than any other important political group in modern China, and all Party leaders, regardless of class origin, have lived an austere, proletarian sort of life in their struggle for power.

The leadership of the Party has had greater unity and solidarity than most Communist parties in other countries. There have been no fundamental internal schisms or dramatic purges since the 1930's, when Mao Tse-tung assumed control, and even Li Li-san, Party leader who was discredited in the 1930's, returned to China via Manchuria with the Russians in 1945 and is now a member of the Central Committee, subordinate to Mao.

Mao is still the undisputed leader of the Party. Chu Teh, the top Communist military chief, is always ranked second, but he is aging and becoming less active. At present, the two most obvious contenders for succession to Mao's position are Liu Shao-ch'i and Chou En-lai. Liu, seldom in the limelight, is described as a theoretician, labor expert, and Party organization man. Chou, Premier and Foreign Minister of the Chinese Communist Government, is Mao's most effective political aide and the Communists' most experienced negotiator.

Led by these men, the Communist Party organization reaches down to the lowest level of society in fact as well as in theory. Through innumerable branches and cells, which can be formed in any organization or locality where there are three or more Party members, the Communists have established deep grass roots. These local organizations now boast an active membership more than 3 million strong, according to recent claims. Although this is a small minority of the total Chinese population, it overshadows any other political group and represents the dominant minority in a country where all political groups are minorities.

Membership in the Chinese Communist Party, furthermore, is not an avocation; it is a career. It is difficult to join the Party, and a new member is fully accepted only after the most intensive kind of indoctrination. A member is bound by oath to obey Party decisions. His lifework can be determined by Party leaders, and his livelihood is often dependent upon the Party. In short, his life is similar to that of a professional soldier, except that "combat" duties are political as well as military.

The organizational structure of the Party, based on the principle of "democratic centralism," is such that authority is highly concentrated. Participation in Party work is spread over a wide base, but policy-making power is held by a few men. The pinnacle of authority is the Central Committee, whose forty-four members (three of whom have died) and thirty-three alternates hold most of the key political positions both inside and outside the Party hierarchy. The influence of these men is omnipresent, and their decision-making power is well-nigh omnipotent. They are linked with the Party's grass roots, however, by a hierarchy of congresses, executive committees, and powerful branch bureaus in key areas of the country which are responsible for carrying out their will. This organizational hierarchy keeps the leaders in touch with the Party's mass membership without fundamentally restricting their power, because the Party organization is one in which "the individual obeys the organization, the minority obeys the majority, the lower ranks obey the higher ranks, branch organizations unitedly obey the Central Committee."

The leaders of the Communist Party are a remarkable group of men. Intellectually tough, they have purpose and determination, are unswerving in their devotion to their beliefs, and are incorruptible to a degree previously unknown in modern China. They are doctrinaire in their basic beliefs, but flexible in adapting means to achieve their ends, and willing to learn in new situations— within the limitations imposed by their Marxist preconceptions. These men have established the over-all character of the Party, and their zeal is shared by most of the Party members whom they control and direct. The membership as a whole, moreover, shares the belief of the leaders that the Communist Party makes up an elite acting in the interests of the Chinese masses. The Communists assert that their Party "is the highest command for the leadership of all organizations" in China.

The main instrument of Communist revolutionary success in China, however, has not been the Party itself but the Chinese Red Army, now called the People's Liberation Army, created by the Party. Political and military power are inseparable in modern China, and the Red Army has spread over the country as the spearhead of the Communist movement. This fact must be understood if one is to understand the mechanics of the Chinese Revolution. Military conquest—what the Communists call "armed revolution against armed counterrevolution"—has been an integral part of the revolutionary process. The Communists did not win their struggle for power by popular uprisings throughout China. They built a military machine by carrying out an agrarian revolution in one part of the country—rural north and northwest China—and then proceeded to conquer the rest of the country and destroy the old regime. Outside of rural areas in a limited part of China, therefore, most of the Chinese population has played a relatively passive role in the transfer of power. The majority of Chinese have not rebelled against the Nationalists; they simply have not supported them. They have not directly caused the political change; they have merely accepted it.

However, the creation of the Red Army as an effective and powerful military machine has been one of the most remarkable accomplishments of the Chinese Communists. It is a new kind of army in China, one that is thoroughly imbued with political consciousness. Recruits gathered from the countryside and absorbed from destroyed Kuomintang units have been drilled in slogans as well as in military techniques; political training has been almost as important as technical training. Like the Communist Party, the Red Army has been well organized, and it has maintained a higher degree of unity and discipline than any other large army in modern Chinese history. Communist military leaders also have evolved effective tactics of fast movement and attack. They have accumulated good equipment from captured Japanese and Kuomintang stocks. They have cared for the troops and their families, maintained fairly equalitarian relations between officers and men, and strictly regulated relations between soldiers and civilians. All these factors have contributed to the success of the army and the Communist movement as a whole. The transfer of power from the Kuomintang to the Communist Party has been accomplished by this military force.

The reaction of the Chinese people to events now taking place in their country is one of the most difficult things for an on-the-spot observer to describe to those who have followed events from afar. The difference in perspective for those engulfed by a revolution and for those who view a revolution with the detachment of distance is vast. During the past two years, I have attempted to analyze Chinese reactions at first hand in both Nationalist and Communist territories. The possible margin of error in determining the psychology of a foreign people is great, but the following analysis is at least an attempt to interpret these reactions on the basis of observation as events unfolded.

In many areas that have been under Communist rule for a few months, there are already signs of developing disillusionment and dissatisfaction. But these sentiments have emerged only after an extended period of Communist rule. The dominant reaction of Chinese people at the time of political changeover has been simple acquiescence, combined with relief that fighting has come to an end.

The Communists themselves claim that they are "liberating" the Chinese people. In a negative sense, there is some truth in this claim. There have been few regrets about the demise of the old regime, and the Communists' catch phrases—defining the things they wish to eliminate or change—do strike a responsive chord among many Chinese. Popular acquiescence to the Communist takeover does not mean, however, that the great mass of Chinese have embraced Communism or even that they approve of the Communists in any definite, positive way. Few Chinese outside of the ranks of the Communist movement itself know what Communism really means. They have accepted a change of regime because of the feeling that conditions could not get much worse and might possibly improve under new rulers, regardless of their political coloration.

Acquiescence has been mixed with various other attitudes in the cases of different people. Many have reacted with a fatalistic, pessimistic acceptance of what has seemed to them to be the inevitable. Others, impressed with the Communists' energy and honesty, have been hopeful that a new regime might bring order out of chaos and achieve some measure of economic stability and improvement. A wait-and-see attitude is widespread. The Chinese as a rule are more interested in practical problems, such as the price of food, than they are in abstract political ideas, and many are skeptical of all political groups and governmental authority. The majority undoubtedly will judge the Communists over a period of time on a pragmatic basis after seeing what Communist rule can accomplish and how it affects them personally.

A small but vitally important minority of the Chinese population, however, have accepted Communist rule in a much more positive, even enthusiastic way. This minority consists of intellectuals and organized, politically conscious peasants, workers, and students. They and the Communists themselves are the only people in China today who have strong political convictions of any sort.

The effect of Communism on its believers and most of its fellow travelers in China can only be understood by analogy with religious faith. Political credo and dogma are accepted uncritically, and the act of conversion seems to release a tremendous amount of kinetic energy and vitality. The believers devote themselves wholeheartedly to the job of carrying out a revolution designed to change all aspects of Chinese society, and they follow their prophets—Marx, Lenin, Stalin, Mao Tse-tung, and others—with naïve confidence. They either do not see, consciously overlook, or consider "necessary" the objectionable characteristics of the new regime. They are the in-group under Communist rule.

On the fringes of this in-group there is an important segment of Chinese "liberals"—educators, writers, artists, technicians, professional people—many of whom also have accepted Communist leadership and the program of "New Democracy," but with a more restrained enthusiasm. Generally, they have not gone the whole way of accepting Communist dogma or subjecting themselves to the discipline of Communist Party membership. At present, however, very few of them are expressing any independent opinions on political affairs. Either out of hopefulness about the possibilities of developing China under the Communists, or because they are anxious to establish themselves under the new regime, they rationalize developments they may not like and echo the Communist Party line.

The allegiance of many Chinese intellectuals, probably the majority, to the Communist cause indicates the ideological as well as political vacuum that the Communists are filling. Chinese "liberal" intellectuals have generally attempted to combine Marxist economics with Western conceptions of civil liberties, but they have floundered and been ineffective between the two monolithic Chinese parties struggling for power. Disillusioned and repressed by the Kuomintang, intellectuals drifted steadily to the Left. This was the only direction in which they could drift, because Western liberalism has never found expression in an organized movement of significance in China, despite the fact that it has influenced many individuals. Since political power has shifted to the Communists, most of these intellectuals have not found it too big a leap to offer their support to the new regime. The Communists have shrewdly put them to work in all sorts of activities, and many politically conscious intellectuals feel for the first time that they are playing a real political role. For most of them, the only alternative would be to stay aloof and risk being classified as "reactionaries"; few have chosen this course.

The acquiescence of the majority of Chinese to Communist rule, and the enthusiastic pro-Communist feeling of a minority—including most intellectuals, as well as some groups of organized, politically conscious workers and peasants—do not mean that there is no antipathy to the Communists. Many Chinese dislike both the Communists' methods and their long-range program. It is significant, however, that even these people have generally tried to effect a quiet adjustment to the new situation and make the best of what they consider a bad situation. They have nothing positive to offer as an alternative. There is no leadership or idea or program to which they give support. In short, there is no significant organized opposition. Some Kuomintang remnants have gone underground, but lacking popular support they are not an important factor in the situation. An opposition requires an organizational basis, ideological focus, and effective leadership, all of which are lacking among those who dislike the Communists. These prerequisites for an opposition may develop eventually, but they can do so only over a long period of time. The Kuomintang has been so completely discredited through its failure that opponents of Communism within China no longer look to it as a possible alternative to the Communists.

During the past year, the Communists have consolidated their power in the territory their armies have won, and step by step they have established formal governmental organs under firm control. The entire governmental structure is authoritarian in form. This is true at all levels of government and is particularly striking in the case of the Central People's Government established in Peking.

The Organic Law of the Central People's Government states: "The People's Republic of China is a state of the people's democratic dictatorship led by the working class, based on the alliance of workers and peasants and rallying all democratic classes and various nationalities within the country."

In his essay "On People's Democratic Dictatorship," Mao Tse-tung puts himself in the position of a critic of the Communists and answers several questions to clarify the Communists' political position:

"You are dictatorial?" Yes, dear gentlemen, you are right, and we are really that way. The experiences of several decades amassed by the Chinese people tell us to carry out the People's Democratic Dictatorship. That is, the right of reactionaries to voice their opinion must be deprived, and only the people are allowed to have the right of voicing their opinion. Who are "the people"? At the present stage in China, they are the working class, the peasant class, the petty bourgeoisie, and the national bourgeoisie. Under the leadership of the working class and the Communist Party, these classes unite together to form their own state and elect their own government to enact dictatorship over the lackeys of imperialism—the landlord class, the bureaucratic-capitalist class, and the Kuomintang reactionaries and their henchmen representing these classes—to oppress them, and only allow them to behave properly and not allow them to talk and act wildly. If they talk and act wildly, they will be prohibited and punished immediately. The democratic system is to be carried out among the people, giving them freedom of speech, assembly, and association. The right to vote is only given to the people and not to the reactionaries. . . . "Don't you want to eliminate state authority?" Yes, but not at present. We cannot eliminate state authority now. "Why?" Because imperialism still exists, the domestic reactionaries still exist, and classes in the country still exist. Our present task is to strengthen the people's state apparatus, which refers mainly to the people's army, people's police, and people's court, for national defense and protection of the people's interests, and with this as a basis to enable China to advance steadily, under the leadership of the working class and the Communist Party, from an agricultural to an industrial country, and from a New Democratic to a socialist and Communist society, to eliminate classes and realize world Communism.

This statement is, among other things, a Marxist way of stating that no opposition to the Communists will be allowed, because anyone who disagrees fundamentally with the Communist program or contests the Communists' right of leadership is classified a "reactionary."

At present the Communist government is made up of a nominal "coalition," but it is a coalition of people who agree, rather than of people who differ, in their political points of view. The Chinese People's Political Consultative Conference (CPPCC), which assisted the Communists in creating their Central Government and which will be the only "representative" body in that government until the election of an All-China People's Congress at some future time (still undetermined), is made up of Communist-picked delegates from fourteen political groups and parties and representatives of various geographical regions, army units, and organizations of workers, youth, women, racial minorities, religious circles, and overseas Chinese. All these people have accepted the program of the Communist Party and have publicly pledged themselves to follow the Party's leadership. There are no competing political ideas represented, and in many cases the non-Communists seem to be trying to outdo the Communists in pushing a Marxist program. The motivation behind the non-Communist parties' adherence to this coalition is probably mixed. Some of the support is based on the honest conviction that the Communist program holds out hope for improving the situation in China. But opportunism also seems to play a significant role. In any case, none of the minor parties—the most prominent of which are the Kuomintang Revolutionary Committee, the Democratic League, and the National Reconstruction Association—is a political party in the real sense of the word. Rather, they fit the traditional Chinese pattern of political cliques. Their membership is small, their platforms are vague, and their power is almost nonexistent.

Apart from providing window dressing for the Communists' coalition, however, these non-Communist groups play a minor role in the present situation. For the Communists, they offer the means to sound out the attitudes of key groups, such as industrialists and intellectuals, to receive their suggestions—which may be heeded or disregarded as the Communists wish—and to attempt to obtain their support or cooperation under the new regime. The members of these groups are given an opportunity to participate in political affairs, and although they have little authority or power, the mere fact that they are put on committees and called upon for consultation makes many of them feel they are playing an important political role.

Only a relatively few people are connected with these minor coalition groups, however, and ordinary people have played no part at all in the establishment of the Central People's Government. Those familiar with the situation in China would not expect much direct participation by the public at large, because the potential electorate in China lacks the literacy, political consciousness, experience, and organization to play an active political role, but the

Communists have not even kept the average citizen informed of developments. The process of setting up a government was largely secret until it was announced as a *fait accompli*. This was in line with the Communists' policy of restricting the process of decision-making to a select few and then encouraging public interest and participation in activities connected with the implementation of decisions after they have been made.

The structure of government organization, as of Party organization, under the Communists follows the principle of "democratic centralism," characterized by the extreme concentration of authority. Power in the Central People's Government is concentrated in the People's Government Council. This body—which consists of a chairman, six vice-chairmen, and fifty-six members—combines legislative and executive powers. It both enacts laws and interprets them, promulgates decrees and supervises their execution. It determines administrative policies, directs the activities of all other government organs, makes treaties, decides questions of war and peace, controls the budget and state accounting, and appoints all key government personnel. In short, it is a power unto itself except for the fact that it theoretically derives its authority from, and is accountable to, the Political Consultative Conference, which may "submit proposals on fundamental policies." This is a system of "legislative and executive powers in one," which the Communists themselves contrast with the system of checks and balances, with the separation of powers.

Under the People's Government Council, and appointed by it, are four bodies that are responsible for actual governing duties under the Council's direction. The Government Administration Council (GAC) is a sort of super-cabinet consisting of a premier, several deputy premiers, a secretary-general, and an undefined number of members. The Administration Council selects four main committees: the Committee on Political and Legal Affairs, the Committee on Finance and Economics, the Committee on Culture and Education, and the Committee on People's Supervision. These coordinate the activities of various government ministries and commissions, the heads of which are all directly appointed by the Government Council. The Administration Council also appoints the administrative heads of the geographical areas into which the country is divided, down to and including the *Hsien* (counties) and municipalities, and one of its jobs is to "direct the work of local people's governments throughout the country."

The other three major bodies appointed by the People's Government Council are the People's Revolutionary Military Council, the Supreme People's Court, and the People's Procurator-General's Office. The Military Council and the Court are the highest army and judicial organs. The Procurator-General's Office, which checks "all government institutions and government functionaries as well as nationals of the country" to see that existing laws are observed, is the Communists' version of a traditional Chinese institution and a comparable Soviet institution.

The extreme centralization of power in this government in a sense merely legalizes and formalizes the Communists' monopoly of power in China. It is clearly authoritarian, yet there are quite a few people in China who are convinced that the Communists' "People's Democracy" is the real thing, and that by contrast the Western form of parliamentary democracy is fraudulent. The reasons for this attitude must be understood if one is to make any sense out of many of the things going on in China today.

The word "democracy" as used by the Chinese Communists and those who support them is virtually a synonym for "equalitarianism," and today the Communists are definitely equalitarian. They aim to eliminate all special privilege and to level classes. They have introduced a cult of the common man and make a fetish of proletarianism. They have glorified austerity and simplicity, and in this respect Communist officials contrast sharply with traditional Chinese officialdom. Most of them wear drab cotton clothes, eat simple food, are willing to get their hands dirty, and emphasize social and economic equality. It is this equalitarianism more than anything else that has convinced the Communists' active supporters that they are democratic, for it is something dramatically new in Chinese life. The Communists' authoritarianism is merely an extreme form of something with which the Chinese have long been familiar. Political democracy in the Western sense of that term has never developed very far in China, and consequently most Chinese do not even know what it really is.

To understand the semantic content of the phrase People's Democracy as it is now used in China, it is also necessary to make a distinction between political authority and political participation.

The Communists have narrowed the base of political authority by concentrating ultimate policy-making power in the hands of a few key Party leaders, whose decisions are executed by a highly centralized Party and government bureaucracy. On the other hand, the Communists have broadened, or are broadening, the base of political participation. More and more people are brought into political meetings, rallies, and demonstrations. There is provision for elected "people's congresses" at every level of government; not many of these have been established so far, but no doubt they will be in time. These congresses are theoretically the basic organs of government, but they have no real legislative power, and practically their only function is the election of legislative-executive bodies which do the governing. There is not much danger of control passing to those who oppose the Communists, because such people can easily be disenfranchised as "reactionaries." The real power of the congresses, therefore, is not great, but they do increase mass political participation. Another way the Communists achieve this is by organizing as many people as possible into groups, under Communist direction, set up along functional or occupational lines. Among the most important organizations of this kind already established are the Peasants' Associations, Poor Peasants' Leagues, All-China Federation of Labor, All-China Democratic Youth Federation, All-China Democratic Women's Federation, All-China Democratic Students' Federation, and New Democratic Youth League. All these groups have a political character, and they greatly increase the number of persons participating in political activities. The Communists also organize thousands of "study groups," which include people of all sorts. The purpose of these groups is to increase political consciousness and to indoctrinate people with Communist theories and policies.

The Chinese Communists are not averse to using violence if it is necessary to achieve their ends. In the past, they have shed considerable blood when they have encountered stubborn opposition, particularly in dealing with landlords in rural areas. At present, however, they are finding it possible to minimize the use of violence, once their armies have achieved control, and they are emphasizing methods of persuasion, organization, and social pressure in administering their rule.

One of the greatest contrasts between the assumption of power by the Chinese Communists and the rise of new rulers in upheavals such as the French and Russian revolutions is the relative absence at present of vengeful killing. The Chinese Communists are not carrying out bloody mass executions of their defeated enemies. Instead, they are depriving them of all power and then, in a remarkable number of cases, proceeding self-righteously with the task of "reforming" them. A "war criminals" list of Kuomintang leaders has been drawn up, but to date those who have stayed in Communist territory have generally been forgiven their past political "sins" on the basis of public recantation, and a few have been given powerless but face-saving jobs in bodies such as the Political Consultative Conference. This policy helps to explain why defection from the Nationalist side has increased, in a kind of geometrical progression, with every Communist victory. The principal motive of the deserters is self-preservation; the Communists' objective in accepting them is to reduce and undermine opposition.

There is, however, another side to the picture. Arrests have not been lacking. Police techniques of control have, in fact, gradually increased once the Communists have stabilized their rule in any area. Anyone suspected of attempting sabotage directed against the new regime and its policies is ferreted out by the secret police and dealt with harshly. And the threat of force is always in the background, even when it is used sparingly.

A number of factors help to explain why the Communists have been able to exercise a minimum of force after the takeover of power. One is the impact of the Communist movement itself, its monopoly of both physical and moral power. Another is the effectiveness of nonviolent methods of control which the Communists have developed. Perhaps most important of all is the lack of any extensive organized opposition. Where active, organized resistance exists or develops, the Communists use force to combat it, but in most places they have taken over this is the exception rather than the rule.

This is not to imply, however, that the Communists do not apply force in more subtle forms. Social pressure and intimidation are used with great effectiveness and are probably felt by ordinary Chinese to a degree they have never experienced before, because the Communists not only control the instruments of power—the army, Party, bureaucracy, and police—but have also developed propaganda techniques and methods of social manipulation as powerful political weapons.

Many things the Communist authorities require people to do are "voluntary" in theory but are brought about by pressures of various sorts. Direct pressure is applied by political workers who make house-to-house visitations. If individuals are uncooperative, political workers may devote hours or days to questioning, persuading, indoctrinating, and "reforming" the persons involved. These political workers are generally polite, but they have the backing of the regime, they can produce stock answers to most evasions and objections, and they usually get results. Through them, Communist influence reaches far deeper into the lives of ordinary people than has that of any past regime. People who do not co-operate are often ostracized by public criticism that marks them as politically contaminated and dangerous elements.

The pressure of propaganda is tremendous. Some propaganda contains direct or implied threats; some of it is persuasive. Verbal vitriol in the form of constant propaganda attacks against "enemy agents" and "reactionaries" contains implied threats for everyone, because these are loose terms and tend to be applied to opposition and obstruction of any kind. Such attacks run as a constant theme throughout Communist propaganda and create an atmosphere in which people fear that any disagreement with, or criticism of, the Communist line is dangerous. For the Communists there is only one "correct" line on any important question.

In a more positive sense, the Communists' persuasive propaganda is an extremely intensive tool. It constitutes a colossal sales-promotion campaign in which the product is ideological. The Communists are trying to sell Marxism-Leninism and Mao Tse-tung's New Democracy to the Chinese people, and their field for propaganda is all-embracing. Every form of artistic or cultural expression is used, together with all media that convey the spoken word.

Popular songs, group dances, radio programs, motion pictures, plays, paintings, posters, and woodcuts all carry a political message. Everyone is exposed; it is impossible to escape from the constant stream of political propaganda in one form or another. According to the Communists, "Art for art's sake . . . does not exist. . . . Proletarian literature and art are a part of the entire revolutionary cause." Their goal is complete thought control, attained through an ideological and cultural revolution, directed toward the achievement of a "New Democratic culture."

The written word is the most important vehicle of propaganda, and all publications are politically screened or controlled. A few non-Communist publications are still tolerated, but only so long as they do not oppose the Communists or contradict the propaganda official publications are disseminating. News is selected, slanted, and distorted to define good and bad, friend and foe, and to support the current propaganda "campaign." The Communists are not apologetic about this lack of impartiality in their "news"; they say, "So long as there are different classes in our society, the press will remain a weapon in the class struggle and will be a part of the machinery of state." Official regulations concerning the press clearly state that one objective is that of "depriving counterrevolutionaries of freedom of the press and speech."

There are no outlets for criticism of the regime, and as a consequence the weight and force of Communist propaganda on the public are overwhelming. The Communists encourage "self-criticism" among themselves, but this is merely a kind of religious confession—concerned with sins and failures and not with first principles. Ideological controls, moreover, are gradually eliminating all sources of non-Communist points of view. There has been no "burning of the books" of the old regime to date, but everything now being published follows the Communist line, and all else is being slowly displaced.

High-pressure indoctrination is another Communist ideological weapon used to mold the attitudes and control the actions of large numbers of people. Intensive indoctrination obviously cannot encompass the entire population, but millions of people within the Party and in all organizations and institutions under Party control are exposed to it. The prime emphasis is placed on ideological conformity and orthodoxy. Perhaps the most effective technique is a method of group indoctrination that might be called "collective autoindoctrination." Small groups are formed to study Communist ideas and policies. They are provided with books, pamphlets, or speeches on which to work and are expected virtually to memorize the material. Each member discusses it with the others, is criticized by the others, and carries out self-criticism in front of them. This continues until everyone achieves a "correct" understanding of the Party's policy or point of view. The social pressure exerted for orthodoxy by this method is amazingly effective, particularly since "individualism" is considered a cardinal sin.

However, in spite of the Communists' successes, China is far from being a Communist nation. It is still only a nation ruled by a Communist Party. This may seem an unimportant distinction to people outside China, but it is a significant one to people in China.

The Chinese Communists have won their struggle for power on the basis of a program called New Democracy. In identifying the Communist Party with specific policies, most Chinese people have thought of New Democracy, not Communism. In acquiescing in Communist rule they have accepted New Democracy rather than Communism. Even many of the Communists' most active supporters are believers not in Communism but in New Democracy. The Communists themselves have always stated in clear terms that they consider New Democracy to be merely a transitional period on the road to Communism, but few other than the Communist leaders seem to have looked into the future and to have realized the full significance of this fact; most people are preoccupied with the immediate present.

The theory of New Democracy seems mild enough for the majority of Chinese to accept. Its agrarian program calls for an increase of private land ownership, on the basis of small holdings, to be achieved by confiscation of the holdings of landlords and "old-style rich farmers," and redistribution of this land to agricultural workers, tenants, and poor farmers. Neither collectivization nor socialization of agriculture is part of the program for this transitional period. The industrial program of New Democracy calls for state enterprises in transportation, communications, and large-scale business and banking, extensive government planning and control, increased labor organization and participation by labor in industrial management, the development of cooperative enterprises in small-scale industry and trade, increased benefits and social insurance for workers, and rapid over-all industrialization of the Chinese economy. All small-scale private industry and commerce, the Communists say, should at present be not only tolerated but encouraged. They consider this necessary because industrialization, and the formation of an industrial proletariat, must precede the establishment of real Communism. The compromise nature of this New Democratic economic theory appears in slogans such as "Benefits to both public and private industry" and "Consider the interests of both labor and capital."

In a general way, the Communists are now merely attempting to carry out the economic program of New Democracy. They have taken over all industries and enterprises formerly controlled by the Nationalist Government and prominent Kuomintang members—"bureaucratic capital"—but they have not initiated over-all nationalization of economic life. They have attacked basic economic problems—rehabilitating the economy, increasing production, raising the standard of living, developing industry and transportation—with a tremendous amount of drive and energy, and even though their accomplishments to date have not been spectacular, they are trying.

But there is an important difference between the approach of the Communists and that of the businessmen, merchants, and ordinary Chinese with whom they must deal. The attitude of the latter is that the program of New Democracy should define the maximum limits of government interference in, participation in, and control over the economic life of the country. The Communists look upon New Democracy as a minimum program, and they do not hesitate to expand the government's influence over the economy whenever and wherever they consider it necessary or feasible. There is constant tension, therefore, caused by the conflict of these different points of view, even though evidence of it seldom comes out into the open.

The Communists are attempting to achieve some of their economic aims by pressing for harder work, austerity, punctuality, and the avoidance of waste. They are attempting to increase incentives by instituting Stakhanovism, competitions, and awards for "labor heroes." They are also trying, without complete success, to keep down the pressure for wage increases. The spectacular rewards they promise are in the future, not the present. They propose that China lift itself up by its own bootstraps, the hard way, for the benefit of the nation and future generations.

However—despite the theory of New Democracy—the logic of the present economic situation and the Communists' desire to progress steadily toward a socialized economy are forcing a fairly rapid expansion of government enterprise and economic controls. Some critical economic conditions have become progressively worse. The economy the Communists have inherited is chaotic to begin with, and the confusion of political readjustment has added to existing problems. In addition, China during the past year of Communist takeover has been stricken with a series of major natural disasters—drought, pests, and floods—that have reduced agricultural production to its lowest level in years. The Kuomintang blockade has disrupted foreign trade, and food imports have been cut off while imports of needed industrial raw materials have dropped. These factors have caused economic stagnation in large segments of China's urban economy. Added to these special problems are the chronic problems that haunt any government in China—one of the most important being inflation, caused by heavy government expenditures (largely for military purposes), an unbalanced budget, and the issuance of unbacked paper currency.

However, the Communists, by stopgap measures, ingenious improvisation, and great energy have managed to mitigate the effects of some of China's basic economic problems. In the major cities, for example, they have kept up food supplies remarkably well in view of over-all national shortages. Their genius for organization has been applied to the collection and distribution of grain to accomplish this objective. But there is no doubt that they have squeezed the countryside to support the cities. Heavy grain requisitions to feed not only the major cities but also the Communist armies of 3–4 million men have eaten into subsistence food stocks in many rural areas, and this winter there will be serious food shortages and perhaps starvation in many parts of the country.

Inflation has been attacked with more imagination and with more success by the Communists than by their Kuomintang predecessors. Wages, salaries, and bank deposits are now computed in terms of cloth and grain values, putting the economy on a "millet standard" in north China and a "rice standard" elsewhere, and necessities have been periodically dumped on the market by government agencies to keep prices down. The fundamental causes for inflation remain, however, and prices continue to rise in spurts which are becoming progressively more violent.

In short, the Communists have not yet been able to start the Chinese economy on the road toward recovery, to say nothing of real development. But they have greatly increased their role in the economy. The pressures of critical, almost insoluble, problems, coupled with the Communists' desire for ultimate socialization, have led them to expand government planning, control, and ownership continuously. Government monopolies in trade and industry are growing. Government-directed cooperatives are steadily expanding their operations. Large state trading companies are taking over an ever-increasing share of internal wholesale trade, and government retail businesses have been started in some areas. Foreign trade is already rigidly controlled and is rapidly being monopolized by state trading companies. The remaining private industries are being affected increasingly by labor, wage, and price regulations as well as by direct supervision. Many private industries are becoming hopelessly indebted to the government because of loans required to pay the wages of idle laborers whom they are not allowed to discharge. Heavy taxation, often unreasonable and sometimes close to confiscatory, is further undermining both large-scale and small-scale private entrepreneurs. These trends are taking place despite the fact that the Communists do not want to take over all private industry now, because they are unable to manage and run it, and even though in individual cases help and encouragement are given to a few private industries. Under the circumstances, the role of government in economic life will probably expand rapidly even in the period of New Democracy.

Thus, many factors raise grave doubts as to whether the Communists, in spite of their victory, will be able to solve China's basic problems. And in the long run their survival will depend on their ability to solve such problems by methods tolerable to the Chinese people. If they fail, the revolutionary pressures that have worked in their favor in recent years will in the future work against them.

In one fundamental respect, the Communists' entire position in China may be undergoing a process of change at the present time. In the past their strength has rested on rural China, or at least on one important rural area, but now they have shifted their attention and the "center of Party leadership" to the cities. The primary goal of their present economic program is rapid industrialization. The full significance of this fact is not yet clear, but it raises many questions. The Communists' industrialization program now emphasizes two points—speed and an autarchic kind of self-reliance. If they are to push a program of rapid industrialization on the sole basis of their own capacities, together with whatever limited assistance may be forthcoming from the Soviet bloc (top Chinese Communist leaders propose the ambitious goal of making the Chinese economy 30 to 40 per cent industrial in ten to fifteen years), then the economic burden of the process must fall on China's peasants, whose position may become worse rather than better. Such a policy would risk alienation of China's agrarian masses. If the Communists eventually begin socialization of agriculture, moreover, they will inevitably encounter strong peasant resistance, regardless of how desirable or necessary such a policy might be in the Communist leaders' minds from a purely economic point of view. Already the Communists are meeting increased peasant opposition to the heavy grain levies required to support an expanding army and bureaucracy. Isolated peasant uprisings have taken place in many scattered places during the past year, and although they generally seem to have been uncoordinated and nonpolitical, they may be a portent of things to come.

In the cities, too, a slow process of disillusionment and passive resistance has already begun. There are many reasons for this: The general slump in business and trade is one, the Communists' constant interference in people's ordinary lives is another. The Communists want to break down old social values, arouse political consciousness, and revolutionize everyone's livelihood, but the average Chinese is probably basically anti-government—whatever government is in power—and resents the intrusion of government into his family and individual life. The discrepancies between the Communists' promises and the bitter facts of life breed cynicism. The Communists, moreover, now get the blame for insoluble economic problems—blame that was formerly heaped on the Kuomintang. These and other reasons seem to have caused a growing amount of psychological opposition and passive resistance to the regime.

New problems have also affected the Communist movement itself. Reliable, qualified Party personnel has been spread thin over many areas where the Party has no organizational roots and little active popular support. Responsibilities have grown out of proportion to the number of persons capable of dealing with them. Party and army have been diluted by rapid expansion. To date, it has been remarkable that this process has not visibly weakened Party solidarity or changed the character of the Communist movement, but the threat that this may take place is ever-present. As their responsibilities have expanded, moreover, the Communists have been forced to cooperate with an increasing number of political allies of dubious long-range reliability from their point of view. Many intellectuals, among their strongest supporters at present, may in time react against Communist methods. Compromises have been made with a number of warlords and local leaders who, although stripped of military power, still have influence of various sorts. The alliances between the Communists and other groups may prove temporary. The Communists' entire "class coalition" may turn out to be unstable when they push beyond New Democracy, attempt to achieve Communism, and try to eliminate some of the classes to which many of their present supporters belong.

In short, the mere fact that the Communists have won their struggle for power does not mean that Communism has yet succeeded in China. The real problems still lie before the Communists, and their difficulties may continue to increase. The slow growth of disillusionment under Communist rule, however, should not be confused with an organized opposition. There is almost no nostalgia about the Kuomintang regime. Even those who are most disillusioned with the Communists would probably not help in any attempted Kuomintang restoration. There is no organized opposition to the Communists because there is no leadership or program on which it can develop at present, and the Communist Party is the one efficient, effective political machine with a positive program in China. The only alternative is breakup, disunity, and chaos—and these are not inspiring prospects for the tired Chinese people.

For the foreseeable future, therefore, the Communists are the only ones who can rule China. An opposition may develop in time; the Communists will do everything they can to suppress it, but the Chinese have a genius for secret organization as well as for passive resistance against any regime they cannot tolerate. The growth of an organized opposition, however, would be a slow and gradual process (it took the Communists almost thirty years to win power in a struggle against a weakening government), and whether or not it develops will depend on how successfully the Communists solve basic problems, particularly in the field of economics.

It is still too early, in fact, to predict what reaction the Communists themselves will make to their environment, to critical problems, and to "public opinion." Possibly they will try to adapt and modify their program to fit the changing needs and realities of the Chinese situation. If they do, they may succeed on the basis of a moderate social, political, and economic system. On the other hand, they may try to ram Communism down the throats of the Chinese in a doctrinaire fashion, with an increasing use of violence and police-state methods. If so, there is little likelihood that they can succeed in the long run.

PART II

POLITICAL AND SOCIAL CONTROL

MASS POLITICAL ORGANIZATIONS

September, 1951

The Chinese Communists have developed a pattern of political organization, modeled on that in the Soviet Union, which has been a major factor in their successful achievement of power. This pattern, which they are now attempting to establish as the institutional foundation of their regime, has been exceptionally effective in arousing, activating, and mobilizing—as well as in controlling, coercing, and intimidating—large numbers of the Chinese people. One of the top-priority aims of the present regime is complete reorganization of the Chinese body politic according to the Communist pattern, and this aim remains constant despite periodic redefinition of the Party's other policies and programs and occasional reorientation of other elements in the Party's ideological line. In short, political organization per se is both a basic instrument of Chinese Communist power and a primary objective of Chinese Communist policy.

The central pillar in the structure of political organization under the regime is the Chinese Communist Party itself, a fairly large but well-disciplined hard core of professional revolutionaries, and the direct rule of the Party is exercised through two principal chains of command: the army and the government. CCP members still comprise a numerical minority of both the People's Liberation Army and the People's Government, but these two bureaucracies function effectively under Communist direction as the military and civil props of Party rule. In addition to these three basic pillars of political power, however, the Chinese Communists are energetically constructing a fourth: "mass people's organizations."

In many respects, mass organizations—including those for peasants, labor, youth, and women—are the most unique element in the structure of Chinese Communist power. They are the principal agencies through which the weight of the Communist apparatus makes itself felt upon the average individual and the means through which the Communist Party has its widest impact. Although political in character, they are not, strictly speaking, elements in the bureaucratic "organizations of state power," but in countless ways they are tied to the Party, the army, and the government, and they form an essential part of the organizational matrix of Chinese Communist rule. They are the organizational link between the bureaucratic ruling agencies and the masses.

According to most recent official Communist claims, the professional hard core of Chinese Communist rule—the Party itself—had a membership of 5 million at the end of 1950. This is a large figure when compared with Communist groups in most countries, but it is a tiny minority (somewhat more than 1 per cent) of the total Chinese population. By early 1950, official estimates of the number of people on the payroll of the Chinese Government ranged between 9 and 10 million. Disregarding overlapping membership, this adds up to a total of perhaps 15 million. It is the mass organizations, however, that bring the largest number of people into direct organizational contact with the Communist regime; the membership of these groups, according to official claims, totals several tens of millions, all of whom are indirectly subject in varying degrees to Party discipline and control. These organizations act as affiliates or subsidiary organs of the Party. Their members join "voluntarily," but the control exerted over them is more direct and undoubtedly more effective than the type of control exercised over the population as a whole through the government bureaucracy.

The ties between the mass political organizations and the Party, the army, and the government are extremely complex and often subtle, but in many respects the nexuses by which these organizations are formally integrated into the structure of the regime are People's Congresses or Representative Conferences of All Circles, which are organized at every level of government. According to the Common Program—a general statement of the Chinese Communist regime's present policies adopted on September 29, 1949, by the Chinese People's Political Consultative Conference—People's Congresses are eventually to be elected as representative groups at every regional level of government; in the interim, some of their functions are to be performed by appointed Representative Conferences of All Circles. Premier Chou En-lai reported that by October, 1950, while only "a few cities and counties" had convened People's Congresses, all other cities and 1,707 *Hsien* (counties) had organized Representative Conferences of All

Circles, and "most" *Hsiang* (administrative villages) had established one or the other.

Although these congresses or conferences are labeled the "organs for exercising state power by the people," they are simply advisory bodies with a symbolic role, described by Premier Chou as one of "uniting various strata, parties, groups, and nationalities among the people, and enabling both the government to hear the opinions of the people and the people to understand and supervise the work of the government." The character of representation in these bodies indicates, however, the great importance the Communists place upon mass people's organizations in their political system. For example, of a total of 510 appointed members in the CPPCC (the highest "representative body" in the Chinese Communist regime at present), 206 represent people's organizations and groups, as compared with 142 representing political parties and groups, 102 representing the administrative regions of the country, and 60 representing army organizations or units.

An analysis of people's organizations' representation in the CPPCC gives an indication of which ones in the Communists' eyes have the greatest political significance. Apart from miscellaneous representatives of educational circles, industrial and commercial circles, and Shanghai people's organizations, the CPPCC representatives come from the "All-China" headquarters of the following organizations: Federation of Labor, Peasants' Associations, Democratic Women's Federation, Democratic Youth Federation, Democratic Students' Federation, Federation of Literary and Art Circles, Conference of Scientists, and Association of Journalists.

Many types of organizations included in the Chinese Communists' over-all network of organization are not on this list. For example, there is no direct representation for cooperatives (in August, 1950, the Communists claimed that the All-China Federation of Cooperatives had 20 million members in 38,000 cooperative units), paramilitary organizations such as militia, or many other sorts of organizations with political significance. But the CPPCC list reveals those mass organizations considered to be most vital in a political sense to the Communist regime, and these organizations alone are said to contain tens of millions of members. By October, 1950, it was officially claimed that the Federation of Labor had more than 4 million members, the Democratic Women's Federation more than 30 million, and the Democratic Youth Federation more than 7 million; and by mid-1951, it was alleged that Peasants' Associations in four of China's six major administrative areas (east, central-south, northwest, and southwest China) had a membership totaling more than 84 million.

These figures may be overestimates, and the effectiveness with which the membership of the mass organizations is actually controlled is difficult to measure and may vary from place to place and time to time; but from the writer's own observation, in north China during 1949, the Communists have been exceptionally successful by Chinese standards in getting large masses of people into these organizations. To understand how the regime functions, therefore, it is necessary to know something of how these people's organizations work—the underlying philosophy, the structural basis, and the complicated ties integrating them into the over-all system of political organization in Communist China.

The Chinese Communists' philosophy of organization is summed up in the principle of "democratic centralism," the basis upon which all Party, government, army, "people's," and other Communist-sponsored and Communist-controlled organizations are established. Two antithetical principles are combined in "democratic centralism" in a formula that makes possible authoritarian control of organizations that have a wide base of mass membership. The "people's democratic dictatorship" is carried out, therefore, by combining maximum mass participation in political organizations with maximum centralization of policy- and decision-making authority. The "broad masses" and the Party elite are equally essential elements in this system of organization. The Communist elite rules, but instead of separating itself from the masses and ruling over them, it takes a large percentage of the masses into its fold and rules through them. Efficient minority rule is thereby exercised through an impressive façade of majority rule.

The basic unit of most important mass political organizations under the regime is the local branch. Organization starts, therefore, at a real grass-roots level. This distinguishes political organizations sponsored by the Communists from almost all previous efforts in China to organize modern political groups; for the first time, active political groups are being formed at the lowest levels of Chinese society.

The basis for the branch varies: It may be a geographical district, such as a village or a city street. It may be an institutional, occupational, professional, or organizational group within the basic geographical district—a factory, a shop, a school, a company, a government office, a hospital, a group of carpenters, butchers, writers, or artists. Or it may be an arbitrary class or social grouping within the geographical district—"urban workers" or "agricultural laborers, poor peasants, and middle peasants." In any case, every member of society is categorized—usually a single person will fall into several different categories—and mass political organizations are based on a combination of these categories and administrative-geographical districts.

A portion of the population falls into ostracized groups—"reactionaries," "feudal elements," and so on—which are disfranchised, barred from all active political life (unless they recant their past, are reindoctrinated, and then are reaccepted into society in a new class or social status), and prevented from combining for joint, organized effort. Most people, however, are eligible for and subject to organization on the basis of at least one, and usually several, of the geographical, class, social, institutional, occupational, and professional categories to which they belong. If the Communists are able to carry through their conception of mass people's organizations successfully, the majority of the people will be brought into one or more of these organizations.

Although the local branch is the basic unit for all organizations, a large branch is usually subdivided into small groups or cells, each of which is headed by one leader. These small groups are extremely important in the Communist scheme of organization because they are the real basis for indoctrination and collective action. The Communists have found that a small group—almost never larger than twenty to thirty—is the most effective basis for thorough indoctrination, mutual surveillance, and cooperative action. A single orthodox, reliable leader can direct, control, mobilize, and stimulate a small group, and the members of the group act upon each other to produce discipline and unity under firm leadership.

Apart from cell subdivisions, each branch is usually organized into a general assembly or congress of all members and a small executive committee which provides active leadership, as well as several functional committees to direct work of different sorts.

With the branches forming a grass-roots base spread all over the country, each important organization is constructed into a pyramidal national structure according to a hierarchical system which includes a congress and an executive committee at each administrative-geographical level into which China is divided: district, county, special commissioner district, special municipality, province, and administrative region. The congress at each of these levels is composed of representatives "elected" by the organization's units at the lower level. This provides a continuous link from the grass roots to the top of the hierarchy, which enables the central authorities to keep a finger on the pulse of the organization as a whole. It provides a route along which a few leaders recruited at the bottom can work their way up the organization to positions of responsibility. It also provides a channel through which "suggestions" and "criticism" from the mass membership can filter up through the organization to the national leaders.

The real chain of command runs from the top downward, however, through the committee system. The executive committee at each level, which is the actual directing body, is theoretically elected by the congress; but (and this is essential to the organizational scheme) the committee's membership must be approved by the executive committee of the next higher regional level, and is subject to discipline and orders coming from above.

At the top of each organization there is a national congress and a central committee which usually has a standing committee, a secretariat, and various functional subcommittees attached to it. The congress meets only once in two or three years; it is the central committee of each organization that is the real center of authority in this system of "democratic centralism." Every major "decision," "order," "program," and "policy" originates with the central committee and is passed through regional committees down the chain of command to the grass roots, where the mass membership is expected to follow and implement it. In addition, the central committee usually links the organization to the international Communist movement not only through its ties with the CCP and the government but also through direct contacts with similar organizations (for labor, youth, women, professionals, and so forth) in other Communist-ruled countries.

Several key principles or ideas cement this organizational structure into an effective institutional framework under Communist direction. One is the idea of leadership. The Chinese Communist Party is specifically designated as the "highest command for the leadership of all organizations" in China. Every organization is subordinate to the Party and must look to it for leadership, orders, and direction.

Another key idea is that of iron discipline and loyalty. The whole system of organization is geared to produce unity and to suppress heterodoxy, and each organization is designed to translate the ideas of a handful of leaders at the top into acceptance and implementing action on the part of the masses at the bottom. Because of this emphasis, all the organizations, in varying degrees, operate under a sort of quasi-military discipline.

Another essential idea is the Marxist dogma that there is only one "correct" line of thought and action in any particular situation. Once the central authorities have defined what is correct, the entire mass membership of any organization is expected to think and act "correctly."

Still another extremely important principle may be labeled the necessity of activism. It is not enough for a person merely to belong to an organization; he must play an active role in carrying out the organization's functions and achieving its aims. Good faith has to be proved with good works.

This pattern of people's organizations through which the CCP exercises much of its influence and control over millions of Chinese might be represented as a series of wheels within wheels. The hub, the Party, is the only organization that is composed entirely of reliable professional workers directly subject to the Communist Party Central Committee and the Party's "iron discipline." In all other important organizations, however, a nucleus of Communist Party cadres or members provides direction, and all the organizations not only are pledged to accept Communist leadership but also in various ways are organizationally linked to the Party. The larger the organization, the less tightly it is organized, but every organization is nonetheless tied to the Party.

Chapter IX of the CC Party Constitution, entitled "Party Organizations Outside the Party," states that a "Party nucleus," which shall be "under the direction of the corresponding Party organizations, and shall enforce their decisions," shall be established in all "government organizations, labor unions, peasants' unions, cooperatives, and other mass organizations," and "the duty of the Party nucleus shall be to direct the work of the members in the leading organ for the purpose of strengthening the Party's influence and carrying out the Party's program and work."

Furthermore, not only are all the mass organizations linked to the Party, but they are themselves interwoven into a complicated network of relationships designed to produce mutual support for the joint aim of "carrying out the Party's program and work." Youth organizations, for example, are expected not only to support the Communist Party's program directly, but also to support Communist-sponsored labor unions, Peasants' Associations, women's groups, and so on, in their activities in support of the Party's program.

Another striking feature of the intricate web of organization under the Communist regime is the extensive system of interlocking directorates, in which a few Communist leaders at any level in the organizational structure, or in a particular region, hold concurrent positions in the executive committees of many of the most important mass organizations as well as in the Party, the government, and the army. At the national level, the leading figures in many if not most of the important mass organizations are prominent leaders of the Communist Party, often members of the Party Central Committee.

The functions the mass organizations are expected to perform are myriad. Certain ones are common to all: to support the Communist Party and its program, to educate the membership in Marxism-Leninism and the "thought of Mao Tse-tung," to "unite the masses," to "struggle against imperialism, feudalism, and bureaucratic capitalism," to imbue the membership with political consciousness, to stimulate the membership to collective action to "build a New Democratic China," and so on. Other functions vary according to the type of membership, and involve the responsibility for carrying out the Communists' program as it relates specifically to the groups included in the membership. The Peasants' Associations, for example, are designated the "legal organizations for reforming the agrarian system" and for implementing the Agrarian Reform Law; and the Federation of Labor's unions "observe that management or the capitalists actually carry out the regulations and directives concerning labor protection, labor insurance, wage standards, the regulation of factory hygiene and safety devices, and other matters as laid down in government decrees."

The relationship between the hierarchy of these mass organizations and their membership is a subtle combination of coercion and cooperation. In every mass organization, there are members who are enthusiastic about the aims and functions of the organization, but there are also members who are either passive or hostile and have joined because of strong pressure or a recognition that failure to join would be held against them. (There is no place for political neutrality or "freedom of silence" under the Chinese Communist regime; nonsupport is considered to be almost identical with opposition.) Every organization performs functions that are considered highly desirable by the majority of the membership; for example, undoubtedly most of the members of the Peasants' Associations actively support land redistribution. But, in addition, the organizations are responsible for functions that are onerous and unpleasant to most of the members; the Peasants' Associations, for instance, also help to enforce tax regulations.

This mixture of "good" and "bad," of positive support and negative control, makes it difficult to generalize about the mass organizations. When there is a basis of popular approval for elements of the Communist program, these organizations arouse, activate, and mobilize support; the result is dynamic collective action which is much more effective in producing results than unorganized activities on the part of isolated individuals or small groups. When there is general disapproval, however, the mass organizations serve as one of the Communists' instruments for controlling, coercing, and intimidating the masses, and for pushing through their program despite opposition. The mass organizations serve the dual purpose, therefore, of mobilizing support and suppressing opposition.

It may serve to clarify these generalities if a few details are presented as to how the Communists are organizing one particular population group, the Chinese youth.

Young men and women have played an extremely important role in the revolutionary upheaval that has been in progress in China for the past several decades. Perhaps because they are particularly susceptible to new and radical ideas, and are more active and dynamic than their elders, youths often come to the forefront at such times. The Chinese Communists have recognized this fact, and during the past thirty years have made every effort to influence, win over, and organize Chinese youth—particularly Chinese students. "It is a fact," says Feng Wen-pin, the Communist Secretary-General of the New Democratic Youth League, "that in the history of the Chinese revolution the youth movement in China, and especially the student movement, has always functioned as the vanguard and spearhead of the revolutionary movement." This is one of the reasons the Communists place great emphasis upon effectively organizing and gaining maximum support from youth. Another reason is the fact that youths, still in the formative years and relatively malleable, are the raw material out of which they hope to create an entirely new society cast in the Communist mold.

Prior to their takeover of power, the Communists were not able to capture complete control of China's youth or the student movement in China, but they did exert a strong influence upon them and drew upon them as an important source for recruits. Most available evidence indicates also that since the Communists have assumed power, organized youth and student groups in China have become a major supporting prop for the regime.

The Communists' first efforts to organize youth groups in China predate by a year even the formal organization of the CCP itself. A Socialist Youth Corps was organized in China in 1920 and, in the words of Jen Pi-shih, a late member of the Chinese Communist Politburo, "played a preparatory role in the establishment of the Communist Party ideologically and organizationally." This was followed by a succession of other Communist youth organizations: the Communist Youth League, the National Liberation Vanguard, the Youth National Salvation Association, and others. These Communist groups represented only a small minority of active youth groups in China, however, and actually the most important groups were broadly based student organizations connected with the Chinese student movement, which began to organize throughout China in 1919 and were active from that time on, principally in Nationalist-ruled territory.

In 1948, as Communist forces gradually took control of more and more territory, however, the Party Central Committee started planning to amalgamate and reorganize Chinese youth groups into an integrated organizational setup covering the whole country. The New Democratic Youth League was established in that year, on an experimental basis, in north China. Then the Central Committee, on January 1, 1949, announced its decision to establish the League nationally as the "nucleus for mobilizing China's youth, serving as both assistant and reserve strength of the Communist Party." There followed, in the spring of 1949, a series of national conferences which set up three "All-China" youth organizations designed to encompass and merge all existing youth groups and to expand the membership of these organizations. These were the All-China Democratic Youth Federation, the All-China Democratic Students' Federation, and the New Democratic Youth League.

The interrelationship between these youth organizations clearly illustrates the method by which the Communists exercise their influence and control over large mass groups in which Party members account for only a small minority of the membership.

The largest, and most loosely knit, of these three organizations is the Democratic Youth Federation, headed by Liao Ch'eng-chih, who is forty-three and is an alternate member of the Party Central Committee. Membership in this body is composed of organizational units rather than individuals, and, according to its constitution, "any nationwide organization established by Chinese youth, including overseas Chinese youth, or youth organizations in various provinces and cities" can be included, if approved by the federation's leadership. The constitution states:

> The aims of the Federation are to unite youth bodies throughout the country, to promote the welfare of youth, to strive with the people to win a complete victory for the New Democratic revolution, to accomplish the tasks of constructing a New Democratic country, and to struggle in cooperation with democratic youth all over the world for lasting peace and People's Democracy.

All the member organizations are pledged to carry out the decisions of the Federation, and the Federation is constructed on the principles of democratic centralism.

The Students' Federation is a similar organization, and, in fact, its constitution is almost identical with that of the Youth Federation. Undoubtedly the Communists have set up a separate student organization because of the special importance of students as the most active and literate element among youth in China, and because the Chinese student movement has traditions and a history that would make it difficult to merge it completely with a more broadly based youth group. The basic units in the Federation are student associations in all middle schools (high schools) and institutions of higher learning. These associations are organized regionally in the hierarchical pattern of democratic centralism, and their functions are essentially the same as those of the Youth Federation. They, also, must carry out all the decisions of the Federation.

These are the largest mass organizations for youth under the Communist regime, but the most important organization is the New Democratic Youth League, which is linked directly to the Party. Youth League members are under tight discipline, occupy key positions in almost all other youth groups (including the Youth Federation and the Students' Federation), and under the direction of the Party exercise "leadership" and control over the entire organizational structure encompassing youth. The Youth League was headed, until his recent death (at the age of forty-six), by Jen Pi-shih, a member of the CCP Politburo; in October, 1950, its membership was claimed to be more than 3 million.

The organizers of the Youth League in any specific locality are specially trained young cadres from the Party in that locality. How this responsibility is assigned is clearly spelled out in official Party directives. In north China, for example, the Party requires each of its regional committees to assign three persons, each county committee three to five persons, and each district committee two persons to work solely on youth organization, without other responsibilities. In every district, the Party committee sets up a working group of about ten persons to establish the League, and at each level the Party's youth workers are responsible for organizing and picking the leaders of local League units. The Party specifies, furthermore, that the secretary of a district committee of the Youth League must be a member of the Party district committee, and qualifications for League committeemen at higher levels are also laid down by the Party. In factories, special youth departments are set up by the Party branch in the factory to do this work; in schools, the school Party committee bears the responsibility; and so on.

The Youth League also is organized in accordance with the standard Communist hierarchical system and the principles of democratic centralism. According to its constitution, "a branch is set up in each factory, enterprise, company, school, office, street, or village (or administrative village) which has more than five League members." Branches are subdivided into cells of three to ten members. Where there are more than 100 members, a general branch is organized and subdivided into sub-branches. Where there are more than 500 members, a League committee is organized. In every district where there are at least three branches, a district committee is established. On this base is constructed the regular committee hierarchy going from district to county to special commissioner district to province to administrative region, and culminating in a National Congress, which meets every two years, and a League Central Committee, headed by members of the Communist Party Central Committee.

League organization in army units is defined by special rules. The constitution states: "The organization and work of the New Democratic Youth League in the People's Liberation Army are drawn up separately by the League Central Committee and the Political Department of the Chinese People's Revolutionary Military Committee."

This indicates the League's relationship to the Party. Equally important is its relationship to other groups and organizations.

The League's constitution states that members must "organize youth to accomplish positively the various important work and missions determined by the Communist Party of China, the People's Democratic Government of China, the higher levels of the League organization, and the branch itself." The League, in short, serves as an instrument for extending the Party's discipline and control throughout all youth groups. As stated by Jen Pi-shih:

> The leaders as well as all the members of the New Democratic Youth League must correctly and thoroughly recognize the absolute necessity of accepting the leadership of the Chinese Communist Party, resolutely carrying out and obeying all decisions and policies adopted by the Chinese Communist Party, learning and studying the theories of Marxism and Leninism and the ways of the Communist Party and guaranteeing that all members of the Youth League, as well as the vast multitude of the masses of youth, will have complete faith in the Chinese Communist Party.

Specifically:

> The Youth League in factories, besides accepting the leadership of the Party branches, should maintain a correct relationship with labor unions.
>
> Organizationally, both the Youth League and the labor unions should follow the leadership of the Communist Party, but the Youth League is to conduct its work among young workers so that these young workers will self-consciously and voluntarily obey and respond to various regulations and appeals of public enterprises and factories as well as the labor unions.

In rural areas:

> Members of the Youth League in farm villages where land reforms have been introduced should become energetic elements in increasing production (including that of secondary enterprises) and in leading the vast multitude of young farmers to cooperate with adult farmers in labor exchanges. . . . They should moreover energetically participate in the cooperative movement in farm villages.

In schools, "they should energetically participate in the various activities of the student associations" and "systematically develop the work of the Youth League."

And so on.

The members of the Youth League, therefore, function as a sort of secondary elite acting under the direction of the Party elite and extending the Party's influence throughout the entire web of youth organizations. League members must be boys and girls between the ages of fourteen and twenty-five (League leaders are specifically exempted from age limits by the constitution) "who support the policies of the Communist Party of China" and who are vouched for by members of the League or the Party, approved by the League hierarchy, and successfully serve a probationary period ranging from three months to one year for different types of persons. (Fully qualified "laboring youth, young revolutionary soldiers, young revolutionary intellectuals, and revolutionary functionaries" are not required to serve a probationary period.)

The size of the elite in relation to the organized masses can be illustrated with two examples. A qualified non-Communist foreign observer who left Peking early in 1951 estimated that in one of the leading universities in Peking, which then had a total enrollment of 1,100, there were approximately 200 to 300 members of the Youth League and perhaps 20 members of the Communist Party. According to this observer, the activities of the 1,100 in the student association were determined by the 200–300 League members, who were controlled by the 20 Party members.

Another example is contained in an analysis of the graduates of the People's Revolutionary College in Peking. This institution is one of many established by the Communists all over the country to train political cadres (particularly for rural work); according to official figures, these schools graduated more than 200,000 political workers from six-month courses during 1950. Of the 6,000 members of the 1950 spring graduating class of the Peking school (one-third of whom are ex-students, the rest being workers, government employees, professional people, and so on), 1,578 qualified for membership in the Youth League and 155 qualified as candidates for the Communist Party.

In short, the influence and control of the Party is extended through the Youth League to larger organizations such as the Students' Federation, the Democratic Youth Federation, and other mass groups, and through them to youth in general. The ratio in both of the examples cited was roughly one Party member to ten League members, and one League member to four members of the larger organizations.

All of this organization generates a tremendous amount of activity, and it provides a stimulus and outlet for the energies of youth. Much of this activity takes the form of collective group study or work. The members of youth organizations hold endless meetings and parades, carry on group discussions and study Marxism-Lenin-ism and the thought of Mao Tse-tung, propagandize other elements in the population, help organize groups of all sorts and push the Party program, carry on political agitation, and take part in manual labor of many kinds. "Learning," "criticism," and "self-criticism" are virtually a way of life for the members of youth organizations, and every effort is made by youth leaders to achieve universal and complete orthodoxy, as defined by their interpretation of Marxism-Leninism.

The Youth League is particularly active. It publishes an official fortnightly called *China's Youth*, runs a Central League School to train cadres for the youth movement, manages an Arts College for Chinese Youth, and leads an organization for children nine to fifteen years old called the Pioneers. There is a weekly "League day" which all members devote to political study, exchange of "criticism and encouragement," lectures, short plays, mass singing, group recitations, and so on. League members put out newspapers and other publications, prepare radio programs, encourage physical exercise, and promote health, sanitation, and literacy drives. They take an active part in unions, cooperatives, labor exchanges, and so on. And above all, they "learn" and "study" the dogma passed down to them, and prepare themselves to play an active adult role in the Chinese revolution under Communist leadership.

These youth organizations illustrate the pattern the Communists aim to apply as widely as possible to different categories of the population. They are not entirely typical because among Chinese youth, particularly students, there is a higher degree of voluntary support of the Communists than among most other population groups, and youths are consequently more easily organized and directed. But the principles followed in organization of youth are applied generally, in varying degrees and slightly different forms, to other categories of the population.

The success the Communists thus far have had in using these techniques of organization to gain and consolidate power does not indicate, however, that their organizational pattern is now already firmly established in Chinese society. There is no doubt, as the writer can testify from personal observation, that the Communists' techniques are more effective, and influence the lives of more people, than previous efforts toward political organization in China. But it is nonetheless difficult to evaluate official claims that tens of millions of people are already effectively organized. The Communists attempt to convey the impression that the structure of their regime is already solid and monolithic, but it is almost impossible to estimate how many of the millions claimed to be members of mass organizations are really well integrated into the pattern the regime is attempting to establish.

There are reasons to believe, as a matter of fact, that the Communists have a long way to go before they can successfully reorganize the entire body politic of China, despite their accomplishments to date. The new pattern of organization has been instituted extensively, but very rapidly and probably not very deeply. Traditionally, furthermore, Chinese society has been extensively but not tightly organized, and the Chinese have exhibited a genius for passive opposition to radical changes in the organization of society, particularly to excessively rigid discipline and control. This tradition is one reason the Communists' forms of organization are so striking in China today, but it is also a reason to ask whether they will be successful ultimately in establishing such a new and thorough organizational pattern in Chinese society.

What the Communists have already been able to accomplish is to superimpose their new pattern upon the traditional organizational structure of China; the guilds, secret societies, and other legacies from the ancient and recent past have been temporarily eclipsed but not yet supplanted. It remains to be seen whether the Communists can fully and permanently impose their political organization upon Chinese society as a whole, or whether the traditional Chinese resistance to strict discipline, tight organization, and rigid control will assert itself in the long run.

3

SOCIAL CONTROLS

April, 1953

The first three years of Communist rule in China have been a period of consolidation of power. Many, if not most, of the Chinese Communists' policies during this phase of their program have been frankly transitional. Land distribution has been carried out to achieve the "elimination of the landlords as a class" and to pave the way for steps toward collectivization. Industrial production has been restored, and controls have been established over private enterprise, to make possible comprehensive state planning. And, as prescribed by the Common Program in 1949, the "people of all circles have been fully organized," preliminary to introduction of a more regularized, permanent system of government based upon people's congresses.

The task of organizing and achieving effective social control over the entire populace has received top priority, because in the last analysis this has been a prerequisite for implementation of all the other policies. The recent announcement that People's Congresses are to be elected during 1953 is a significant indication that the Communists themselves now believe that their controls are adequate and dependable enough to permit this step.

The myth, formerly accepted by many people, that no regime could effectively organize and discipline the Chinese people seems to have been exploded. Reports from refugees and persons expelled from China since the Communist takeover give a startling picture of regimentation. It appears that in three short years the Chinese Communists have in fact accomplished what must rank with the most phenomenal feats of social organization in history.

The control the Communists have established over the Chinese people is not a remote type exercised only at the top levels of administration. They have constructed an organizational apparatus that reaches deep into the grass-roots levels of the country and into the privacy of people's lives. Although our knowledge of this apparatus is still incomplete, the general outlines are sufficiently clear.

The Party itself is, of course, the controlling nerve center in the body politic of China today, and its cells and ganglia are located in every part of the country. The quarter-million basic Party branches, with approximately 6 million members, are distributed among villages, factories, and organizations, and they direct the control apparatus at every level.

The creation of a disciplined Party—an effective Leninist elite organized according to the principles of democratic centralism—has been one of the Communists' most remarkable accomplishments, for they have succeeded where others in China have tried and failed. How have they been able to achieve disciplined unity and to suppress or control the factionalism that has plagued other Chinese political groups? There can be no simple answer, but two important factors are worth mentioning. Despite rapid expansion of the Party, they have maintained tight controls over membership through careful selection, screening, indoctrination, and probationary testing. In addition, the concept of inner Party struggle has been extremely important. This process might be described as a ceaseless purge—not in the sense of physical liquidation, but rather of ideological purification, with the weapons of criticism and self-criticism, designed to maintain standards of loyalty, discipline, and orthodoxy.

The controlling position of the Communist Party in China, and of its members in any situation in the country, is sanctioned by the principle of leadership, according to which all other groups must defer to the alleged superior wisdom and authority of the Communists or risk being classified as reactionaries or counterrevolutionaries. The sanction of force is also essential, however. The Party came to power by military means, and the role of military force has continued to be important. Public Security army units garrison key centers throughout the country and provide support to the political functionaries of the Party even when the military remains in the background.

The controlled use of violence, terror, and class warfare in the Communists' mass campaigns during the past three years has also clearly indicated to the Chinese people that the members of the Party are backed by effective weapons of physical coercion, even when they rely on persuasion to achieve many of their aims. The hundreds of thousands of "undesirable elements" publicly executed during the "Agrarian Reform" program of 1950–52 and the Campaign Against "Counterrevolutionaries" in 1951 do not represent a large proportion of the Chinese population, but the execu-

tions have created an atmosphere of fear and an attitude of submissiveness which affect the majority of the population, and they
have removed many of the potential leaders of opposition. Class
warfare in both countryside and city, furthermore, has undermined
the solidarity of local interests that might have joined in opposition to the Communists.

The legal vacuum in which the Communists have operated since
their takeover has also reinforced their controlling position. Upon
assuming power, they abolished "all laws, decrees, and judicial
systems" previously existing in China, and although a few laws
and many decrees with the force of law have issued from the Communist-controlled Central People's Government since then, no
general codification has yet been completed. In this situation,
there has been no possibility of appeal to previous laws, customs,
or traditions against the policies of the Communist Party or the
will of its local functionaries. The Communist-established People's
Courts have been responsible for enforcing policies more often
than laws, and the regulations establishing the courts specifically
state that "Where no [legal] provisions have been made, the policy
of the Central People's Government [i.e., Chinese Communist
Party] shall be adhered to."

The few definite laws that have been promulgated merely provide "legal" justification for the revolutionary policies of the CCP,
and are generally applied *ex post facto* to the period prior to the
Communist takeover. The vague terminology in many of the laws,
furthermore, leaves ample room for interpretation according to the
whims of local Party leaders. The regulations concerning counterrevolutionaries, for example, authorize severe punishment, including even the death sentence, for such vague crimes as "conducting
counterrevolutionary propaganda and agitation" and "fabricating
and spreading rumors."

All these factors—the discipline within the Party, the unchal-
lengeable principle of Party leadership, the ever-present backing
of military force, the selective use of terror, the elimination of
potential opposition leaders, the social disruption of class warfare,
and the use of law to support revolutionary political action—help
to explain how a minority of 1–2 per cent of the population has
been able to carry through the organizational, propaganda, and
indoctrination programs through which it has established effective
social control over the most populous nation on earth.

The Communist Party does not rely solely upon its membership,
however, for the role of non-Party *kanpu* (cadres or political work-

ers) is extremely important. Recruited largely from youth and from
the "activists" who emerge in every locality during Communist-
conducted mass campaigns, these political workers are supported
by the Party and subject to its discipline. Huge numbers of them
have been mobilized during the past three years.

After these workers have been indoctrinated, trained, and organized into small groups, they are sent on assignments all over the
country, to work in direct contact with the masses and to help
implement Communist policies. They are, in effect, a tremendous
corps of political extension workers who help bridge the gap
between the making of high-level decisions and implementation
at the grass-roots level. In short, the Chinese Communists, when
they want to carry out a policy, do not merely issue orders and
instructions or rely solely on the established bureaucracy to carry
them out. They also dispatch specially trained groups of Party
members and non-Party political workers to assist the regular Party
and government hierarchy. There has been no shortage of volunteers for this political work. For youth, the work provides an outlet
for energy and enthusiasm and a sense of participation in important
activities. For anyone, furthermore, virtually the only stepping
stone to prestige, influence, and power in China today is political
work of some sort.

One of the principal responsibilities of Party members and
political workers is the development of mass political organizations,
and these organizations are an important element in the apparatus
of control. It is not an exaggeration to say that the ultimate aim
is to bring all people, except for elements branded as political
pariahs, into mass organizations under Party control, and considerable progress has already been made in that direction. All these
organizations carry out propaganda, agitation, indoctrination, and
other activities, and they are undoubtedly the agencies through
which the Party apparatus has the strongest impact on the average
individual. The mass political organizations serve a dual purpose.
On the one hand, they mobilize the energy and enthusiasm of
supporters of Communist policies and direct them into channels
considered important by the regime. They also facilitate surveillance, intimidation, and control of nonsupporters.

Supporting organizational control measures of this kind, the
Communists have established extremely effective ideological controls and have progressed very far toward their aim of complete
thought control. In many respects, their techniques of propaganda
and indoctrination, utilizing mass psychology, are the most dis-

tinctive feature of the regime. For the Chinese Communists, at least at this stage, seem to rely more on the control of people's minds, and less on crude police repression, than their mentors in the Soviet Union.

The volume of propaganda output in China today is staggering. Radio, motion pictures, the press, and other publications are devoted wholly to propaganda purposes, but the Communists do not confine themselves merely to these modern means of communicating ideas. In addition, propaganda themes, slogans, and symbols are injected into entertainment media such as operas and rural story-telling, into the arts (painting, drama, music, and dancing), and even into industrial products (for example, machine-knitted garters bearing slogans such as "Aid Korea and oppose America").

Great stress is also placed upon meetings, parades, demonstrations, and oral propaganda. A propaganda network of oral agitators, who work directly under the Party's propaganda machine and are fed ideas and material by it, is responsible for carrying the Party line directly into people's homes. One of the mottos proclaims, without a trace of humor, that they are to "replace family gossip with talks on current events." There are already more than 2 million propagandists in this network.

Even more important than propaganda as such in its possible long-run implications is the method of indoctrination through small discussion groups, now being widely used by the Communists to indoctrinate not only active political elements but also the masses of ordinary people in China. The aim is to introduce Marxism-Leninism and the thought of Mao Tse-tung as a universally accepted ideology, supplanting traditional Chinese ideas and values.

The indoctrination in these groups varies in intensity and is given various labels (it is most commonly called *hsueh hsi* [study] or *szu hsiang kai tsao* [ideological reform]), but certain basic principles are characteristic of the process in all its forms. The groups are small, usually with fewer than a dozen members. Almost always one or more members have been previously indoctrinated, and a designated group leader reports attitudes and opinions to higher authorities. Meetings are held at regular fixed periods, often for an hour a day, and they are generally convened at one's place of work. The subjects for discussion and the material to be discussed are given to the groups, whose members are then expected to discuss thoroughly all aspects of the question under consideration.

Discussion of a single question may be extended over several weeks, or even months.

One aim of the discussion process is to have aired all possible heterodox views and then to have the group demolish them through criticism and self-criticism. A premium is placed on confession of past errors. No one can be a passive participant in such a group, and discussion on a question is not ended until each member expresses acceptance of the "correct" Party line. If, after prolonged discussion, a member persists in holding out against the orthodox viewpoint, he runs the risk of punishment—which may be more intensive indoctrination or something worse. Perhaps the most distinctive aspect of this group indoctrination is the way in which intense social pressure is generated within the group, by the participating members themselves, to force complete conformity, at least on the surface, to the Communist-approved line.

So far, I have not even mentioned the hierarchy of government itself as an instrument of social control in Communist China, although obviously the government bureaucracy, controlled by the Communist Party, is extremely important. And during the past three years this bureaucracy has expanded both in its size and in its functions.

Two general categories of controls over the population exercised by the government bureaucracy at the lower levels of society deserve mention here. Since their takeover, the Communists have transformed and adapted traditional forms of neighborhood organizations which have a long history in China. They have also adapted and refined modern techniques of police-state control which are a more recent innovation.

The *Pao-Chia* system reintroduced by the Chinese Nationalists to organize and control the population was a major target of Chinese Communist denunciation prior to 1949, and the system was abolished when the Communists took power. But in its place a new system of an almost identical nature has been set up in China's cities. The principal change has been a simplification of the structure in which one level of organization, the Residents' Committee (*Chu Min Wei Yuan Hui*), has been substituted for both *Pao* and *Chia*. If anything, however, the new neighborhood associations seem to be under more effective control than their predecessors, owing to an expansion of the number of Public Security police outposts (*P'ai Ch'u So*) which closely supervise them.

In the countryside, the situation is somewhat different, but the result appears to be about the same. In each village, the Peasants'

Association, which at least for a period of time possesses extraordinary powers and serves as a revolutionary junta to carry out land reform, and the village militia units, organized on a permanent basis, seem to have taken over the control functions of the old *Pao-Chia* system. In both city and country, the government bureaucracy at all levels has Public Security bureaus whose responsibilities include general political control as well as maintenance of order.

Secret police organizations exist in Communist China under both the Ministry of Public Security of the government and the Bureau of Social Affairs of the Party's Central Committee, but not a great deal is known of their operations. They do not appear to be as omnipresent as their counterparts in the Soviet Union. One important public manifestation of police-state controls, however, is a system of so-called Public Security committees, established on a nationwide basis in 1952. These committees, composed of three to eleven members each, are to be organized in every village, factory, institution, and organization in the country "to organize and lead the masses to help the government and public security organs to denounce, supervise, and control counterrevolutionary elements" and "to protect the state and public order." In short, a nationwide system of police informers has been organized. Anonymous denunciations have also been legalized and systematized by such devices as "people's opinion boxes" run by the local representatives of the Committee on People's Supervision. These and similar measures have contributed to a general atmosphere of mutual suspicion which effectively inhibits the expression of any opinions in conflict with the official line.

The total web of organizational and ideological controls in Communist China appears to have brought the entire population under control of the ruling group to an unprecedented degree. A situation has been created in which there seems to be little likelihood of successful organized opposition to the Communists within China, regardless of the state of "public opinion," so long as the Communists can maintain their control apparatus.

The Communists are now using their control over the population not only to maintain their power but also to engineer one of the most thorough revolutions of modern times, for, as Mao stated in the summer of 1949, the Chinese Communist leaders regard the conquest of power not as the final aim of their revolution but rather as the "first step in a long march of 10,000 li."

4

PARTY CONSOLIDATION

December, 1953

After fifteen years of rapid growth during its revolutionary struggle for power, the Chinese Communist Party—the ruling bureaucracy in China today—has slowed down its organizational expansion and is now engaged in a process of consolidation. In some areas of China, the Party has temporarily stopped, or limited, recruitment of certain types of new members. In other areas—particularly south China, where a shortage of Party personnel exists—expansion of Party membership is still being promoted, but there is evidence that the Communists have not had spectacular success during recent months in attracting large numbers of new members.

The hasty expansion of the Party in earlier years created many problems, and the Chinese Communists are now trying to weed out undesirables, improve training and indoctrination, and tighten up Party discipline. The change in the Party's status, from a growing revolutionary elite achieving success after success to a relatively stabilized ruling bureaucracy facing problem after problem, has created new organizational and morale problems. In general, the psychological atmosphere in which the Party works—as well as one can sense it from Hong Kong—seems to have undergone some subtle changes. The high pitch of emotional fervor has waned perceptibly, and there is more talk of overwork and bureaucratic ossification.

Nevertheless, the unity, discipline, and basic strength of the CCP seem unimpaired four years after its rise to power, and the Party is continuing the process of consolidation. No major ideological schisms are visible, at least from the outside, and the Communists are still able to cope with the Party's internal problems primarily by indoctrination and organizational methods. Moreover, they still maintain unprecedented control over the entire country. Hong Kong, a refugee haven with a 22-mile common border facing Communist China, has received no important political defectors from the CCP during the past four years.

At the start of the Sino-Japanese War, the Chinese Communist Party was a relatively small organization, with perhaps 40,000 members concentrated in northwest China. But the political vacuum that Japanese invasion created in north China and the effectiveness of the Communists' guerrilla tactics and rural program led to a phenomenal expansion after 1937. By 1945, the Chinese Communists had 1.2 million members. The momentum continued, and even increased, during the ensuing civil-war period, and by the time the Communists achieved a predominance of power in China, in 1949, Party membership had more than doubled over the 1945 figure. Rapid growth continued during the Communists' first two years in power, and by mid-1951 the official figure for Party membership had reached 5.8 million.

This figure had been accepted, for lack of more up-to-date information, until an announcement made this July by An Tzu-wen, Deputy Director of the Organization Department of the Chinese Communist Party, placing membership at a total of 6.1 million. In short, the net increase in membership during the past two years has been roughly 5 per cent—as compared with an increase of almost 50 per cent during the previous two years, immediately after the Communists came to power in China.

Actual trends within the CCP are not indicated simply by these over-all membership figures, of course. The figures do not even reveal the total numbers of persons recruited during the last two-year period, because more than a half-million Party members were ousted in the same period during a single major purge, in an effort to improve Party discipline and efficiency.

Shortly before the Communists formalized their conquest in the fall of 1949, top Chinese Communist leaders began to show considerable concern about the effects of rapid Party expansion and political victory. In March of that year, Mao Tse-tung made a speech on the subject which is still constantly quoted:

In view of our victory, there may appear within our Party such phenomena as conceit, pride, self-complacency, and lack of desire to advance, aspiration only for personal welfare and pleasures, lack of desire to struggle further against difficulties and lead a frugal life.

In view of our victory, the people will be grateful to us. The bourgeoisie will flatter us. The enemy cannot defeat us, this has already been proved. But weak-willed people in our ranks may succumb to the flattery of the bourgeoisie. There may be such Communists, who had never bowed to an armed enemy and who in the struggle against the enemy had proved worthy of being called a hero, but who now will not be able to resist those who attack them with "sugar-coated" bullets, and will succumb to them.

During the following two years, more and more questions were raised by Party leaders about the quality of Party membership. It was asserted that standards for joining the Party had often been lowered, applicants had not been properly examined or indoctrinated, and "alien elements" had penetrated the apparatus, creating a "serious threat to Party organizations."

As a result, in March, 1951, a special conference called by the Party Central Committee decided to launch a "Rectification" campaign throughout the entire Party. Today, over two years later, the campaign is still in progress. (A study recently made by the Union Research Institute, a Chinese research organization in Hong Kong, provides many details on this campaign; what follows draws heavily on this study.)

This campaign is one that involves a recheck and reregistration of every member of the Party. Carried out by basic Party branches, it involves first a review of the ideological development and actual work record of each member, a process carried out by criticism and self-criticism. If a member is found to be not fully qualified, he is subjected to re-education designed to correct his "erroneous views" and shortcomings. A member who is labeled an "alien element" is expelled from the Party. This label is applied to eight types of persons: elements of an "alien class," former members of "reactionary parties or reactionary religious sects" who have not severed "organizational or ideological ties" with them, persons "suspected of being enemies of the Party," speculators, former betrayers of the Party who have reinfiltrated, persons hiding serious offenses in their political past, violators of state laws and discipline, and corrupt elements.

To date, this campaign has been completed in basic Party organizations within the government, and has been "completed for the most part" within urban Party branches such as those in schools and industries, but it still has a long way to go in rural villages, where it is scheduled for completion next spring.

In 1952, the Chinese Communist Central Committee also launched an intensive "Three-Anti" campaign against corruption, waste, and bureaucratism, which ran simultaneously with the Rectification campaign but was applied to all government institutions, mass organizations, and army units as well as to the Party itself. This frenetic movement, "to purify" Party organizations and "to defeat the attacks of the law-breaking elements of the bourgeoisie," resulted in the expulsion of many people from the Party, as well as the reindoctrination of others, and a reregistration was carried out for all Party members involved in the campaign.

One result of these two campaigns has been the purging of about 10 per cent of the total CCP membership, or more than a half-million persons. Of this total, 3–5 per cent were expelled as "alien elements," while 5–7 per cent "admitted lacking the qualifications required of a Communist and have voluntarily resigned" (some were "advised to resign"). There is no doubt that the two campaigns have accomplished a good deal in tightening up centralized Party control and discipline.

Another result, of perhaps equal importance, has been the reindoctrination of Party members and the furtherance of ideological conformity within the Party. This emphasis upon conducting ideological struggle within the Party and "re-educating" as many wayward members as possible (instead of simply executing or exiling deviationists) seems to be one of the distinctive characteristics of the CCP. Ever since the wartime Cheng Feng movement launched by the Communists in 1942, there have been periodic special campaigns for "Ideological Reform" within the Party in China, and in many respects there has been an almost constant struggle for ideological uniformity. The philosophical basis for this approach to internal Party problems is most clearly expressed in a book (first given as a lecture in 1941) called *On Inner Party Struggle*, by Liu Shao-ch'i, one of the top Chinese Communist leaders. Liu advocates continuous ideological struggle within the Party against all deviations, stating: "The upholding of Party discipline and Party unity does not in the main depend on the punishment of comrades (if they have to be upheld in such a manner it signifies a crisis in the Party), but rather on the actual unity of the Party in ideology and principle, and on the consciousness of the vast majority of Party members."

The process of Party consolidation, of which these campaigns are a part, is one of the most important aspects of Party developments in Communist China at the present time, and it is likely to continue to be so, at least until completion of the current Rectification campaign.

The slowdown of Communist Party organizational expansion has been most noticeable in the northern part of China. This is not surprising. The main growth of the Party took place in the north, for it was there that the Party first established its power. As a result, there are many more northerners than southerners in the Party, and despite broad distribution of members all over the country during the past four years there are still more of them working in the north than in the south.

In addition, since the Communists shifted the "center of gravity of Party work" from the countryside to the cities in 1949, they have wanted to increase the proletarian element in their basically peasant organization. Consequently, the admission of new Party members in the villages of "old liberated areas," which are in the north, has been "temporarily stopped," and even in "newly liberated areas" where personnel shortages are not acute, admission of new peasant members has been "limited."

At present, great stress is being placed on the need to recruit industrial workers for Party membership. However, although there are reports of quite a number of industrial workers joining the Party, the total urban working class in China is so small, relatively, that the Communists' possibilities along this line are limited. The basic character of the CCP as an organization of primarily peasant origin is still unchanged, therefore, although the significance of this fact can easily be overestimated since there is no doubt that most of these ex-peasants have been, in a sense, "proletarianized" and seem to act like quite a different breed from the majority of peasants.

The Party's situation in much of south China, the "backward area," is quite different from that in the north. "Liberated" last, the Central-South Administrative Region and Southwest Administrative Region are still behind most of the rest of the country in implementing many Communist policies. And one of the basic problems in these regions is the shortage of Party members and other qualified political workers. Therefore, when the Party Central Committee issued instructions last May to strengthen Party-building, the problem of expanding Party membership applied particularly to areas in China south of the Yangtze.

As the recruiting campaign got under way, particularly in the central-south and southwest, many official reports revealed the existing weakness of Party organization in various areas. Discussing the central-south, the Wuhan *Yangtze Daily* stated that in some government organs Party members constituted only 10.9 per cent of the staff, that in some universities there were few or no Party members among the teachers, and that it had been impossible to set up strong Party branches in some business organs. The *New China Daily* in Chungking cited similar facts about the southwest and admitted that among more than 20,000 *Hsiang* in the region, 93 per cent still had no Party branches.

The Party expansion campaign to rectify this situation was carefully organized. The priorities for recruiting new members were defined as follows: "progressive elements" from among urban workers, "peasant activists" in rural areas where land reform had been completed, and activists in government organs and schools. Instructions were issued that responsible Party members should be designated as both full-time and part-time organizers in the campaign. Propaganda accompanying the campaign was extensive. And detailed stipulations were made on the qualifications for membership and the methods for selecting, examining, training, and finally initiating new recruits.

Apparently, however, there was no general rush to join the Party. Perhaps this was partly because the Party makes very heavy demands on its members. The discipline of the CCP is demanding, to say the least. One of the "eight qualifications" for membership adopted by the Party in April, 1951, requires a recruit to prove that he is "determined to carry on this revolutionary struggle heroically for the rest of his life." Others require pledges to "carry out faithfully the resolutions of the Party and observe strictly the discipline of the Party" and to put "the interests of the Party above their own private interests."

The rather discouraging initial results of the campaign led to inevitable recriminations. One explanation of the disappointing showing (this one appeared in the *New China Daily*, but similar statements were published in official organs in other regions) was as follows: "In the first place, many Party Committees did not recognize the importance of Party expansion work and did not want to participate in the practical leadership of the work; and, in the second place, many Party members did not want to take the trouble and the responsibility of acting as the sponsors of active elements."

The final results of the campaign last year were never officially revealed, but it is clear that the drive did not solve the problem of personnel shortages; Party expansion is still considered an important task in many southern areas, and there are still numerous complaints of too few Party members and inadequate recruitment. Undoubtedly, the Communists in time will be able to fill the gaps in their Party's ranks in south China, but the difficulties they have been having are an indication not only of the special problems they still face in the south (which often in the past has been a difficult region for Chinese central governments to control and rule), but also perhaps of a certain weariness and the inability of some members of the Party to maintain their ardor at peak intensity.

Although the Three-Anti campaign against corruption, waste, and bureaucratism last year purged large numbers of Party members and gave the entire Party a vigorous shaking up, the struggle against these trends, and particularly against bureaucratism, still continues. It seems almost inevitable that the longer the Communists are in power, the more tendencies there will be toward bureaucratic hardening of arteries, but they are still strongly resisting such tendencies. An Tzu-wen (in the same statement cited earlier) said: "The Three-Anti movement was directed mainly against waste and corruption. The struggle against bureaucracy demands a much longer period, since the bureaucracy that exists now in China has deep historical roots and a broad economic foundation, and cannot be eliminated in one blow."

Another source of current concern to the Communist leaders is what they call "commandism"—the inclination of Party members increasingly to employ arbitrary force and compulsion in their dealings with people. It is admitted that many Communists "rudely insult and beat up people." The Chinese Communists would not admit that their entire revolutionary program rests basically upon compulsion—which seems clearly to be the case if one recognizes the coercive element in the many methods of "persuasion" they use—but they apparently are worried about the possibility of alienating people by excessive use of crude methods of compulsion and arbitrary exercise of power by Party members.

When problems of this sort come to the fore, the Communist leaders respond almost automatically by starting a new campaign. The Rectification campaign, already described, is not the only inner Party struggle of this sort now going on, therefore. Combined with it is a Campaign Against "Bureaucratism, 'Commandism,' and Violation of Laws and Discipline," which was inaugurated this January by the Party's Central Committee and is still being carried on.

Struggle (*Tou Cheng*) is the keynote in the life of a member of the CCP; as soon as he starts to relax, his leaders begin to get worried and think up new things for him to struggle against—including his own tendency to relax.

Some observers of developments in China have wondered how long the Communists can maintain this state of exhausting tension without some real relaxation. To date, there has been no indication of any general let-down. In the past few months, there have been hints, however, that in some areas the Communists realize they have piled too much onto Party members, and steps have been taken to lighten the load.

One of the most interesting indications of this is the current movement against "Five Too Many," started in June of this year in rural north China. "What stands out most strikingly this year," stated the Peking *People's Daily* in an article on the movement soon after it started, "is the fact that too many urgent tasks assigned by superior organs have given rise to a series of problems such as 'Five Too Many'—too many meetings, too many documents and forms, too many training courses, too many organizations, and too many posts for *Hsiang* and *Ts'un* [village] cadres. This phenomenon has not only added numerous difficulties to the *Hsiang* and *Ts'un* cadres but has hindered peasants' production efforts." The article admitted that this situation has "caused discontent among a section of the peasants," and it urged that steps be taken against "blind enthusiasm," impatience, and overzealousness on the part of leading Party organs responsible for this state of affairs.

None of these trends indicates any real internal weakening of the Chinese Communist Party, however. All evidence points to the fact that the Party remains an effective totalitarian instrument which, by and large, has maintained the "iron discipline" and unity that Lenin prescribed as essential for any Communist Party's organization. But the trends do suggest that adjustments and changes are taking place as the CCP moves slowly toward becoming a relatively stabilized ruling bureaucracy, increasingly subject to all the problems of "bureaucratism."

5

FORCED LABOR

January, 1955

Last November, a European newspaperman who had just completed a quick tour of Communist China came across the international border to Hong Kong and reported to the world, confidently: "I feel entitled to say that neither labor camps nor concentration camps exist in China today. No one talks about them, whispers about them, or even assumes they exist."

This claim, apparently made in good faith, unfortunately had been contradicted by the Chinese Communists themselves two months earlier when they publicly stated that four out of five convicts in China were then engaged in forced, unpaid labor for the state under a system called "Reform Through Labor."

In September, the Chinese Communists published their "Regulations on Reform Through Labor," which describe in detail the system of forced labor that has steadily been put into effect during the past five years and is now legally applicable to the entire Chinese penal system. On the day these regulations were published, September 7, the official Peking *People's Daily* carried an editorial which said:

> During the past few years, we have achieved great results in the work of reform of criminals through labor. According to statistical returns from different areas, of the criminals in confinement throughout the country, more than 83 per cent have participated in agricultural and industrial production, or have been organized into various engineering corps for the felling of timber, construction of buildings, restoration and construction of conservancy works, and the building of railways and highways.

Some of the difficulties and pecularities of studying present-day Communist China are illustrated by this case. Observers living outside China's borders are gravely handicapped by their inability to view situations on the spot; consequently, they search eagerly for eyewitness reports of conditions and developments within China. But observations made by persons visiting China are frequently of limited value; sometimes, they are either of dubious reliability or clearly erroneous. Many aspects of life under Communism in China are not easily observable, and the best one can hope for is fragmentary evidence about them. Forced labor fits into this category. During recent years, quite a few refugees coming to Hong Kong have reported observing, or participating in, forced labor, but there has been no basis for obtaining an accurate picture of how extensive the system is throughout the country or exactly how it is organized. Now, however, the evidence has been provided by the Communists themselves in official publications. The bureaucratese of the Regulations on Reform Through Labor adopted by the government in Peking last August 26, and the official reports and newspaper editorials that heralded publication of the regulations, reveal more about forced labor in China than all the fragmentary reports of refugees and visitors during recent years.

An interesting commentary on legal concepts in Communist China is provided by the fact that forced labor has gradually been put into effect during the past five years, prior to promulgation of any formal law regulating it. During this long period, the "legality" of the system has rested upon a flimsy basis consisting of two brief references to Reform Through Labor, one in an article written by Mao Tse-tung in his capacity as Chairman of the Chinese Communist Party and the other in a general statement of government policy made by the Communist-appointed People's Political Consultative Conference when the Peking Government was first established.

In "On People's Democratic Dictatorship," published July 1, 1949, Mao Tse-tung wrote:

As for those belonging to reactionary classes or groups, after their political power has been overthrown, we will also give them land and work, permitting them to make a living and to reform themselves through labor into new persons—but only on condition that they do not rebel, sabotage, or create disturbances. If they do not want to work, the people's state will force them to do so. Furthermore, the propaganda and educational work directed toward them will be carried out with the same care and thoroughness as the work already conducted among captured army officers. This may also be spoken of as a "benevolent" policy, but it will be compulsorily imposed upon those originally from enemy classes.

It would have been difficult to predict that this rather vague statement would be used to justify a general system of forced labor applicable to all inmates of penal institutions.

Article 7 of the Common Program was only a little less vague:

> The People's Republic of China must suppress all counterrevolutionary activities, severely punish all Kuomintang counterrevolutionary war criminals and other obdurate arch-counterrevolutionary elements who collude with imperialism, commit treason against the fatherland, and oppose the cause of People's Democracy. Reactionary elements, feudal landlords, and bureaucratic capitalists in general must, according to law, also be deprived of their political rights within a necessary period after they have been disarmed and their special political rights abolished; but at the same time they shall be given a means of living and compelled to reform themselves through labor to become new men.

On the basis of these two somewhat cryptic statements, forced labor has developed in China to the point where it involves more than 80 per cent of all prisoners of the state—ordinary as well as political prisoners, and "criminals" awaiting trial as well as persons already convicted. Now, however, in the words of the Peking *People's Daily*, the recently adopted regulations "have affirmed in legal form our state's policy and measures for the enforcement of compulsory labor service."

The system of forced labor sanctioned by these regulations is modeled on the system in the U.S.S.R.—"Soviet legal experts" helped to draft the regulations—but there are some differences in details. As in the Soviet Union, compulsory labor is applicable to all persons convicted or detained in penal institutions, at the discretion of the state; the regulations cover not only "counterrevolutionaries" (a broad term that is applied flexibly), but also all "other criminals." A person does not have to be convicted of a crime to be included; the regulations apply to "criminals not yet sentenced." In one respect, the Chinese system goes further than its Soviet model. All prisoners in China can be put to work without pay under Reform Through Labor, whereas in the U.S.S.R. the system provides, on paper at least, for a sliding scale of wages based upon the seriousness of offenses.

Altogether, there are seventy-seven articles in the Chinese Communists' regulations. They deal with the general principles of Reform Through Labor, describe the penal institutions that implement them, and outline in some detail the rules and practices that are now to be put into effect on a nationwide basis.

The fundamental policy of Reform Through Labor, it is stated, is to "coordinate punishment and control with ideological reform, and to coordinate labor production and political education." There is no doubt that the system does aim at "reform" of prisoners—to "make them new men" in the Communist sense—as well as exploitation of their labor. The Communists are determined to make every prisoner "bow his head and confess his sins" as well as to "earn merits and expiate sins." This self-righteous, moralistic theme is a constant one in their approach to criminology as well as in measures of social control applied to the entire population. The Regulations on Reform Through Labor make clear, in fact, that the release of any prisoner, even at the end of his term, depends upon his having acquired acceptable attitudes; anyone's term of Reform Through Labor may be extended by the authorities if he has "failed in getting reformed." Although prisoners are given political indoctrination throughout their period of imprisonment, however, it seems probable that their "reform" is less important to the regime than the value of their free labor. While the regulations require that "study" generally "shall not average less than one hour a day," they specify that the "period of labor for criminals shall generally be from nine to ten hours," and may be as high as twelve hours, per day.

Four different types of penal institutions in Communist China, all of which function as forced-labor organizations, are described in the regulations: detention houses, prisons, Reform Through Labor corps, and institutes for juvenile delinquents. The last three are set up not only by the Central Government but also by governments at provincial and municipal levels. Detention houses are even more extensive; they are maintained by all governments down to and including the *Hsien* and in some cases the subdistricts within cities.

Detention houses are "used mainly for the custody of criminals not yet sentenced," but they are also used to hold convicts with short sentences, of two years or less, who cannot "conveniently" be sent away to a Reform Through Labor corps. Prisoners in these detention houses can all be "organized for appropriate labor service." They provide a very large number of penal laborers, scattered in small groups all over the country, who are used by local governments for many projects including the construction of public works.

Larger prisons are designed primarily for convicted prisoners who are "not suited to labor service in the open"—either because they are important persons and must be confined for security reasons, or because health considerations are involved. Included are "counterrevolutionary criminals" sentenced to life imprisonment or given a "suspended death sentence." Exemption from "labor service in the open" does not free these people from work, however. On the contrary, they are under particularly severe discipline and are made to work within prison, at things such as handicraft manufacturing.

In the institutes for juvenile delinquents, special emphasis is placed upon "education in politics, in the new moral code, and in basic cultural subjects and production technique." But the inmates, whose ages range from thirteen to eighteen, are also "made to perform light labor service."

The Reform Through Labor corps are perhaps the most important element in the system. These are working groups, often containing many thousands of men, which are subdivided into branches and large, medium, and small divisions. Their members are convicts who can do "labor service in the open"—that is, outside of prison but under guard—on farms, in factories, or on public-works projects. It is clear that the regime considers most prisoners as falling into this category.

The entire system is organized and run by police under the Ministry of Public Security and its local organs. However, People's Procurators are responsible for general supervision over it; People's Courts are involved in numerous related judicial matters such as decisions on the release of prisoners or extension of their terms; and relevant economic organs in the government take part in determining the use of convict labor.

The economic importance to the regime of Reform Through Labor is clearly revealed in the regulations on the system and in other writing about it. The production of prisoners is, in fact, integrated into the government's general economic plans. Reform Through Labor, say the regulations, shall "serve the interests of national construction and be included in the state's over-all production and construction plans." Decisions on how convict labor will be used are made by top economic bodies in the government, with guidance from departments of agriculture, forestry, industry, finance, communications, water conservancy, and commerce. At each of the higher levels of government administration, special committees are established, with representatives of financial and economic bodies as well as of the police and courts, to manage the production of forced labor.

By and large, most prisoners are put to work on projects in local areas, but they can be transferred as needed to remote parts of the country. Plans for such transfers are drawn up by the Ministry of Public Security, but all moves except temporary and small-scale ones must have the approval of the Central Government's cabinet.

The prisoners can be made to do virtually any type of work, including farming, lumbering, manufacturing, construction, road work, and so on. The economic value to the state of this controlled, unpaid labor force was given great emphasis in a general report on Reform Through Labor made in August by the Minister of Public Security, Lo Jui-ch'ing. After reporting that criminals in China have been organized to "carry out production on a considerably large scale," Lo said:

> During the past four years, we have established many farms for re- form through labor, and among them are many larger farms of over 10,000 *mow* [over 1,600 acres] of land each. We have also estab- lished considerable numbers of industrial production units, and many engineering corps for the repair of conservancy works, build- ing of railways, felling of timber, and construction of buildings for the state. These production enterprises have not only benefited the development of the state's various construction enterprises, but also produced a considerable savings in the expenditure of the state and created wealth to a definite amount.

Just how much the thousands of forced laborers in Communist China have contributed to the national economy to date was placed in doubt, however, by another statement made by the Minister of Security in his report. He said that after deduction of the living costs of the convicts and other "necessary expenses," "the income from production of Reform Through Labor . . . has been accumulated, in the form of fixed capital and fluid capital, to an amount approximately equal to the expenses appropriated by the state for Reform Through Labor." It is difficult to know exactly what he meant by this, but if he meant that the net value of the production of forced labor just balances the over-all costs of maintaining the system, one would conclude either that the labor is relatively unproductive or the costs of administering the system are remarkably high. It is startling that immense net profits are not shown from a system providing free labor in such huge quan- tities.

No statistics have ever been published on the total number of prisoners in penal institutions in Communist China, but the total is certainly in the hundreds of thousands, probably in the millions. Each of the major campaigns in Communist China—Agrarian

Reform, the Campaign Against Counterrevolutionaries, the "Five-Anti" campaign—has sent thousands of victims into places of detention, and China's convict population undoubtedly includes more political and class enemies of the regime than ordinary criminals. When one adds persons classified as counterrevolutionaries, reactionaries, bureaucratic capitalists, bandits, local despots, unreformed landlords, secret agents, members of antagonistic classes, and deviationists to the more standard criminal categories of gangsters, robbers, swindlers, arsonists, rapists, and murderers, as well as "other undesirable characters left over from the old society," it seems probable that the total in Communist China is in the millions. And at present 83 per cent of the total are reportedly engaged in forced labor.

There is no doubt that the leaders of Communist China hope that penal labor which is "forced, unpaid, and subject to strict control" will in time make a large contribution to "national construction." The few criminal laws that they have drafted so far guarantee, in fact, that the supply of forced labor can be almost limitless—or rather limited merely by practical rather than legal considerations. The vagueness of their "Regulations on the Punishment of Counterrevolutionaries," and of their whole approach to law, makes it possible in effect for the state to arrest anyone it chooses, and all prisoners are subject to forced labor. Furthermore, the Regulations on Reform Through Labor provide that any prisoners' sentences may be indefinitely extended, while those who are released can still be kept under state control. These last features are undoubtedly the worst ones in the regulations from the prisoners' point of view, because they raise the prospect of perpetual detention. If it is alleged that a prisoner "fails to engage actively in labor service, frequently violates prison regulations, and is factually proved to have failed in getting reformed," his sentence can be extended. Even if a prisoner is "released," he still "may be accommodated by an organ enforcing reform through labor and be placed in employment" if he "desires to remain" in a labor corps, or has no home or job to which to return, or is "in a place extensive in area and sparse in population" where "there is need for him to participate in local resettlement measures." In the last instance, a prisoner shall "go through the procedure of being released," and thereafter he receives wages for his work, but he is still under the strict control of the state. In short, the state can decide to retain the services of any convict in China, even after the end of his sentence.

These, in brief, are a few of the most important features of the system of forced labor now operating in China, as described in official documents and publications.

But these few facts are cold and barren; the human element is entirely lacking in the regulations, reports, and newspaper articles from which they are gleaned. What actually happens to the hundreds of thousands, or millions, of unpaid prisoners who now spend their days working in labor gangs all over Communist China? What sort of places do they live in? What do they eat? What sort of people are they? What sort of men are the policemen who keep them under constant guard? How are the convicts really treated? What is their attitude toward "reform"? What is their attitude toward work? What do they think? What is the effect of Reform Through Labor on them? These and a thousand other questions cannot be answered.

It is in the hope of learning something of the human element of situations and developments in Communist China that observers in Hong Kong eagerly search out travelers from the mainland and question them on what they have heard and seen. But travelers have not been able to throw much light on the Reform Through Labor system. Most of what we know comes from analysis of the dry, bureaucratic, and lifeless prose of the Chinese Communist publications that come across the border.

PART III

PROPAGANDA AND
INDOCTRINATION

6

PROPAGANDA

November, 1952

"The aim of all our efforts," Mao Tse-tung wrote in "On New Democracy," published in 1940, "has been the building of a new society and a new nation of the Chinese people. In such a new society and new nation, along with a new political organization and a new economy, a new culture must arise."

To achieve this "new culture," the Communists are conducting an all-out ideological assault on the minds of the people of China, and probably more time, effort, and energy are devoted to the task of influencing what people think than to any other activity in China today. The goal is complete thought control, and the propaganda apparatus established by the Party and state is tremendous and pervasive.

Marxist dogma maintains that any society's economic and political systems determine its culture, but the Chinese Communists, while asserting their Marxist orthodoxy, seem to believe that they must first revolutionize attitudes, opinions, and ideas in order to create a firm foundation for their planned economic, political, and social changes.

Several important premises underlie the way in which the Chinese Communists operate. They believe that everything the people feel, think, and do is of concern to the Party and the government. Nothing is "nonpolitical." For example, whether a peasant plants wheat or cotton can be a political matter because the state usually has a definite opinion on which he should plant—depending on the time and place—and therefore the peasant's attitude on this question reflects his attitude toward the state. If a man beats his wife, this is not merely a personal problem but a political offense because the man obviously is opposing the Communists' policies on emancipation of women. A professor who wants to spend all his time on laboratory research, and balks at attending time-consuming political meetings, is showing dangerous "bourgeois" traits of "individualism," "separating theory and practice," "divorcing himself from the masses"; these traits cannot be ignored.

In China today there is an officially sanctioned, "correct" line defining almost all human attitudes and behavior, and if a person violates the line, serious ideological implications are involved. Such a person must not only correct the specific actions and attitudes that are out of line (i.e., he must plant cotton, stop beating his wife, or attend political meetings, and must proclaim that he fully realizes that this is the right thing to do), but must make every effort to improve his understanding of fundamentals—i.e., he must study, or restudy, Marxism-Leninism and the "thought of Mao Tse-tung" to understand the nature of the Chinese Revolution, the "leadership" of the Communist Party, the "line demarcating friend and foe," and so on.

In short, virtually everything one thinks or does in China is analyzed in terms of "right" or "wrong" by the authorities. And the incentive to be right is very strong. At best, a person who is wrong, even on seemingly unimportant things, will probably be subjected to public criticism, propaganda attacks, or well-organized social pressure to make him recant and reform. At worst, a person who is wrong may be punished by the "instruments of state power."

There are several primary sources for the final word on the correct line regarding any question. Most important are the fundamental scriptures, which include all the writings of Mao Tse-tung as well as those of Marx, Engels, Lenin, Stalin, and similar luminaries. These are supplemented by the interpretations of prophets of the second rank, including such men as Liu Shao-ch'i. On most questions, however, these serve mainly as basic reference works, and they are further interpreted in more specific terms by the statements, speeches, and articles of other Communist leaders, and by the decrees, laws, and regulations issued by both the Party and the government.

Once the line is defined, it is disseminated by the tremendous propaganda apparatus of the regime through every conceivable medium capable of conveying ideas to the people.

"News," all of which is disseminated through the official New China News Agency (NCNA), is one of the most important propaganda instruments. News is frankly and unapologetically propagandistic, and the "bourgeois concept of objectivity" is not tolerated. Foreign news comes largely from Soviet sources such as *Pravda* and *Tass*. Domestic news is gathered from all over the country, from reports sent in by NCNA branches; it is then re-edited and distributed through the same network. A very high percentage of the news carried in local papers everywhere in the country originates in the capital, and the texts of government decrees, reports, speeches, and the like take up a large part of the space of the average newspaper.

The editorials of the Peking *People's Daily*, the principal central organ of the Party, play a particularly important role in propagating the official line on current issues. These editorials frequently are reprinted in full in newspapers all over the country, and they always provide the cue for what local editors should write. Editorial "opinions," in short, spread by a chain-reaction process. When the question involved is not of national interest or fundamental importance, the original source may be one of the Party's organs at a regional level, but the process of dissemination is the same. The importance of the *People's Daily* editorials in this scheme of things, however, can be illustrated by one incident. On the day when the results of the recent Sino-Soviet Moscow talks were released in China, all morning newspapers in Shanghai were held up for over twelve hours; they reached the streets only in the evening, after the text of the *People's Daily* carrying the official line had been received by the Shanghai editors.

All Party members, political workers, and activists are expected to read newspapers daily, and failure to do so is criticized as dereliction of duty. As the official Party organ in Canton recently put it, "Neglect of newspaper reading is neglect of politics. The neglect of politics is not an ordinary trifle but is a serious manifestation of bourgeois decayed mentality infiltrating into the minds of our working cadres." Everyone else is "encouraged" to read newspapers, too, and various devices are used to get them to do so. Postal personnel, for example, solicit subscriptions. All mass organizations consider it part of their duty to foster newspaper reading. Another very effective means by which readership is increased is the formation of collective newspaper reading groups, which meet at regular intervals and are usually led by professional propagandists. Such groups are particularly useful in extending the audience of newspapers to illiterates, and they have been organized in China on a large scale. The Chinese Communists claim, for example, that 40,000 such groups have already been organized in the East China Region alone.

The outreach of the press is further extended by a radio monitoring network that covers rural areas not served by large newspapers. In every *Hsien* and town, the government assigns full-time monitoring personnel to copy dictation-speed news from Peking. This channel is used for the rapid distribution not only of news and editorials but also of important decrees, regulations, laws, and policies. The monitoring stations reproduce this material so that—in theory, at least—it reaches virtually the entire population. Some of them mimeograph local newspapers; others send the most important material to personnel maintaining thousands of "blackboard papers" and "wall newspapers" (handwritten local sheets) in local areas. In some villages, "megaphone broadcasts" by propaganda personnel are held daily to reach the masses.

In addition, of course, the news is broadcast orally over an extensive network of regular government-run radio stations which blanket the country. But the number of radio receivers, particularly in rural areas, is so limited that the more primitive forms of dissemination via the monitoring network reach a larger number of people. The outreach of regular radio programs is gradually being enlarged, however, by several methods. One is the organization of collective listening groups. To date, this has generally been restricted to special events, but it is a method that can mobilize a huge listening audience when desired. This spring, for example, special broadcasts of trials that took place during the anti-corruption campaign were reportedly heard in the city of Canton alone by more than 600,000 residents, who were organized by roving propaganda teams to listen to the available receivers. The establishment of village and town systems of wired loudspeakers, attached to central receivers, is being pushed by the authorities, but it probably has not yet developed very far because of equipment shortages.

Books and periodicals of all sorts are naturally another principal propaganda medium used by the Communists. More are being published in China today than ever before in history. And more people are reading what is being printed.

There are now sixty-two state-owned publishing houses, and the Communists claim that during 1952 five times as many books and periodicals will be published in China as in the peak prewar year, 1936. The Peking Government's Publication Administration states that 886 million books and 180 million copies of periodicals are scheduled to roll off the presses during the year. These publications, regardless of the type, all carry a propaganda message. Even purely literary works, such as poetry, plays, and novels, cannot be nonpolitical; widespread "rectification studies" carried out by Communist-organized artists and writers associations have attempted to overcome remnant nonpolitical tendencies. The Communist-sponsored national association of scientists has done the same with its members, as have other mass organizations.

When any "deviations" from the correct political line occur in publications, this merely provides an occasion for enthusiastic self-criticism and reinforcement of orthodoxy by prolonged discussion of errors. This year, for example, *Hsueh Hsi (Study)*, China's top official magazine dealing with ideological questions, got slightly off the beam in its analysis of bourgeois thought; as a result, it was suspended from April to August (by what Olympian authority it is difficult to know), and when it reappeared it was filled with humble confessions and elaborate definitions of the correct line.

A great many of the books now being published deal with politics, economics, and philosophy, all from the Marxist point of view. New textbooks, many of which are adaptations of Soviet volumes, are coming out in great numbers, as are scientific and technical volumes of practical use. It is perhaps significant, however, that the best creative writers in China have been notably unproductive during the past three years.

In the book-publishing field, one development, paralleling similar developments in other fields of creative expression in China, has been the debasement of literary values under the banner of popularization. The two best-sellers during the past year, for example, have both been simplified, illustrated editions of books dealing with current government policies; one on the new marriage law sold 11.5 million copies, and another on the suppression of counterrevolutionaries sold 10.6 million copies. Pocket-size cartoon books have also been promoted on a big scale, and since the Communist takeover several thousand titles, and millions of copies, have been sold; the majority of themes and stories are overtly political.

Although there has been no dramatic destruction of pre-Communist literature in China, a process of eliminating old titles has taken place steadily and quietly. Libraries have weeded out "bad books" in which "there are ideological mistakes." Many plays and operas have been banned, while others have been revised. The flow of "undesirable" books from abroad has been cut off. And even the old-style cartoon books have slowly been withdrawn and destroyed.

A flood of new periodicals has appeared in China. The best seller of them all has been one called *Current Affairs Handbook* (*Shih Shih Shou Ts'e*), a fortnightly propaganda guide which in a single issue during the past year reportedly sold 3.5 million copies. The other best-sellers are mainly in the field of slick mass pictorials, such as *People's Pictorial* (*Jen Min Hua Pao*), and magazines such as *Cartoons* (*Man Hua*), But probably the majority of magazines are specialized, official house organs of the myriad government, Party, and mass organizations in China; these specialized magazines aim at such specific target groups as children, youth, women, artists, movie workers, scientists, and the like. They translate the general Party line into terms relevant to specific audiences, and many are virtually required reading for thousands of people.

The development of a new literature for the semiliterate rural population is another important development. Many pamphlets, books, and even newspapers are being published in colloquial, simply written language to reach peasants and workers who have never been readers before. At the same time, a national program of literacy training has been undertaken. The system currently being promoted is the so-called "Chi Chien-hua short-course literacy method," devised by a teacher in the army. This method is actually based on ideas developed many years ago by Chinese linguistic experts but never tried out on any large scale. The Communists now claim that illiterate soldiers, workers, and peasants can be taught 2,000 basic Chinese characters (enough to read popular newspapers and books) by this system through intensive study in the relatively short period of 300 hours.

A national anti-illiteracy forum in Peking in September of this year defined the targets for the present campaign being developed all over the country as follows: "to eliminate illiteracy among cadres of all organs and bodies in the country within two years; to eliminate illiteracy among all industrial workers within three to four years; to eliminate illiteracy among young peasants and workers of all trades within six to seven years; to eliminate illiteracy entirely in China within the next ten years." The Chinese Communists are not averse to ambitious projects. Their primary motives for the large-scale plans to promote literacy are practical ones. "The starting point of culture now is literacy," Teng Tzu-hui, Deputy Chairman of central-south China, said in a speech last July. "After they are literate, the masses of workers will be able to go a step further by studying political theories systematically and learning advanced industrial techniques. The short-course literacy method is a prerequisite for such studies. Once the mass of workers and peasants have mastered the cultural tool, their progress will be rapid, and they will easily catch up with the requirements of national construction."

In conjunction with their publication and literacy programs, the

Communists have also developed further the mechanics of distribution and sales. State bookstores have been opened in all areas of the country. The New China Publishing Company, a state enterprise, centralizes distribution, and it now has more than 1,000 branches throughout the country; from these, it sends out circullating teams that penetrate towns and villages. Rural libraries have been fostered, and it is officially claimed that there are already more than 13,500 of them in existence. The organization of "culture centers" in both villages and urban factories has been pushed; almost a year ago, the Communists asserted that 700 had already been set up. Through these channels, as well as through schools, organized indoctrination classes, and mass organizations, publications of all sorts filter down to the grass roots, and strong pressures are applied to induce people to read them.

It is not possible to describe in detail the entire range of propaganda media the Communists employ, but a few more should at least be mentioned. All motion-picture studios in China are now grinding out propaganda films, and Soviet films are shown with Chinese subtitles. Films are scarce, because productions from the U.S. and other Western countries, which formerly dominated the China market, have been banned. But the few films now available are fully used. In the cities, they normally rotate until they have been shown in all theaters; block sales of tickets to members of various mass organizations ensure attendance, however dull a motion picture may be. Many rural projection teams have also been organized to tour the countryside. In addition, simple slide projectors are being produced on a fairly large scale, together with appropriate slides, for showings in rural areas.

These are merely the most obvious and conventional propaganda media, however, and the Chinese Communists do not confine themselves to the obvious. In the big cities today, for example, one cannot go anywhere without being exposed to some sort of propaganda. Tall buildings have long cloth streamers bearing slogans (the current emphasis is on the Communists' "peace" campaign). Wall space is covered with written slogans. A group of workers going to their factory in a truck may be carrying flags and banners enscribed with slogans. An old man reading on a park bench will probably have a bookmark bearing Communist maxims stuck in the back pages of his volume. A young girl writing in her diary at night undoubtedly will read a Communist thought for the day on each page. School children in a singing class will learn songs about how China must "Resist America and Aid Korea." Middle-school children during recess may well be going through the motions of a dance with political significance. An old-fashioned couple who prefer Chinese opera to Communist propaganda films are likely to find their favorite opera modified to carry a political message on current affairs. The calendars in restaurants, if new, no longer bear portraits of pretty girls; instead, they depict scenes of land reform or the "People's Volunteers" in Korea. Portraits of Communist leaders are everywhere.

Although the villages are less highly organized, the situation there is comparable. Even in the traditional "New Year pictures" which plaster the doorways of most homes, the old gods are being replaced by modern figures representing revolutionary heroes. Paper cutouts decorating windows are used to convey a political message. Itinerant storytellers are being indoctrinated with new story material.

To produce the huge volume of propaganda in all these varied forms, virtually all persons in China working in creative literary and artistic fields have been organized into mass organizations, which operate under the direction of Communist propaganda agencies, and they are in effect tools of the Communists' propaganda machine.

A simple listing of the propaganda media the Communists employ gives only a partial picture of the extensive propaganda system in China today, however. In fact, perhaps the most important element in the system is agitation and personal contact by trained propaganda teams and individuals.

On January 1, 1951, the CCP Central Committee issued a "Directive for the Establishment of a Propaganda Network for the Masses Throughout the Party." The system now being organized on the basis of this directive reaches down to the lowest levels of Chinese society, and the trained propagandists working in the system are responsible for oral propaganda even in individual homes.

By the start of this year, twelve months after the original directive, the Communists stated that in this Party-run network they had already organized almost 2 million "propagandists" and more than 50,000 "information officers." The numbers are undoubtedly much larger now. The immediate aim is to bring at least 1 per cent of the general population into the network (this would amount to perhaps 5 million people), and up to 5 per cent of the personnel in key places such as factories.

The propaganda network is organized and run by Communist

Party committees at all levels. Party propaganda departments, co-operating with the cultural and educational bureaus in local governments, select and train the personnel. They also provide them with propaganda plans, directives, and material. Although present evidence indicates that the system is not yet completely standardized, it is planned that provincial and municipal Party committees will issue detailed propaganda plans and directives bimonthly or monthly, while the basic Party branches will hold planning and briefing conferences fortnightly or weekly.

"Information officers" are generally found only at the level of district committees and above and are, for the most part, "responsible leaders" of the Party. Their function is to make periodic speeches and reports on important issues, not only to Party personnel but also to mass gatherings in villages and factories. The propagandists are the real workhorses, however. They are usually Party members, but some Youth League members and trusted activists are also included. Responsible for all activities at the grass-roots level, they not only distribute available propaganda materials but also must carry on extensive oral propaganda. Their manifold duties include the following: making speeches and delivering reports; spending time with selected individuals and indoctrinating them; storytelling; organizing slide showings, picture exhibitions, puppet shows, singing sessions, and dramatic performances; maintaining "wall newspapers" or "blackboard newspapers"; and giving "megaphone broadcasts from the rooftops." They must "deliver propaganda to the door" and conduct "propaganda on the kang" (a kang is a bed in north China, often used also as a couch). They are urged to "talk to anybody you meet" and to "form the habit of propagandizing whenever and wherever you can."

In many places, there are local "propaganda stations" or libraries managed by the propagandists, who must also mobilize assistance from among local activists drawn from the ranks of the masses. The aim is to have "people's propaganda teams," composed of activists organized by the professional propagandists, in every village and in every urban street. These teams can be used to reach into all homes. The Communists claim that this aim has already been accomplished in some areas and that in isolated places up to 15 per cent of the population can now be mobilized for propaganda activities—to work on the other 85 per cent.

Apart from Youth League members and leaders of mass organizations, a major population group mobilized for propaganda activists is the rural teachers. The Communists estimate that there are more than 700,000 primary-school teachers alone in rural China, and they call them a "formidable force in our propaganda corps." "A scrutiny of the school teachers' experiences has shown that propaganda by teachers in public places has been very effective, and the school children will carry the propaganda deep into the families, to the women and their young friends. The combination of rural teachers and primary-school students can form a huge propaganda force indeed."

This nationwide Party network of information officers, propagandists, and propaganda activists is a permanent system, supplemented from time to time by other special propaganda teams. It is a system by which the Communists can ensure that their propaganda reaches people throughout the country on a continuing basis, and it guarantees that the current Party line can be projected into every home.

In addition to this highly organized regular propaganda setup in China, the Communists have developed a system of group indoctrination that is probably even more effective in influencing the minds of the Chinese people than the regular flow of propaganda. Not only are the schools centers for indoctrination, but a large percentage of the adult population in China have been subjected to intensive indoctrination in small *hsueh hsi* groups during the past three years. In these groups, the Party line is hammered into people's minds by methods that deserve the attention of psychologists and psychoanalysts; group pressure is used to break down any individual resistance or nonconformist tendencies until every group member expresses full acceptance of the ideas the Communists wish to get across.

There is no doubt that Communist propaganda techniques are extremely effective. On the surface, China appears to be rapidly becoming a regimented country of "yes men" who simply parrot the Party line. Surface appearances may be somewhat deceiving, however. Ideas can go underground, and probably a significant number of people, especially educated adults, have resisted Communist propaganda with varying degress of success. But the question of what is happening to the minds of illiterates and youths who lack a sound basis for judging and evaluating Communist propaganda is a different matter. It is these groups—particularly the youth—who are most important in Chinese Communist eyes. And the Communists will undoubtedly be able to inculcate a great many of them with their "new culture," because before many years pass they will not remember or know anything else.

7

MOTION PICTURES

May, 1954

Moviegoers interested in the fairer sex have a variety of films to choose from in Hong Kong this week. At the Lee Theatre, Jane Russell dances in Technicolor and "3-D," in a movie called *The French Line*. The "giant wide" Cinemascope screen at the Oriental Theatre is dominated by Marilyn Monroe, Betty Grable, and Lauren Bacall, who demonstrate, also in Technicolor, *How To Marry a Millionaire*. The Star Theatre outdoes the others, however, by showing a film starring ten young women; entitled *Woman Locomotive Driver*, it is strictly black-and-white and two-dimensional.

This last film, imported from the Chinese Communist mainland, might well have been given another title by its Shanghai producers—perhaps *The Party Line* or *How To Become a Locomotive Driver*. It is doubtful, however, if a change of title alone could have added much in the way of color or dimension to the moralistic political propaganda of the story itself, which is representative of the general run of films now being produced in Communist China. Hailed as a "heroic story of New China's first women locomotive drivers," it attempts to fulfill the aims of China's reorganized movie industry, as defined by leaders in Peking.

"Our cinema," stated an editorial of the Peking *People's Daily* early this year, "has in the main followed Comrade Mao Tse-tung's guidance on literature and art. It reflects the life and struggle of the laboring people, manifests their noble spirit and quality, and correctly explains the purpose of life to the people." Entertainment is subordinated to "education," and art is sacrificed to politics and morals.

Mao defined the basic purpose of all Chinese Communist literature and art in a speech made in 1942: to "become a constructive part of the whole revolutionary machine" and to be a "powerful weapon for uniting and educating the people and for crushing and destroying the enemy."

81

During the past four years, the political arbiters of art and morals in Communist China have attempted energetically to remold the motion-picture industry into a political "weapon" of their "revolutionary machine." Rigid standards of orthodoxy for themes, plots, and characters have been defined, and production has been brought under the quota system. Fitting the creative talents of artists and entertainers into a political strait-jacket is not without its difficulties, however, and the movie industry in China has undergone a steady decline as a result of stifling controls. Official reports indicate that despite the importance placed upon films as a major propaganda medium, the motion-picture industry now encounters difficulty producing a dozen or so movies such as *Woman Locomotive Driver* each year.

Perhaps it would be revealing to examine one of these films closely. *Woman Locomotive Driver* describes how several young Chinese volunteers were trained to become the first women locomotive engineers in China. The setting is a technical school established in Dairen in 1949 by the Chinese Communists with the help of Soviet advisers.

The principal heroine is a not-very-bright girl named Sun, who is admirably eager and hard-working and aspires to be a model worker. She is one of ten girls taking the training course. Another, an extremely bright but proud and self-centered girl named Fung, comes closest to being the villain in the piece.

The other main characters are all administrators or teachers in the school: Lu, an old-time railway man whose job is to teach the girls how to shovel coal; "little Chiang," a smiling young railway worker who assists with the teaching; Kao, a technical instructor on locomotives; Sedov, Soviet adviser at the school; and the Communist Party school administrator.

As the movie opens, the girls are trying to learn how to shovel coal. They are awkward, and Lu is convinced that woman's place is in the home—or at least not in locomotive cabs. Sun and several of her classmates are in danger of failing this course in coal-shoveling, but "little Chiang" comes to the rescue. Late at night, Chiang teaches Sun the proper technique, and Sun, elated, wakes up two of her friends and teaches them.

The next crisis occurs when the girls begin to study the workings of a locomotive. Kao explains locomotives to the class, but all the girls except Fung are mystified. Although Kao is discouraged, Sedov hits upon a solution, proposing that they build a simple mechanical model of a locomotive; he and Kao stay up all night working on it, so that it will be ready for class the following day.

The model proves a great help, and almost all the girls learn enough to pass their examination. But not Sun, who fails. Kao, although sympathetic, advises her to try some other work, and Sun is crushed. She broods on her cot in the barracks and stares at pictures of labor heroines on the wall. Finally, she determines not to give up.

The Party administrator of the school, who sits with a portrait of Mao Tse-tung behind him and a bust of Mao at his side, is moved by Sun's plea for another chance. Her attitude of struggling to overcome all difficulties is the right approach, he says, and Sun is given another chance.

During the next month, Sedov and all the girls except Fung pitch in and help Sun. Then comes her makeup examination. Everyone gathers around to watch, tensely, as Sun works over a model locomotive. A clock ticks off the minutes, and for a while it looks as if Sun will fail again. But at the last moment she is able to repair the model, and everyone cheers. This is really the emotional climax of the film.

From classwork, the girls graduate to field training on locomotives of the Dairen–Port Arthur line. They start as firemen, and Lu is in charge. Lu's skepticism about women is at first confirmed when Fung, the brightest girl in the group, is careless, wastes coal, and delays the locomotive by her slow oiling, but he begins to change his attitude when he sees how hard-working and conscientious Sun is.

Finally, the girls take, and pass, examinations in solo runs as locomotive engineers. A huge celebration, which coincides with the New Year, follows, and there are dancing and singing, and congratulations are made all around. The ten girls show their gratitude to Sedov by presenting him with a group picture, but he tells them that he deserves no personal thanks, that he is merely a representative of the Soviet Union and its aid to the Chinese people. The party ends when Fung and Sun challenge each other to a labor competition.

The dramatic high point of the movie comes when the girls make their first actual run between Dairen and Port Arthur. Fung, at the throttle, sets a fast pace—too fast, in fact, and too careless. When a peasant's cart, which has broken down on the tracks, looms up, Fung is paralyzed. But Sun steps into the breach, the train is stopped (the audience cheers wildly), the cart is moved, and the train moves on.

The picture ends with the girls' formal graduation ceremony. They line up, holding bouquets of flowers, in front of three festooned locomotives bearing portraits of Mao. Then they scramble onto the locomotives and move off under a hail of flowers. The sides of the locomotives are emblazoned with large placards inscribed with such slogans as "Oppose aggression."

This brief story outline indicates the barren simplicity of the theme. The actual production, however, shows some skill. The photography is quite good, and the acting acceptable. The characters are shallow stereotypes, but at times they seem human, and the girls do not entirely lack feminine charm. The deadly earnestness is relieved at two or three points by light touches of humor.

Woman Locomotive Driver, however, is basically neither art nor entertainment. It is a political morality play, designed to teach the audience some of the standards and values propagated by the Communist regime. Perhaps the most important ideas it glorifies are the equality of women, the dignity of labor (particularly manual labor), and the importance of struggling to overcome difficulties; also glorified are machines, Soviet advisers, and model workers. Criticism is directed at self-centeredness, carelessness, and unwillingness to change old ideas, while hard work, the simple life, perseverance, and patience are praised. Determination and group cooperation are elevated above individual brilliance. These are all values the Chinese Communists believe are essential if the Party and the state are to carry out their program of collectivism.

It is interesting that although the stars of *Woman Locomotive Driver* are ten young women, there is not one trace of romance in the film. Romance is not considered important in a society dedicated to "socialist industrialization."

The Chinese Communist motion-picture industry is currently undergoing a serious crisis as a result of the intimidation and stifling of creative talent caused by stringent political controls. Last December, the Peking regime's Government Administration Council held a meeting to discuss the crisis, and this past January it released a document admitting that a "serious shortage of film scripts" has created a situation in which "both the quantity and quality of the films presently produced are inadequate to cope with the demand of the broad masses."

The main cause of this situation has been the effect upon the movie industry of the furor in 1951 over a film called *The Story of Wu Hsun*. Produced in 1950 by some of China's leading film artists, it had its premier in Shanghai on the last day of 1950 and received wide praise. By April, 1951, however, Party-controlled organs began to criticize it, and by May a tremendous campaign of "ideological education" centered on the movie had begun. This campaign lasted for over a month, during which time the Chinese Communist press devoted primary attention to the film, and many magazines published special issues on the case.

The Story of Wu Hsun was about an actual nineteenth-century Chinese figure—well known and widely admired—who started as a beggar, decided to devote his life to establishing schools for poor children, and adopted "Begging to set up a school" as a personal slogan. Eventually, through begging and moneylending, he became a landlord and was able to set up several schools.

The film portrayed Wu Hsun in a very favorable light, but before the campaign against the film ended, Wu Hsun had been thoroughly denounced in Communist terms as a feudalistic money-lender and landlord, a nonproletarian rogue who depended upon support from wealthy gentry and officials, and a nonrevolutionary "capitulationist." The producers of *The Story of Wu Hsun* were bitterly chastised for their ideological backwardness in producing a favorable movie about him.

This campaign had a paralyzing effect on the Chinese movie industry, and the ghost of Wu Hsun still hangs over film writers. During the past three years, political control of movies has steadily been tightened, and a Government Administration Council directive of January this year prescribes a detailed system of complete Party and government control.

Top responsibility for planning and supervising the motion picture industry in China rests with the Cinema Bureau of the Ministry of Cultural Affairs (this agency also coordinates the work of several other organizations). The planning of stories, and the organization of writers to produce specific scripts, are handled by the Bureau, with the help of the Union of Chinese Writers and local Federations of Literary and Art Circles. A general four-year plan has already been outlined, and this is filled in with specific one-year plans which are more detailed.

During the planning of stories and the organization of script writing, assistance and guidance are obtained from relevant government departments, the Political Department of the army, the trade unions, and the Youth League, whose advice is necessary to ensure that the films will be a "vigorous propaganda medium."

After scripts are completed, the Cinema Bureau gives them a "strict preliminary examination" and then passes them on to the

Ministry of Cultural Affairs for further "examination and approval." Only then can shooting begin.

During the actual production process, the Bureau must subject the shooting to "strict scrutiny, so as to ensure that no major revision will be needed when the film is completed." Final approval must be given by the Bureau before any film is released.

In addition to this step-by-step control exercised by government agencies, the Communist Party maintains a further censorship check. The annual plan for film stories, and the "scripts or shooting programs of films of major political significance," must be submitted to the Party's Propaganda Department for examination. It is not surprising that centralized political control of this sort, plus planning of stories and supervision of scripts, has discouraged creativeness on the part of the movie industry in China.

According to a recent editorial in the Peking *People's Daily:*

> The crucial problem of present film work is to increase the number of feature films and to elevate their quality. During the past four years, the production state of our film enterprise has been unsatisfactory. Work had to be partially suspended by the film studios because there were no films to shoot. Many directors and actors and actresses had for prolonged periods no chance to show themselves, while the audience complained of the small number of new films.

The exact output of feature films in Communist China during recent years is not certain, because of conflicting official claims, but it is clear that the figure is remarkably low. According to one recent statement, only 15 features were completed in all of mainland China during 1952, and last year the total dropped to 10. Production plans for this year call for only 13 feature films. (As a basis for comparison, the tiny colony of Hong Kong alone produced 188 feature films in the Chinese language last year.)

The 10 feature movies produced in Communist China during 1953 were not the total fare presented to Chinese audiences. They were supplemented by numerous Soviet-bloc films (shown with Chinese subtitles) and a few newsreels, documentaries, and other "shorts" produced by the Chinese themselves.

More than 40 Russian and satellite films were circulated through China during 1953 alone, and the total during the past four years has been more than 200—several times the number of Chinese movies produced and shown during the same period. These Soviet-bloc films have taken over the entire market for foreign films in China, since "nonprogressive" Western movies have been banned.

The production of various types of "shorts" and features in Communist China during 1953 included 10 full-length and 16 short documentaries, a weekly Chinese newsreel and semiweekly international newsreel, and 10 scientific-education films. All these were even more frankly "educational" than feature films like *Woman Locomotive Driver*. The newsreels were produced as "visual political essays," and the scientific-education films, called "visual popular talks," were about subjects such as childbirth, exercise and health, train operation, eclipses, water conservancy, insect pests, zoological gardens, splenic fever, food and nourishment, and science and technology. The 10 full-length documentaries included *Stalin Will Live Forever in Our Hearts, Resist America and Aid Korea,* and *The Great Land Reform*. The closest approach to pure entertainment was in *Ballads and Dances* and *Puppet Show of South Fukien*.

This meager fare was all that was provided to more than 750 movie theaters and roughly 2,000 mobile projection teams throughout China during 1953.

Last month, the Chinese Communists' Fourth National Cultural Work Conference was held in Peking, and it placed great emphasis on the "importance of organizing creation in the fields of cinema and drama." Apparently, the political authorities are finding it necessary to apply pressure on writers in order to fulfill even the limited production quotas specified for the years immediately ahead.

The current four-year plan for the motion-picture industry, announced by the Government Administration Council early this year, sets surprisingly low goals for movie producers during the remainder of China's much-publicized Five-Year Plan. The annual quota is twelve to fifteen full-length features (plus a few special features for villagers, children, etc.), ten full-length documentaries, more than twenty short documentaries, fifteen scientific-education films, and a weekly newsreel. The plan also specifies that every year Soviet-bloc films and "progressive films of the capitalist countries" should be "equal in number to the Chinese films produced."

The content of the films already planned is very similar to the morality-play pattern so well illustrated by *Woman Locomotive Driver*. The thirteen features announced for this year, for example, include themes described as follows: "a film about the heroic struggle of the North Shensi peasants during the liberation war," "a film using the invention of a steel-press worker to show how members of the working class employ their originality to strive for industrial automation," "a film using the episode of how a worker became a member of the leadership cadre to reflect the advanced ideology of the working class," and "a film about the correct enforcement of the nationality policy by the cadres of a certain Tibetan nationality area in the southwest to unite the various classes and strata and to annihilate the bandits and special agents."

Numerous meetings of writers, directors, actors, and actresses have recently been held, and, according to the Chinese Communist press, "the ideological and professional level of the film cadres and their creative ardor have been enhanced, and film production work is now capable of being carried out in a planned manner."

The Chinese Communists call their movie industry the People's Film Enterprise. They do not mean by this, however, either that the public should be able to dictate what kind of films should be produced or that artists should be given free rein for their creative talents. "The film," they say, "is an important medium for educating the people in patriotism and socialism." In short, the ruling Communist elite, who have established themselves as the dictators of art and morals, as well as politics and economics, determine what they think is good for the public and force the artists to produce "according to plan."

Although the Communists make claims of "enhanced creative ardor," the strangulating effects of political controls on artistic creativeness are clearly indicated by a current crisis in the Chinese movie industry and the "serious shortage of film scripts." It seems likely also that movie audiences in China are far from satisfied with the unrelieved political propaganda to which they are now constantly exposed. Official statistics indicate that the audiences have steadily risen, but this is probably more of a tribute to the Communists' development of mobile projection units and the organization of group attendance at movies than it is to the appeal of the films offered to the public.

This week in Hong Kong, where Chinese moviegoers still have much to choose from, numerous locally produced films are drawing far larger crowds than *Woman Locomotive Driver*. There is no doubt that a large majority of Hong Kong Chinese, from the creative artists to the viewing masses, would definitely vote for the "tyranny of the box office" in preference to the tyranny of the political commissar. It is probable that most of their compatriots in Communist China would opt similarly, if allowed to voice their preference.

8

GROUP INDOCTRINATION

March, 1954

The revolution in China is a process of struggle. It is a struggle not only to "reform" society but also to capture and "remold" the minds of one-fifth of the human race. The Chinese Communists' aim is mass ideological conversion and creation of the "new socialist man"—a man who rejects the past and accepts an entirely new code of Communist "truth" and morality.

Indoctrination, which strikes at the innermost recesses of the mind, is therefore given equal priority with industrialization, collectivization, and similar programs that attack the political, economic, and social structure. The Chinese Communists believe that if minds can be controlled, and basic ways of thinking changed, their revolutionary struggle can be won.

Considerable attention has been devoted by the Western press to the intensive "thought reform" carried out by the Chinese Communists on a few imprisoned foreign missionaries, businessmen, and prisoners of war. Some of these men, whose minds and wills were broken by the strains of powerful mental pressures, have described how they were forced or persuaded to make false confessions.

Much less attention has been given, however, to the methods of indoctrination the Communists are using to assault the minds of their own people—not only the imprisoned minority who are considered "enemies" by the regime, but the mass of ordinary people of all sorts: workers, students, government employees, intellectuals, business employees, housewives, and farmers.

The Chinese Communists use many methods of thought control. Formal education is, of course, important. The entire educational system in China has been reorganized and its content changed. A new generation is being nurtured on strictly controlled fare rationed by the Communist leaders. Propaganda media of all sorts are important, too. The Communists attempt to control everything that is capable of conveying ideas and symbols. This control is designed to place strict limitations upon the ideas to which people are exposed, and since thought does not take place in a vacuum, the elimination of heterodox ideas from the intellectual marketplace is an important means of thought control.

One of the most distinctive and successful means the Communists are using in their ideological struggle, however, is group indoctrination. It is group indoctrination that they employ to give political training to the new elite of the country—the students, *kanpu*, government workers, and Party members. Group indoctrination is the basis for campaigns to change the outlook and attitudes of entire classes—campaigns such as the "ideological reform" of the intellectuals carried on during 1951–52. And it is also used in prisons to "reform" or at least to cow the actual or potential "enemies" of the regime—"reactionaries" and "counterrevolutionaries." In effect, virtually everyone in China is exposed to group indoctrination in some form or other. Primary attention is devoted to youth and "intellectuals" in the broadest sense, and the urban population is more thoroughly organized for indoctrination than people in the countryside, but no group is exempted.

The term used throughout Communist China for group indoctrination is *hsueh hsi* or "study" (literally, *hsueh hsi* means "to learn and practice"). The origin of this phrase is traceable to Confucius, who says, in Chapter I of the Analects (using the words *hsueh* and *hsi*): "Is it not pleasant to learn with constant perseverance and application?" But the phrase was little used in modern times until the Communists adopted it for their indoctrination methods, and it now has harsher, sterner connotations. Actually, the Communists use *hsueh hsi* to refer to all political study, including individual "self-study," but in common usage it has become almost synonymous with collective group study, which is given primary stress by the regime.

Hsueh hsi has become an essential part of the fabric of society and the way of life in Communist China. Every day, millions of Chinese gather together in small groups of a half-dozen to a dozen people—in factories, shops, schools, and offices—to *hsueh hsi* the ideology and policies of the Communist regime. These organizational cells are a direct link between the Communist rulers of China and the brain cells of masses of ordinary people.

During the past three years, I have talked with many Chinese refugees in Hong Kong who have taken part in *hsueh hsi* groups in Communist China. What they describe is not "study" in any sense in which the word is understood in non-Communist countries; it is a unique process of manipulating minds and organizing social pressure to force acceptance of the new philosophy and ideology sponsored by the Communists. The individual in a *hsueh hsi* group must think, but he does not think independently; his mind is shaped by the pressures within the group. Clearly, the Chinese Communists have hit upon a method of indoctrination that reveals great intuitive insight into subtle psychological principles and principles of "group dynamics," applied to political purposes.

"You can't think clearly, even if you think you can, when you are taking part in intensive *hsueh hsi*," one former newspaper editor, now in his forties, said to me. "You instinctively realize that your real thoughts will some day pop out of your mouth and that therefore to be safe you either have to change your real thoughts or not think at all."

"Most students began to change after undergoing *hsueh hsi*," said a young girl who had just been graduated from a university in Communist China. "Only a small percentage stuck to any old beliefs. That doesn't mean, however, that this 'change' was really 'conversion' in many cases. For most students, there wasn't much to convert; they had no firm or well-developed ideology; they were an ideological blank. The 'change,' therefore, was an acceptance of new ideas which filled a vacuum."

"It is difficult to know how much the Communists are able really to change people's thinking," another *hsueh hsi* participant said to me, "but there is no doubt that at least they break down almost everyone's resistance to the new ideas."

A young man who had actually joined the CCP after his indoctrination told me: "*Hsueh hsi* is very effective. I was impressed by the theory and the ideas I learned. It was only later, when I began to see differences between theory and practice, that I became disillusioned."

From these and other persons who have belonged to *hsueh hsi* groups in Communist China, one can learn how *hsueh hsi* groups operate—in what way they are organized, how they function, what they study. There are many variations in details; at one extreme, these groups are used in special training courses where *hsueh hsi* is carried on six or eight hours a day for many months; at the other extreme, in some offices or organizations, the groups may meet for a weekly one-hour session only. But there are certain basic principles that seem to apply to all *hsueh hsi* groups.

One of these, an essential, is the principle that the "study" is collective, a group effort. Not only is it possible for the regime to reach and control much larger numbers of people through groups than it could individually, but the fundamental nature of the Chinese Communists' indoctrination methods requires group action. The Communists do not trust the individual, or believe that the individual can be allowed to function as an independent unit, even in his thinking.

Hsueh hsi groups are small: sometimes as few as six members, rarely more than twelve. The groups have continuity. There is definite membership, and the same people meet together over an extended period of time. Their meetings are regular and periodic, whether several times daily or only once every few days. One of the most common practices of *hsueh hsi* groups, particularly in large organizations, is to meet for an hour a day, either before or after regular working hours.

Although participation in *hsueh hsi* groups is sometimes described as "voluntary," the pressures to take part make it compulsory in fact. If a person shows reluctance, he is criticized as being "backward and unprogressive," and he is not left in peace until he shows a more cooperative attitude. Often, however, there is no attempt to maintain the fiction of voluntariness; all members of a large organization are simply assigned to small *hsueh hsi* groups.

Hsueh hsi groups do not function as isolated or independent organizations. They are always established on the initiative of higher authorities. (In any particular area, ultimate responsibility for them usually rests in the hands of educational organs in the government and propaganda organs in the Party.) Each group is tied into a network of similar groups and is responsible to a hierarchy of leaders or committees which exercise direct supervision and control over it. In many organizations or local areas, for example, about ten small groups (*hsueh hsi hsiao tsu*) are grouped into a larger unit (*fen tui* or *ta k'o*), and above these larger units are committees linking them to the ultimate local authority for *hsueh hsi*. Instructions are passed down to the small groups on their schedule of meetings, subjects to be discussed, material to be read, lectures to be attended, and so on. And the small groups submit regular reports to the organizational hierarchy above them. When the members of any one small group gather for their regular meetings and discussion, therefore, they know in most cases that thousands of other people like them are meeting simultaneously in similar groups, discussing the same topics. They are merely one small unit in a tremendous, organized "captive audience."

Each *hsueh hsi* group has a leader, and sometimes there is also an assistant leader. In most cases, the group leader is "elected," but people who have participated in the groups report that "the Communists have ways of getting the people they want into positions of group leaders." If the group contains a Party or Youth League member, an "activist," or a known "progressive" (and where possible, they are organized so that at least one such person is included in each group), this person usually emerges as the leader. If a clearly undesirable leader is elected, the authorities veto him; in extreme cases, they may break up and reorganize a group that shows its "backwardness" by choosing a suspect leader.

The group leader is a direct link with authority, through the organizational hierarchy above the *hsueh hsi* groups. He carries out instructions from above. He supervises discussion sessions. He takes notes on the meetings and makes regular reports (sometimes written, sometimes verbal) to those above him. He is supposed to learn everything about each member in his group and watch with care the development of his ideas and attitudes. He represents the eyes and ears of the regime and is a personification of the conscience of the group.

The role of the group leader in the whole scheme of small-group *hsueh hsi* is extremely important. Responsible to the authorities, he symbolizes the power of the regime, and although he is expected to lead and guide in a restrained manner, his mere presence in the group ensures control. On all questions discussed, he is the ultimate arbiter and oracle of the "correct," orthodox "truth"—or if he himself does not have the answer to a question, he is the pipeline to higher authorities who do.

Another basic principle of this group indoctrination is the fact that discussion is the essence of the process. "Studying" is not conceived of as a matter of passively listening to lectures or privately reading books and other written materials. Thoughts and ideas must be expressed verbally, and there must be interchange and interaction among all members of a group. Lectures and reading play a role in the process, but primarily to provide a springboard for group discussion. And even in lectures and reading, the emphasis is upon collective rather than individual activity. Lectures are attended en masse, and very often textual source materials are read aloud in the study groups. (One technique is for the group leader to read a text, paragraph by paragraph, with prolonged group discussion after each paragraph.)

Every member is expected to participate actively in discussion within the groups. This is extremely important. There are no passive observers; there is no neutrality or indifference. If a group member appears to stay aloof, it is the responsibility not only of the leader but also of all other members of the group to arouse and involve this laggard, to criticize his backwardness, to solicit his views. This necessity for active participation means that every member of the group is involved in the indoctrination process in a positive way, must be mentally alert throughout the meetings, and must bare his mental "self" to group scrutiny.

The pattern of discussion in the groups has peculiarities of its own. "Free discussion" and strict control are combined in a unique formula. Abstract theory is linked to personal attitudes and experience. Criticism and self-criticism are used to bring all members of the group into a complicated interrelationship in which they exert a mutual influence upon each other. The confessions involved in self-criticism give the discussion a strong emotional flavor, making it something quite different from a primarily intellectual discussion.

One fundamental premise of all the discussion is that for every problem or question there is a "correct" solution or answer. The "truth" is contained in "scientific Marxism," as defined by the Party, and the problem is to understand and accept the Communists' basic theories of historical and social change, to relate these to current social, economic, political, and international issues, and to adapt one's own behavior to this theoretical frame work. It is also assumed that no one—even old Party members—has progressed as far as is theoretically possible in understanding this "truth" and in fully relating one's personal life to it.

This means that for average members of a *hsueh hsi* group, the whole aim of discussion is focused upon the necessity of repudiating past beliefs, discovering what it is that the Communist regime now requires them to believe, rejecting all competing ideas, and expressing—at least verbally—full acceptance of the "correct" dogma.

Discussion always centers on one, or a few, specific ideas or ideological problems. More often than not, they are quite abstract theoretical or philosophical questions. The following are typical examples, taken from a study outline for one *hsueh hsi* group of university students:

"Selfishness is natural; the working class is also selfish." "If the individual is slightly selfish, that is all right as long as he does not interfere with other people." Why are these thoughts the selfish and self-profiting ideology of the petty bourgeoisie? Are they influenced by feudalistic or capitalistic ideology?

The revolutionary outlook on life is one involving examination of one's life from a revolutionary standpoint. Revolution is the meaning of life. One lives for the revolution. Why? How do you understand this now? In the past?

From a class viewpoint, what is your opinion of internationalism and patriotism? Patriotism is certainly related to internationalism. Why? By what steps did you come to an understanding of this question?

Why do the ideas of "being a sympathizer with the working people" and having a "new viewpoint of showing gratitude" reveal that you really do not yet understand that the laborer is the master of history and the masses are the real heroes? Why are these ideas merely petty-bourgeois humanitarianism and salvationism? Examine yourself to see if you have such thoughts.

Of course, not all of the discussion concerns broad questions of attitude and outlook such as these. *Hsueh hsi* groups also discuss current events, government policies, and concrete problems related to the work of group members. But the broad ideological questions are looked upon as of fundamental importance.

As already stated, lectures and reading of prescribed texts (books, pamphlets, newspaper editorials, or specially mimeographed material) play a part in *hsueh hsi* and usually precede discussion. In some situations, normal procedure is for several *hsueh hsi* groups to meet together and listen to a speech, which may last two to four hours, or for all the group members to read the basic writings on a particular question, either individually or collectively.

The lectures and reading provide the raw material for discussion and pose the problems or questions to be discussed. The presentation is often highly "dialectical"—full of "on the one hand" and "on the other hand," outlining wrong answers and the right one, listing rightist and leftist deviations and defining the "correct" view.

Upon analysis, one interesting fact about this preparation for discussion becomes clear. At the very start, everyone in a *hsueh hsi* group knows what the right answer to the question under discussion is; it is contained, either explicitly or implicitly, in the speeches that group members have heard or in the material they have read. Yet the members of a *hsueh hsi* group then proceed to spend hours, and sometimes weeks, in discussion that will end where it began. In short, the discussion is not a genuine search for unknown answers to difficult questions and problems; it is a process of clarifying and obtaining acceptance of answers that are defined at the beginning.

What happens, then, during the course of lengthy discussion of a topic? Essentially, there is a detailed examination of every conceivable aspect of a question; an attempt to bring into the open and refute all possible objections, counterarguments, and doubts concerning the "correct" line; an effort to get each group member to renounce any reservations about accepting the orthodox view; and finally insistence that each member of the group openly express full acceptance of the officially sanctioned "truth" and try to relate this to his personal life.

Even if every member of a group is inclined to accept the pre-scribed ideas at the start of discussion on a particular subject, the process of discussion cannot be dispensed with. Group members must rack their brains to raise problems and doubts, even if they have to invent them, so that they can be properly disposed of.

If a group member genuinely disagrees with the "correct" line, and persists in resisting conversion, it is the responsibility of all members of the group to criticize him, argue against him, and prove him to be wrong. If they do not speak up, this fact may be interpreted by the group leader as indicating that they share the mistaken ideas of the maverick.

The result, therefore, is mobilization of intense social pressure within the group to achieve total conformity. In a sense, every member of a *hsueh hsi* group is a minority of one being worked on by all the rest. Some of the groups are composed of people who may all be skeptical of the Communist line, yet in these groups a remarkable phenomenon occurs: Eight or ten skeptics all exert pressure on each other to become believers—under the watchful eyes of the group leader.

Persons who have participated in *hsueh hsi* describe a subtle but deep undercurrent of tension, suspicion, and fear that exists, at least in many of the groups. Each group member realizes that the discussion is a test of his ability or willingness to accept the official ideology of the regime. He realizes also that the Commu-nist authorities demand acceptance of their ideology and that in the long run he either must give in or risk subjection to further, more intensive indoctrination. If a person is really stubborn, he may be sent to a jail for "re-education"—or worse—and everyone knows this.

The pressures upon a group member's mind during discussion are by no means all negative, however. Constant repetition of ideas hammers them into one's mind and leads to an increasing willingness to accept and believe. Hearing the other group members argue in support of the "correct" line begins to undermine one's belief in different views; a person begins to think, "Maybe, after all, they're right and I'm wrong." The pressure to verbalize arguments supporting the official line, even if one is skeptical, begins to create a readiness to accept the ideas. And all possible arguments to support the Communist-approved answers to problems are mobilized during the course of the group discussion.

The final aim of discussion on any question is open acceptance, by each and every member of the group, of the official ideas and viewpoint, and this is usually achieved. Even those who have participated in *hsueh hsi* groups, however, find it difficult to assess the real effects of all this upon members of such a group. In some cases, genuine conversion and full acceptance of the ideas are achieved. At the other extreme, verbal acceptance in some cases is obviously a fraud, and people begin living a double life mentally—espousing one set of ideas openly, but clinging to another set privately. Many people probably fall into categories between these extremes. But one thing is clearly and indisputably achieved: open expression of intellectual submission to the official line of the regime. Whether a person is actually converted or secretly persists in maintaining intellectual independence, almost all admit by their verbal acceptance of the "correct" views that they are subservient to the regime.

Discussion of any one major subject by a *hsueh hsi* group usually ends with a summary of all that has been said. In special intensive indoctrination courses, the course comes to a climax when each participant writes what is called an "ideological résumé" (*szu hsiang tsung chieh*). Criticism and self-criticism are essential components of the process of group indoctrination, and they reach their apex in these ideological résumés.

An ideological résumé is usually a long document, of several thousand words, in which an individual recounts his whole past life (childhood, class status, education, work, activities of all sorts) and previous thoughts and attitudes, confesses all those aspects that did not live up to what the Communists define as ideal, and describes how he has now renounced the past and has been converted.

Sometimes, several weeks are devoted to preparation of these documents. Each individual in a group first works alone on preparation of a résumé. The drafts are then circulated among members of the group, who write criticisms and suggestions. They are then revised, and subsequently each member reads his résumé to the group, which critically examines and discusses it in detail. The individual is probed to see to what extent he has completely revealed all of his past, confessed all of his errors, and actually presented convincing proof of having really changed and become a new man ideologically. Almost always, a résumé is rejected by the group after the first reading, and the individual is told to improve it and make it more complete. Sometimes, a person must revise and expand his résumé two or three times before it is finally accepted by the group and then by the hierarchy of authority above the group.

Everyone I have talked with who has written an ideological résumé states that it is a devastating experience, that the necessity of dissecting and denouncing one's past breaks down one's integrity as an individual. The problem of justifying oneself, and supporting the claim that genuine ideological change has taken place, puts a great mental strain upon a person. It is not uncommon for an individual to lose several pounds during the period he is preparing and defending his ideological résumé.

The final approved résumé is kept on file by the authorities, and according to some people it becomes the basis of a permanent dossier on one's thinking, following a person from place to place and job to job. The sincerity of a person's claims about past and present thoughts can be periodically checked by referring to his ideological résumé and looking for inconsistencies between past and present statements.

The most effective indoctrination is obviously achieved in the full-time, intensive *hsueh hsi* schools, whose students are usually persons slated to work for the regime and whose aim is complete "thought reform." In such schools, the small group is the basis of the students' entire life; not only *hsueh hsi* as such but all other activities are carried out collectively. The schedule of activities of the schools, furthermore, is designed to occupy all of the students' time and energy, and for periods ranging from a few weeks to several months the students spend almost the whole of every day in discussion sessions designed fully to "remold" their minds.

The most intensive process of all is that applied to prisoners in Chinese Communist "re-education" jails. The treatment of these prisoners—including Westerners—is rather different in its psychological basis, however, from the *hsueh hsi* undergone by ordinary people. Fear, intimidation, and threats play a much greater and more obvious role here than in ordinary *hsueh hsi*, although they are certainly present in every *hsueh hsi* group. Often a person's mind is broken down in prison by methods that can only be labeled "mental torture." As one American missionary friend of mine who spent eleven months in a jail in southwest China has reported, "One's mind begins to find it difficult to distinguish between what the court has suggested and what one had known to be the facts." The "confessions," obtained from minds that are sick and confused as a result of unbearable psychological pressures and fatigue, are very useful to the Communists' propaganda machine.

In other cases, however, prisoners make false confessions as a result of despair. A missionary who spent over two years in a Chinese Communist jail said to me that he finally reached a point where the desire for release, combined with a realization that he would never be freed until he confessed as his prison wardens required, made him decide to do and say everything the Communists wanted, even to the extent of inventing wild untruths to confess.

The experiences of men such as these indicate that the Communists have developed psychological techniques that can "break" men's minds as well as "remold" them. The emphasis in most *hsueh hsi* is upon remolding minds, however, and this is what the Chinese Communists are trying to do on such a wide scale.

What is the image of the "new socialist man" that the Communists are trying to create by this remolding in China? Briefly, he is a man who has been converted to an entirely new outlook on life, accepts the "truth" of Communist dogma as outlined in Russian and Chinese Communist classics, and lives according to a new code of morals defined by the Party. He is expected to subordinate his own individual will completely to the will of the Party. Self-sacrifice, obedience, loyalty, and discipline are fundamental requirements. He must be willing to struggle actively for the revolution in order to ensure the course of social development which the dogma states is both necessary and inevitable. He is supposed to think in class terms, to differentiate "good" from "bad" and "friend" from "foe," to glorify and imitate the ideal of being proletarian, to be frugal, to live a simple life. He must identify himself with the "masses" and be willing to live a collective group life. He must fight against anything that he is told is "feudal, capitalist, or bourgeois." And he must support all the policies of the Communist Party and the regime it has created. This is a big order, but it is what the Chinese Communists are trying to achieve.

This is why so much attention is devoted to "attitudes" and "outlook" in *hsueh hsi* groups. However, the groups also try to indoctrinate their members in the entire Marxist ideology—that is, Marxism-Leninism and the "thought of Mao Tse-tung"—as well as in the many specific policies of the CCP and the government.

An outline of one course at a twelve-month indoctrination school in Communist China gives an idea of the political content of some of the indoctrination:

First three and a half months.
1. History of social development.
   a. Ancient history.
   b. Modern history.
2. Basic principles of the Chinese Revolution.
   a. The present stage of the Chinese Revolution.
   b. The social foundation of the present stage of the Revolution.
   c. Leadership, etc., of the present stage of the Revolution.

Next four and a half months.
3. History of the Revolution and Chinese New Democratic principles.
   a. History of the Revolution and its principles.
   b. Basic experiences of the Revolution.

Last four months.
4. Establishment of New Democratic principles.

But this is only one course and one general category of the material included in *hsueh hsi*. Actually, there is no end to *hsueh hsi*. It is conceived of as a lifelong process, although its intensity may vary during different periods of one's life, and everyone from old Party leaders to factory workers or store clerks is expected to keep up *hsueh hsi* on current policies and problems and also to keep on improving his understanding of basic Communist-defined "truth."

The reading material used by *hsueh hsi* groups is consequently almost inexhaustible. Actually, all important editorials on policies in newspapers such as the Peking *People's Daily* are texts for *hsueh hsi* groups. So are the major writings and speeches of Chinese Communist leaders, as well as those of Marx and the Russian Communists.

The entire propaganda apparatus of the regime grinds out an unending flow of material, most of which can be, and much of which actually is, used by *hsueh hsi* groups. (The principal theoretical journal published by the Chinese Communists, incidentally, is called simply *Hsueh Hsi*.)

What is perhaps most startling to a non-Communist observer, however, is the emphasis placed upon theory. One would naturally expect the Chinese Communists to indoctrinate the people on political and economic policies, and hence it is no surprise at all to discover that works such as Lenin's *Imperialism*, Stalin's *The Foundations of Leninism*, Mao's "On New Democracy" and "On Peoples' Democratic Dictatorship," the Peking regime's Agrarian Reform Law and Common Program, and many similar writings are widely used in *hsueh hsi* groups. But it is surprising to learn that one of the most universally used texts is a book called *The History of Social Development*, that everyone reads *From Monkey to Man*, that *Dialectical Materialism and Historical Materialism* is inflicted even upon persons with very little formal education, and that abstruse works such as "On Practice" and "On Contradiction" are given high priority. Great stress is placed upon ideological fundamentals.

This effort at mass conversion of the entire Chinese population to a new ideology through intensive group indoctrination raises some questions that are difficult to answer. How did the Chinese Communists develop the program? Where did they learn the technique used?

Although the idea of educating the populace in an orthodox, state-approved ideology is not new in China, it is difficult to find any precedents in Chinese history for intensive group indoctrination of the sort now used by the Communists. Many aspects of the indoctrination, such as the emphasis upon criticism and self-criticism, have clearly been borrowed from the Soviet Union, but the use of intensive group indoctrination to remold the thinking of the mass of the population (not just Party and government personnel) has never been developed or pushed in the U.S.S.R. to the extent that it has been in Communist China. In scope and intensity, group indoctrination in China appears to be a new phenomenon—new both to China and to world Communism.

I have discussed the origin of *hsueh hsi* with Chang Kuo-t'ao, a former member of the Chinese Communist Politburo who now lives in Hong Kong, and he believes that it developed by trial and error during the period in which the Communists were recruiting guerrilla armies. "It started in the army," he says. "The rank and file of soldiers were uneducated peasants. We experimented in explaining commands and then seeing what they understood and remembered. It was difficult to teach them, and we had to teach them all sorts of things—how to work a rifle, how to live together, why they should not steal. The idea of teaching them through group discussion slowly developed." This throws a little light on the origins of *hsueh hsi*, perhaps, but it hardly explains how it has developed to its present stage.

The insight into subtle psychological techniques and group pressures revealed by present methods of *hsueh hsi* also is surprising. It makes one wonder if Communist leaders in their caves at Yenan were reading Freud and Jung as well as Marx and Lenin, although there is certainly no evidence that this was the case.

Undoubtedly, the entire program developed in China slowly on the basis of both Soviet and Chinese experience, but there is no doubt that *hsueh hsi* and the great emphasis placed upon remolding the thinking of the entire population in China are now in many respects unique aspects of the Chinese Communist regime.

How effective is this group indoctrination, and how much success are the Communists actually having in their efforts to accomplish a mass ideological conversion?

One can answer, at the start, that group indoctrination has been very successful in achieving surface conformity in the thinking of the Chinese people. They are being taught the new ideology, and they are expressing verbal acceptance of it. But it is extremely difficult to know what actually goes on in the minds of those indoctrinated. How many genuinely believe the new ideology? How many people's minds are confused by a combination of partial belief and doubt? How many people "believe" only because of the unremitting psychological and social pressures upon them? What would happen if the pressures were lifted? How many have built walls around their minds and have tried to stop thinking? How many cling stubbornly to old beliefs despite the necessity of approving the new ones verbally?

It is almost impossible to answer these questions with any confidence, although undoubtedly there are people who fit each of these categories.

One thing is probable, however. The younger the persons exposed to the indoctrination, and the longer the indoctrination process, the more likelihood there is of genuine belief in the new ideology. And there is no doubt that many of the older generation, particularly those of the educated classes, secretly maintain ideas they can no longer express. The psychological strain of the indoctrination process on many of the older people is very severe, and there is evidence that many are afflicted by psychiatric disorders. In Shanghai, for example, the mental wards of hospitals are more crowded than they have ever been in the past. One hears of cases that lead one to guess that schizophrenia is often the price paid for attempting to lead a double mental life. Certainly, "peace of mind" is not characteristic of Chinese society under Communist rule.

It is too early to predict whether or not the Communists will be able, in their revolutionary struggle, completely to reshape the minds of the inhabitants of the largest single nation on earth. But it is possible to say that through *hsueh hsi* they are now trying very hard to do so, and the degree of success they seem to be having is profoundly disturbing.

9

PRISON INDOCTRINATION

March, 1955

Hong Kong rests on the edge of two worlds. But sometimes one forgets it, because the place is so calm, beautiful, and "normal." Then, unexpectedly, something happens that shakes you emotionally and intellectually, making you realize that the frail wire fence separating Hong Kong from Communist China symbolizes a chasm which is frighteningly wide and deep.

One day recently, a friend of mine told me that I looked pale. I have no doubt that I did. During the previous twenty-four hours, I had undergone a genuinely unnerving experience. I had seen and talked with two young Americans who had just emerged from Communist China after serving three-and-a-half-year "sentences" for "espionage." Both were completely indoctrinated in the ideology and world outlook of their Communist jailers.

When these two young Americans, whom I shall call Mrs. Smith and Mr. Jones, arrived in Hong Kong, instead of being jubilant about their release or resentful against the Peking regime which imprisoned them, they immediately made it clear to the world that they had become dedicated supporters of and enthusiastic missionaries for the Communist cause. Both of them flabbergasted friends and reporters who met their train by openly confessing complete guilt as "spies," expressing deep "shame and remorse" for all their past "crimes against the Chinese people," praising Communism and the Peking regime extravagantly, and announcing that in the future they planned to "work for the people."

Mrs. Smith and Mr. Jones seemed to be under some sort of spell even after crossing the border. As they talked to reporters, the words came flowing out in the clichés and vocabulary of Radio Peking; it was as if they were repeating a Communist catechism rather than describing personal experiences. The whole performance seemed unreal, even though both spoke with obvious conviction. As I listened, the dominant thought that kept running through my head was that their bodies had been freed from jail but their minds were still imprisoned by the narrow dogmas to which, amazingly, they had been converted while behind bars. They were still living in a world created in their minds by years of indoctrination and psychological pressures in prison.

Both Mrs. Smith and Mr. Jones came out of China hypnotized by the Communists' "truths," which they learned not by personal observation or reasoning but by instruction in jail. In conversations, they spoke constantly of the "truth." What a short and simple word! Webster says that it means "conformity to fact and reality." Simple enough, in theory. But Mrs. Smith and Mr. Jones seem to have lost or abandoned their own capacity to make independent judgments on "facts" and "realities" and to have accepted completely the "truths" propagated within prison walls in Peking.

These two young Americans are the most striking examples to date of foreigners successfully indoctrinated within Communist China's jails. They are disturbing testimony to the vulnerability of the human mind to psychological pressures, and striking proof of the effectiveness of Chinese Communist indoctrination methods.

Jones, now in his late twenties, is a native of New York City, where his father, a respected professional man, lives in a fashionable midtown area. Tall and lanky, he looks younger than his years. He was educated at one of the best-known American Ivy League universities. After graduation, during World War II, he joined the army and was sent to China. For the next year or so, he says, he worked for the Office of Strategic Services, before being demobilized and sent home after the war.

More study in the U.S. followed, but apparently the lure of the Orient infected Jones as it did many of his fellow GI's during the war, so he went back to China, this time to study at one of the major Western-supported institutions of higher learning, in Peking.

In early 1949, the Communists entered Peking. At first Jones, like most other foreigners who had not evacuated the city, continued his work undisturbed.

I was in Peking at that time, and although I did not know Jones personally, I heard others talk about him. He was one of the sort who "settle in" abroad, learn the language, live very much as local inhabitants do, and avoid involvement in the somewhat ingrown community life of their fellow countrymen's enclaves. He was immersed in Peking. A few of the Americans there who knew

Jones regarded him as "emotionally immature," but people gave him credit for "really trying to learn about China."

Finally, in mid-1951, Jones was arrested, along with a number of other Americans, and disappeared into a Chinese Communist jail. From that time until last month, little was heard of him. Peking made no public mention of his name, and no charges against him were aired.

A few reports about him did trickle out to Hong Kong, however, from fellow prisoners and other Americans released earlier. These reports indicated that he was a recalcitrant prisoner who for a long time stood up to his jailers and consequently received tough treatment from them. During the early period of his imprisonment, he was seen in chains; later he was observed manacled with handcuffs.

Mrs. Smith is now in her mid-thirties. Her family home in the U.S. is in a suburb of New York City. For a number of years, she has been studying China professionally; she did graduate work in Chinese studies at a leading American university and received an M.A. soon after World War II.

In late 1948, she went to China on a fellowship to continue her study of China and chose Peking as a place to settle down. When the Communists took over, she was working toward a Ph.D. in Chinese studies and teaching English at one of the best-known Chinese universities in Peking on a part-time basis.

The strong arm of the regime descended suddenly in July, 1951. Mrs. Smith was first placed under strict house arrest for over a year, and then she was taken off to jail. No charges against her were publicly announced when she was arrested.

During 1949, in the period immediately after the Communist entry into Peking, I saw something of Mrs. Smith and got to know her fairly well. She impressed me as a highly intelligent, stable American girl whose interests seemed to be more cultural than political. Like most Americans with her kind of educational background, however, she did, of course, have political views. They impressed me as being mildly New Dealish and "liberal" but in no sense pro-Communist. She was, in short, neither radical nor ultraconservative, but somewhere in the middle.

Mrs. Smith was in a basic sense religious, I believe, although she was not a proponent of dogma and did not parade her religious beliefs very much in public. Her personality was one exhibiting quiet self-confidence, friendliness, and warmth.

There was no forewarning of the release of Mrs. Smith and

Jones, just as there had been none of their arrest. Suddenly, on a Sunday not long ago, they simply presented themselves to the police at the Hong Kong border.

Hasty telephone calls from the American Consulate-General notified a handful of reporters and friends of their arrival, and, by the time the afternoon train from the international border to Kowloon station had arrived, there were about a dozen people waiting for them at the station.

When the two of them stepped off the train, it was obvious that they were tired and tense, but neither looked in bad shape. Their clothes were hardly impressive: Jones was wearing faded blue jeans and an old gray shirt, while Mrs. Smith had on black slacks and a checked jacket. But it was clear that they were all right physically—sound of limb and not emaciated. Their friends heaved sighs of relief, and the reporters took note of their condition.

Fifteen minutes later, friends and reporters alike were exchanging questioning glances, shaking their heads in amazement, and looking bewildered. We were assembled in a small station teashop interviewing the two of them, and what we heard seemed unbelievable.

The first question directed at Jones, was a general one: "Well, what has happened to you during the last three and a half years?" Very simple, he said: "I was a spy." From then on, his words tumbled over each other as he volubly described his guilt, his shame, the justification for his arrest, the good treatment he received in jail, his admiration for the Communists, and his support of all the Peking regime's domestic and foreign policies. He spoke rapidly, somewhat nervously, and with considerable emotion. When questions from his listeners revealed doubt or skepticism, he argued heatedly to convince the questioner. He sounded like a spokesman for the Chinese Communist regime rather than an American who had just been released from a Chinese jail.

All the reporters present scribbled furiously. This was turning out, unexpectedly, to be quite a story. No American expelled from China before had talked quite this way. Some had been strongly influenced by indoctrination in jail; many, for example, had believed propaganda such as the germ-warfare charges, or were impressed in general by the strength and dynamism of the regime. But none had turned out to be confirmed partisans and apologists for the Communists.

Mrs. Smith sat calmly on the sidelines while Jones held the

limelight, but finally the interview was switched to her. She was asked, "And Mrs. Smith, what comment would you like to make about the things Mr. Jones has told us?" I'm sure that almost everyone present expected her to disagree with what had been said. Her first remark, therefore, was stunning. "I absolutely echo his statements," she said. Then she proceeded, in her own quiet way, to add a good deal more.

The interview broke up with everyone in a strange mood. Mrs. Smith declined an invitation to stay with an American couple who had been close friends of hers in Peking; she chose instead to take a room in a social institution for women. Jones found a room elsewhere, in a similar institution for men.

I decided that I must have an opportunity to talk with them again, this time alone, so the next morning I telephoned Mrs. Smith. She was friendly: "Certainly, come on over." When I arrived, Jones had already joined her, so I sat down with the two of them in a sun-washed lounge. We talked for a couple of hours. Their answers to my questions were like a conversational fugue— the parts neat, regular, and intertwining, the themes consistent and familiar. It was no act, however; I was absolutely convinced of their sincerity.

It is difficult to describe impressions of people's minds, because such impressions are formed not only from what the people say but also on the basis of how they say it. However, I know of no better way of giving a thumbnail sketch of the present state of mind of Mrs. Smith and of Jones than simply by quoting some of the things they said to me. I cannot attempt to reproduce the full conversation, but even disjoined fragments may give a rough idea of their thinking.

All the following quotes were taken down verbatim during our talk, and they were spoken with what appeared to me to be firm conviction.

The question of espionage charges and guilt came up first. Both Mrs. Smith and Jones were determined to prove their own guilt.

Jones: "When I was arrested, I was absolutely guilty of the crime of espionage."

Mrs. Smith: "My situation was clearly espionage."

Jones: "I knew in the first place that I was guilty. In order to gain self-respect, one has to confess."

Mrs. Smith: "Before I was arrested, in my heart I knew that I was guilty of being a spy, but I wouldn't have admitted it."

Jones: "We are grateful for such light sentences. One has to be penitent to be released."

What did their "espionage" consist of?

Jones said that as a member of the OSS during the war he "did intelligence and espionage against the Chinese Revolution." Then, he said, when he was in Peking as a student during the period of the Communist takeover, he "did another piece of espionage" when he "sneaked through" the "wave length of a spy radio" to an American university lecturer outside Peking who, Jones says, was a "spy" and "not a friend of the Chinese people." In addition, he said that he delivered information on the "Chinese Volunteer Army" to an American girl in Peking; this girl, a student, was also a "spy," according to Jones. In short, he said, "I admit I spied for the U.S. Government. It is a fact. How can I deny a fact?" He then went on to say that previously he had had a "savage mentality" and "did not know" what he was doing. Later, he said, he had come to feel "full of shame and remorse."

Mrs. Smith stated that she had "helped" another American "do espionage work." This, she said, consisted of "military, cultural, and political intelligence." She also asserted that she received $2,300 from the U.S. Government in 1948. "In the beginning," she added, "I was terribly reactionary, refusing to see what the truth was."

On the surface, these confessions, from the "criminals" involved, may sound fairly convincing. Yet I know of no one who talked with Mrs. Smith or Jones in Hong Kong who was convinced. The two of them found themselves in the anomalous position of confessing their guilt to people who did not believe them.

I personally am convinced that neither Mrs. Smith nor Jones was guilty of "espionage" as the term is used in the West. I asked Jones if he had ever, in Peking, submitted regular reports to any agency of the U.S. Government or received any money for information. The question annoyed him, and his answer was evasive. "Espionage has nothing to do with money," he said. I probed Mrs. Smith on the source of the money she said came from the U.S. Government. Reluctantly, she admitted that the $2,300 that she received in 1948 consisted of a scholarship grant.

But both Mrs. Smith and Jones left China convinced that they were guilty of "espionage," as the term is used by the Communists. In short, they apparently came to accept the Chinese Communists' definition of the word, which can be extended to cover acquisition of almost any knowledge about the regime, particularly by persons unsympathetic to the Communists.

Some news reports from the U.S. following Mrs. Smith's release implied that she might be trying to protect others still in jail in Peking. But I am sure in my own mind that this was not the case. She appeared to be sincerely convinced of her own guilt and, like Jones, was "full of shame and remorse."

From the day they were arrested until shortly before their release, neither Mrs. Smith nor Jones was given a trial or convicted of any crime. Then, about two weeks before they left, they were both "tried," sentenced to three and a half years' imprisonment, and "deported" from China "because they had already served their terms." In view of these facts, their opinions on the present legal system in Communist China are startling, to say the least.

Mrs. Smith: "In China today, a person who is not guilty of a crime could never be arrested or convicted."

Jones: "I was together with several hundred people at different times in jail. I never knew anyone who was not guilty of serious crimes. I never met one innocent person."

Mrs. Smith: "They don't arrest you until they have absolute proof that you are guilty."

Jones: "The legal system in the People's Democracies is the most infallible system on earth. Why? It is democracy. Anyone who thinks that anybody else has made a mistake or is capable of making a mistake can express himself on it. That is the essence of democracy."

I asked them if they did not think it strange that their "trials" came at the end rather than at the beginning of their imprisonment. Of course not, they replied. They were guilty from the start. The authorities make no mistakes. The system is infallible.

Jones spent a total of three and a half years in jail in Peking, and, as stated earlier, he was reliably reported to have been in chains or handcuffs during at least the earlier part of that period. Mrs. Smith spent two and a half years of her "sentence" in jail.

Many reports on conditions within Peking jails have been made by persons coming out of China during recent years. They indicate that treatment of different individuals varies considerably. In some cases, the authorities are fairly lenient in a physical sense, and the emphasis is on indoctrination. In others, however, the jailers are very rough, and sometimes prisoners undergo prolonged periods of physical maltreatment. Most foreign inmates seem to get enough food to survive without difficulty, but the diet is meager. The cells are usually overcrowded, and prison life is extremely austere. Many prisoners are made to work. All prisoners live in an atmosphere of psychological harassment, pressure, and fear while they undergo intensive indoctrination and demands for confessions.

What did Mrs. Smith and Jones have to say about their treatment in jail?

Jones: "I was always treated kindly while in jail. Everyone was —not only Americans, but also Chinese. I had pneumonia once and almost died. The doctors treated me day and night."

Mrs. Smith: "The food was good."

Jones: "The Chinese Government gave me two lives. I should have been shot for espionage and wasn't. I might have died of pneumonia in prison and didn't. I am certainly grateful to the Chinese people."

Mrs. Smith: "Our conditions were so good! The People's Government took care of us so well!"

There was no irony in these statements. They were made with genuine emotion.

One of the most significant things about the discussion of jail life by Jones and Mrs. Smith was the fact that they refused to talk at all about their indoctrination. They refused, in fact, to recognize that the "study" and "discussion" groups in which they participated were instruments of indoctrination. The whole process, they asserted, was a voluntary one in which they gradually came to see the errors of their past and accepted "truth."

Mrs. Smith: "In jail, I sometimes studied and sometimes worked, at sewing and such. The study was often in groups, sometimes individual. But don't think it was forced. Usually, the demand for study came from me. It was not placed on me by the government."

Jones: "We could discuss anything we wanted in jail. It was free discussion."

Mrs. Smith: "We had no pressure put on us."

As I listened to such claims, I thought of all the people who previously had described to me the severe psychological pressures of prison indoctrination they had experienced. I wondered how and when Mrs. Smith and Jones had been "broken." But it did not surprise me that they could not admit, even to themselves, that their ideological conversions had been under duress.

When Jones was asked about reports that he had been kept in

chains, he became agitated and said he would not answer such questions.

Everything Mrs. Smith and Jones said provided evidence that in their Peking jail they had undergone a basic emotional and intellectual conversion, and that they had left China believing with religious fervor in Communist "truth."

Mrs. Smith: "In a People's Democracy, after you express your opinion, through the course of discussion you arrive at the truth. There is only one truth. There is only one standard for judgment: what is good for the most people."

Jones: "Everything we read in the newspapers told the truth. The newspapers in China cannot tell a lie. No, we did not see any papers but the Peking *People's Daily*, but it tells the truth. It is not distorted like American papers."

Mrs. Smith: "When I first went into jail, I argued for American democracy. We had many happy discussions. But gradually I realized that I was looking at things from the wrong viewpoint, through the wrong glasses. Gradually, one comes to realize the truth."

Jones summed it up neatly when he said: "A cigarette is a cigarette, a piano is a piano, and truth is truth." How can one question it? There it is—simple, clear, undebatable.

What had happened to the innate skepticism, the insistence on personal opinions and individual judgments, the belief in independent thinking these two graduates of leading American universities must once have held? Wholehearted belief in the "one truth" had superseded all.

After hearing Mrs. Smith and Jones speak as they did of the "truth," I was hardly surprised when I heard them express their political views.

Mrs. Smith: "In the New Democracy today, the government is of the people. It comes from the people."

Jones: "If Lincoln were alive today, he would be a Communist."

Mrs. Smith: "The Communist Party is an organization of the people. Anyone who wants to work for the people can join the Party. The people and the Communist Party are one."

Jones: "It would be perfectly impossible to have democracy without the leadership of the Communist Party."

Mrs. Smith: "There is absolutely nothing you can say to express the new spirit you see in China. Many of the principles of

morality in Christianity are absolutely akin to the principles practiced in People's China."

Jones: "In the whole world, there is nobody so peaceful as the
Chinese Government and the Chinese people."

Mrs. Smith: "The Communists are always against aggressive
war."

Jones: "The United States is filled with poverty at the present
time and is on the road to war. Depression is inevitable in the
U.S. It cannot be avoided. Periodic depression is part of the
system."

Mrs. Smith: "Capitalism is inseparable from poverty and war."

Jones: "I am sure that the future standard of living of the
Chinese people, after they have completed their socialist industrialization, will be much higher than the standard of living in any
capitalist country."

Mrs. Smith: "In the future, America will be a socialist country.
It is not a question of whether the U.S. *should* copy the U.S.S.R.
and People's China. It is a question of whether the U.S. *will*. It
absolutely will; that is the way the whole world is inevitably
going."

Jones: "Taiwan belongs to the Chinese people and does not
belong to the U.S. No evil force can stop them."

Mrs. Smith: "No force on earth can stop the Chinese people
when they want to get what is rightfully theirs."

The whole schematized Communist conception of the world,
phrased in standard terminology, was repeated over and over. If
there had not been such conviction in their manner of speaking,
their contributions to the conversation would have sounded like
the reading of a well-rehearsed script. One of the pair would make
a statement; the other would affirm support for it and then, using
the same terminology, add something in the way of elaboration.
The first would then pick up a cue and continue. And so on. Their
answers to questions were not short and simple. They had to answer every question with the complete version of the catechism;
and even if interrupted, they would insist on continuing to speak
their piece.

One very revealing incident took place while we were talking.
An American woman who had joined our conversation noticed
that Jones was not wearing socks and asked him why. He was
flustered by the question and said: "I am sorry. Yes, I should be
wearing socks, shouldn't I? I will get some." He was like a small
boy reacting to a verbal spanking. I wondered how many, and

how harsh, his verbal thrashings had been during the past three and a half years in jail, and whether he would be able to stand on his own feet again as an independent person, intellectually and emotionally.

The shock of listening to them expressing Communist dogma would have been less if Mrs. Smith and Jones had become members of the Communist Party. A great many things follow from the fact of joining the international apparatus of Communist organizations. But this was not the case with them. Both stated that they had not become Party members—they seemed genuinely surprised when asked if they had—and there seems no reason to doubt their claims. They are ideological converts, not political recruits.

When Jones was asked if he had joined the Party, he replied, "I have not that honor."

Mrs. Smith answered the same question by saying: "How can we join the Communist Party? Only the best people can join the Communist Party. I am not worthy. I have committed crimes."

Both of them, however, indicated that they felt in a vague, undefined way a tremendous obligation to work for the Communist cause, for the new "truth" they had accepted.

Mrs. Smith, when asked of her future plans, said, "I want to return to the U.S. to be an honest person, work for the people, and make up in some way the harm I have done in the past."

Jones said: "I will try to be an honest and upright person, a person who does not harm the people. I will try to apply the morality the Communists taught me—you must not harm the people."

My principal emotions after talking with Mrs. Smith and Jones were pity and shock. I believe this was true also of most others who talked with them here in Hong Kong. There were very few angry reactions.

My pity was based upon realization of the terrible emotional stress they must have undergone during indoctrination in jail, and apprehension about the difficulty they will have in adjusting to a world in which the "facts," "realities," and "truths" they now accept will be in constant conflict not only with attitudes they will encounter but also with the things they themselves will observe and experience. They have traveled a hard road psychologically during the past three and a half years; another difficult road lies ahead.

My shock came from seeing what had been done under pressure

to the mind of a person I knew. After talking with Mrs. Smith, I had the sinking feeling that "if it could happen to her, it could happen to almost anyone I know." The Chinese Communists' methods of indoctrination are not basically esoteric or mysterious. Essentially, the technique is to control all that a person sees and hears, as well as to focus on any individual the full force of authority and social pressure, and to use both persuasion and threat to make a person confess past guilt, renounce previous attitudes, and wholly accept a new faith.

Of course, my conversations with Mrs. Smith and Jones took place only during the first days after they had left China, so it is difficult to judge to what extent they will be able, slowly, to come out of their present trancelike state of mind and adjust to a new environment during the months ahead. Their indoctrination may, or may not, wear off.

But certainly, immediately after their release, both Mrs. Smith and Jones were living in a world far different from the one I know on this side of the flimsy wire fence separating Hong Kong from Communist China.

OLD AND NEW

March, 1954

One of the outstanding characteristics of contemporary China is rapid change. New ideas, technology, and social organization—borrowed to a large extent from various Western cultures—have been superimposed upon traditional Chinese society with a rapidity which, if viewed in historical perspective, is remarkable. This process of change—the essence of the Chinese Revolution in its broadest sense—predates the existence of the Communists, but they have seized control of it, shifting it in new directions and accelerating the pace.

The changes now taking place are so rapid that it is easy for an observer of the Chinese scene to be impressed only by innovation and lose sight of what is permanent and enduring. How deep are many of the changes? To what degree are some of them superficial? In what way are the old and new combined into a complicated mixture? Where and how do strong subterranean currents of tradition continue to exist? These are extremely difficult questions to try to answer.

To what extent, for example, is the modern Chinese, whether Marxist or non-Marxist, really a successful rebel against the past, or is he the captive, consciously or unconsciously, of old Chinese patterns of thought and behavior?

There is no doubt, for example, that the Communists' methods of indoctrination are having a tremendous impact upon the minds of the people; but it is extremely difficult to judge how deep and enduring the changes are. From time to time, one has an experience that forces one to admit that the task of judging real change is enormously subtle, complicated, and difficult.

The case of one young Chinese friend of mine here in Hong Kong is illustrative. Chen Pao-li (not his real name) is in his early twenties. He is a product of Western education in modern China, and although he is a political refugee from Communism, he is, in an intellectual sense, certainly a Chinese revolutionary.

Pao-li comes from a landowning family with a tradition of officialdom and government service, and he was sent to college at Nankai University, in north China. (Chou En-lai started his career with a similar family and educational pedigree.) He was halfway through college when the Communists came to power, and like most politically conscious university students in China he was sympathetic to the Communist regime at the start. He and his schoolmates believed that what China needed was modernization and development, and they felt that perhaps the Communists could press forward toward this aim.

Pao-li became disillusioned with the Communists sooner than most of his schoolmates, however. Within a year, he developed strong objections to the authoritarian controls exercised by the Peking regime and decided to leave the mainland. His family was from south China, and he had relatives in Hong Kong, so there was a place to which he could go.

When he decided to become a political refugee, Pao-li did not abandon his interest in politics. On the contrary, he started to think even more seriously than he had in the past about the problems of development and modernization in China. In Hong Kong, he began to read an increasing number of Western philosophical works and became more and more convinced that Western liberal philosophy should be introduced further in China to serve as the ideological basis of the Chinese Revolution. Philosophically speaking, Pao-li slowly became an intellectual creature of the West. He now knows more about Bertrand Russell than he does about Confucius or even recent Chinese thinkers.

Pao-li has little sentimental attachment to Chinese tradition, at least on an intellectual level, and he believes that if China is to modernize it must be ideologically Westernized. The tragedy, in his mind, is that ideas from the Western liberal tradition did not take root rapidly enough in China, and that Marxism was given the opportunity to fill the vacuum created by the disintegration of old Chinese society and the discrediting of traditional Chinese thought.

Pao-li eventually reached the point of wanting to do something about these new ideas of his. Consequently, he and a group of like-minded Chinese friends in Hong Kong decided to publish a literary-philosophical magazine in order to propagate the liberal Western thought to which they subscribe. They also decided to translate a number of Western books into Chinese, to spread non-

Marxist philosophical ideas among young Chinese in areas not under Communist control.

This publishing enterprise developed slowly. The magazine and books did not have any spectacular success, but the enterprise was at least able to survive—in a place where most publishing efforts are ephemeral.

The next project that took shape in Pao-li's mind was a novel. He decided a short while ago that he wanted to put on paper some of his ideas about the revolution in China, and that the novel would probably be the most effective medium. He formulated a outline, found a publisher, and is now writing the book.

The novel's setting is modern China, and the period covered spans the Kuomintang era and the early years of Communist rule. The story concerns a triangle that involves a father, a son, and a girl who is the father's concubine and the son's lover. The theme in this dramatic thread of the story is the conflict of generations in modern China—a bitter struggle in terms of politics, philosophy, and morals, as well as the psychological competition of father and son. The complicated political theme is intertwined with the personal relationships in the story. One of the fundamental ideas is the conviction that the father's generation was unable to carry out the Chinese Revolution successfully and lost the struggle to the Communists because, despite a veneer of Westernization, it was too much weighted down by outmoded traditional Chinese ideas, moral values, and habits of behavior. The father's generation was semimodern, but not modern enough to be successfully revolulutionary.

Both Pao-li's publishing enterprise and his current novel are an expression of his own revolutionary (in an intellectual rather than purely political sense) attitude—his rebellion against the past and his belief that new ideas and behavior must supplant old Chinese tradition. His novel is also a clue to his reaction against old patterns of personal and family relations—a reaction that has been widespread and deep among youth in contemporary China.

Pao-li—whom I have known well during the past three years— always seemed to me in many respects almost a model of the most Westernized kind of modern, revolutionary Chinese youth. Then, not long ago, he dropped in to pay me a visit, and I suddenly discovered another Pao-li—one I had not known at all.

As soon as he sat down on the couch in my apartment, I sensed that he had a problem and wanted help. It did not take long for it to come out.

"This is very embarrassing for me," he said, "but I am going to ask you for a favor."

He paused and folded his hands, resting them between his knees. He was dressed in Western clothes and had the clean-cut appearance typical of many modern young Chinese.

"I need some money," he went on, speaking in English. "Not a gift, but a loan. I will be able to pay it back in a matter of weeks, as soon as I finish my novel. The publisher has guaranteed an advance as soon as I give him the manuscript."

"Perhaps I can help you with a small loan," I answered. "What do you need it for?"

I asked even though I really knew without asking that his need for money was probably connected with the approach of the Chinese New Year—a time for settling all debts and accounts, and a time also for celebrations, which cost money.

But the thought flashed across my mind: "What does the Chinese New Year mean to someone like Pao-li?" It is an old-fashioned festival. Most of the customs associated with it are survivals of a past era, long predating the modern revolution in China.

"Well," Pao-li said, "you know that New Year is coming. It is going to involve a lot of expenses for me. You see, I am the head of our family."

"You are what?" I knew that Pao-li's father, a former Nationalist official, was alive and was also a refugee from the mainland. I thought perhaps I had misunderstood him.

He saw that I was baffled, and he laughed.

"Yes, I am the head of our family."

I became interested. "How is that possible?" I asked. "I don't understand."

He smiled in a slightly embarrassed way. "It is a long story," he said.

" I have plenty of time," I replied quickly.

So he began. This is what he told me, reduced to the essential facts.

Pao-li's grandfather was a wealthy man and in many respects a typical old-style Chinese family patriarch. He had three sons. The eldest son died young. Pao-li's father was the second son, and his uncle was the third.

Loss of the eldest son was a great blow to Pao-li's grandfather. He wanted the family's continuity to be unbroken, and he felt that the leadership of the family should be passed on through the eldest son of the eldest son. And since his eldest son had died as a youth, this was not possible.

That is, it was not possible in the normal way. But there are traditional means of dealing with such situations, and Pao-li's grandfather decided that he could solve the problem.

He first contacted a friend whose daughter had died when very young, and they agreed to "marry" their dead son and daughter. A ceremony was arranged, and a posthumous marriage performed. Step number one was thereby accomplished; his dead son could be considered a married man. The next problem was to give him a son. This is where Pao-li came into the picture. His grandfather decided that Pao-li should be "adopted" by the dead first son whose marriage he had just performed. In this way, Pao-li would become first son of the first son, and the proper direct inheritor of the family line. A ceremony was arranged, and this was done. Pao-li thenceforth had two sets of parents—his own blood parents and the dead parents by whom he was "adopted."

When the grandfather died last year, therefore, it was Pao-li rather than his father who became the titular head of the family, with theoretical control of family property and all the obligations and responsibilities of family leadership.

I listened with fascination to Pao-li's account of all this.

"Does this mean, then, that you actually do control all the family property?" I asked.

"No," he replied, "that is one of the difficulties. My father and uncle, and all the elder relatives in the family, don't really turn over responsibility for these things to me. But my theoretical position is recognized, and therefore at New Year I am the one who must arrange a family dinner, pay formal visits, and give gifts to all the family members. That is what I need the money for."

"And do you really have to do all these things?" I asked.

"Yes."

I lent him the money.

But for a long time after he left, I thought about the ridiculous anomalies of Pao-li's position.

He is a highly Westernized young man who in many respects is a revolutionary. He believes that new ideas must supplant traditional Chinese ones. He blames the political failures of the older generation in China to a large extent upon the inability to slough off the impedimenta of the past. His writings reflect rebellion against old moral values and social ties—particularly against the family. Yet he finds himself trapped by family obligations imposed upon him as a result of actions by his relatives that he himself considers almost fantastic.

How much is he really a captive of the past against which he rebels? It is doubtful if even he himself knows.

A case such as Pao-li's makes one ponder. To what extent is rapid social change deceiving? What is left of tradition under the surface, and how much is the old intermixed with the new?

In Communist China, for example, where almost everything today appears to be in flux, is the persistence of tradition greater than one might assume at first glance? It is, of course, easier to ask the question than to answer it.

Does all of this mean that *plus ça change, plus c'est la même chose?* No. The process of change is certainly not illusory. Tremendous and real changes have taken place in China in the modern period, and under the Communists the changes are greater and more rapid than ever before.

But people like Pao-li dramatize the difficulty of judging the permanent reality and actual dimensions of the change one observes in China today.

men him, as a result of actions in his relations that he him, of conflict is almost invisible.

How much is he really a captive of the past against which he whom it is doubtful if even he himself knows.

Whichever of these it makes one ponder. To what extent is rapid social change occurring. What is left of tradition under the sur- face and how much is the old intermixed with the new?

In Communist China, for example, where almost everything today appears to be in flux, is the persistence of tradition greater than one might assume at first glance? It is, of course, easier to ask the question than to answer it.

Does all of this mean that plus ça change, plus c'est la même chose? No. The process of change is certainly not illusory. Tremen- dous and real changes have taken place in China in the modern period, and under the Communists the changes are greater and more rapid than ever before.

But people like Fan-li dramatize the difficulty of judging the permanent reality and actual dimension of the change one ob- serves in China today.

PART IV

MASS MOBILIZATION:
SOCIAL AND ECONOMIC CHANGE

THE IDEOLOGICAL REFORM CAMPAIGN

July, 1952

Since achieving power, the Chinese Communists have advanced their revolution through a continuing series of intensive mass campaigns and movements. Each of these has severely shaken the structure of old Chinese society and has pushed the revolution a step further. During the past year, China's intellectuals—and the Chinese educational system—have been the prime targets of an important one of these movements, the Ideological Reform campaign.

"The Chinese Communists are converting the universities on the mainland into political centers and trade schools." That is how an American-educated Chinese college professor (I shall call him Professor Wang), who worked under the Communists in east and south China and recently arrived in Hong Kong as a refugee, sums up the present policy toward higher education. His statement is supported by official pronouncements and reports on current developments in Communist publications.

During the half-century prior to the Communists' rise to power, modern education in China developed under the strong influence of Western ideals of liberal education and academic freedom. This influence, combined with the well-established Chinese respect for scholars, produced, in the modern universities of China, centers of intellectual ferment that played a leading role in the Chinese Revolution. But the revolution is now turning on the universities and attempting to destroy them as centers of independent thought. The universities are gradually being converted into indoctrination schools and technical training institutes for the bureaucracy of the new regime.

For two and a half years after the Communists "liberated" the country, they moved rather cautiously and slowly in their relations with universities and intellectuals. Then, in the fall of 1951, they took off their gloves and started an all-out campaign of Ideological Reform, a campaign that has subsequently developed into a many-sided attack upon intellectual freedom and integrity in China's academic institutions. During recent months, for the first time, educators of outstanding national reputation—men who at one time publicly supported the Communist regime and tried to adapt themselves to it—have been made scapegoats in this attack on the intellectuals. The professors at Yenching University, in Peking, have been a major target.

Yenching, formerly a private, American-supported institution and one of the leading universities in China, is not entirely typical. During the first stages of Communist control, it was treated more leniently than the average government university, and recently, since the beginning of more strenuous efforts to root out what the Communists call "American cultural aggression," it has been treated more harshly. But the process is essentially the same in all universities, despite variations in timing and methods.

When the People's Liberation Army entered the campus of Yenching in December, 1948, it received an enthusiastic welcome. The prevailing atmosphere was one of hope and optimism. I remember a conversation I had there about six months later with the President of the university, Dr. Lu Chih-wei. He said, in effect, "I sincerely believe the Communists will allow universities such as Yenching to continue, and we are going to try to adapt ourselves to the new regime, as long as we can maintain our basic standards and principles." For about two years thereafter, Yenching continued operating without basic change. Then, in April, 1951, the government abruptly "took over" the university and made it a state institution. Other private institutions, particularly those which had received foreign financial assistance, suffered the same fate subsequently. Half a year went by, and then, in November, 1951, the government adopted a "Plan for the Reorganization of All Technical Colleges Throughout the Nation" which transferred Yenching's Engineering Department to Tsinghua University and its Colleges of Arts, Science, and Law to Peking National University. The plan included a sentence that stated simply: "The name of Yenching University shall be abolished." This step was taken after initiation of the intensive Ideological Reform movement in Peking. The final blow, however, came late this spring when President Lu Chih-wei and several outstanding Yenching professors were publicly denounced and removed from their posts. Lu, according to one of the most recent travelers from Peking, is believed to be under arrest.

Recently, I asked Professor Wang what he believed the effect of these harsh measures against Lu and his colleagues would be upon intellectuals elsewhere in China—specifically, the professors whom he knows and was in contact with only a few months ago. "Tremendous," he said. "Yes, tremendous. Lu and the others are universally respected in China. They are representatives of what I would call the cream of China's intellectuals. Lu, particularly, has been admired for his character as well as for his scholarship. If people of Lu's stature can be denounced and discarded, no one is safe; I imagine my friends are thinking that this is only the beginning."

Full reports of developments in Yenching have never been published, but copies of a college publication called *New Yenching* have recently reached Hong Kong, and this journal contains many of the details.

The climax of the attack on President Lu Chih-wei came when he was denounced by his only daughter in a bitter tirade made at a public accusation meeting this past March 11. The daughter, Lu Yao-hua, postgraduate student in Yenching's Biology Department and a candidate for membership in the Communists' New Democratic Youth League, was at one time known to be exceptionally fond of her father, according to friends now in Hong Kong, but she lashed out at him in a merciless attack: "You are a one hundred per cent claw of imperialism and a tool faithful to American imperialism in its cultural aggression." "You have been a hypocrite, and I have been cheated by you." "You are no longer my respectable father." "You are actually a 'Christian with no political sympathy for the Communist Party.'" "No Chinese will ever pardon you." She excused herself for not having denounced him earlier by blaming her weakness on the "love between a father and a daughter," but she went on to say: "Even if this love is true, it is definitely insignificant compared with the love among the broad masses, not to mention the fact that your love is not love but deceit. Why must I be deceived by you and revolt against the people? I want to be with the broad masses and struggle hard for the sake of Communism."

During the course of the Three-Anti campaign which was in progress when he was denounced, Lu Chih-wei himself humbly confessed that he had been "one hundred per cent pro-American, willing to carry out American cultural aggression," had "passively attacked the cultural-educational policy of the Chinese Communist Party," and had "sought to keep the old traditions of Yenching." "I confess my crimes," he said; but apparently his confessions were not sufficient. He was repeatedly denounced and "exposed" for organizing a "reactionary clique" in Yenching and "conniving with the enemy to monopolize school affairs and continuing to carry out his policy of cultural aggression." The "Lu clique," all of whom were denounced, included four of the key figures in the university: Nieh Ch'ung-ch'i, Dean of Studies; Ch'i Ssu-ho, Head of the Department of History and Dean of the College of Arts before its dissolution; Ch'en Fang-chih, Head of the Department of Political Science; and Shen Nai-chang, Head of the Department of Psychology.

In addition to Lu, two other Yenching professors with nation-wide reputations were denounced and removed from their posts at about the same time; there are unconfirmed reports that they as well as Lu are under detention. One was Chang Tung-sun, an outstanding philosopher who for many years was a leader of the Democratic League, the principal pro-Communist "minor party" in Peking's present "coalition." The other was Chao Tzu-ch'en, head of Yenching's School of Religion, who has been a vociferous fellow traveler and public defender of the Communist regime as well as one of the leaders of the Communist-sponsored independent Chinese Christian Church. At the time of their denunciation, Chang was a member of the Central People's Government Council, the top executive-legislative body in China, and both Lu and Chao were members of the People's Political Consultative Conference, the precursor of a People's Congress.

Although Yenching is in some respects a special case, the drastic measures applied there are merely an extreme form of the pressure that is being applied to all universities in the intensive "ideological reform" process that has been carried out during the past year. This process began in Peking, where it has already passed its peak, but it is now being extended to other parts of the country, and in Kwangtung, the province bordering Hong Kong, it has just "begun in earnest" in most universities.

Like so many of the "campaigns" that have taken place in Communist China one after another, in rapid succession, during the past three years, the Ideological Reform campaign started with relatively little fanfare and then, over a period of months, built up into a frantic, violent, and almost hysterical "struggle." (A recent refugee from the mainland has described some of the meetings held during the course of the campaign in Peking, and they sound very much like "holy roller" orgies.) The stated aim of the campaign when it started was to carry out general "ideological reform" through a "study movement" and "criticism and self-criticism." It was initiated in Peking, foremost center of higher education in China, by a nineteen-member, government-appointed Study Committee of Teachers of Institutes of Higher Education in Peking and Tientsin, headed by the Central Government's Minister of Education, Ma Hsu-lun. Under this over-all committee, subcommittees were established in each of the twenty-odd participating institutions, and under the subcommittees the professors were grouped into small discussion groups of approximately ten members each.

The campaign really started rolling on September 29, 1951, when Premier Chou En-lai addressed a mass meeting of more than 3,000 professors, assistants, and instructors in Peking, to define a correct "standpoint" and "attitude" for them. The professors were then put to work reading Communist literature, including Chou's report, holding discussion meetings, and carrying out thorough criticism and self-criticism. A special journal, named *Teachers' Study*, was brought out by the directing committee to guide the campaign, and the committee dispatched reporting officers, coordinators, and liaison men to all the universities to check up on the process. Altogether, more than 6,500 professors and other university teaching personnel in Peking took part. They spent many hours each week in required reading, discussion, and meetings.

Five stages in the campaign were outlined. The first consisted of study of Chou En-lai's report. The second centered upon a report by the local Peking Communist Party chief, P'eng Chen, concerning three previous "major movements" (Agrarian Reform, the Campaign Against Counterrevolutionaries, and the Resist America and Aid Korea movement); it was intended to "expose reactionary thoughts" and "draw a clear line of demarcation between ourselves and our enemies." This was followed by a period of study focusing on the CCP and its history; the aim was to establish the correct "standpoint, viewpoint, and method of the working class" and to criticize the "mistaken thoughts of the bourgeois class and the petty bourgeoisie." Subsequently, the professors studied a report on national economic development stressing the need for training cadres in order to "establish the ideology of education serving the needs of national defense and economic construction." Finally, they went through a "summing-up" period.

The key elements in this process were criticism and self-criticism, which are among the Communists' most effective techniques for thought control and indoctrination. During the latter part of 1951, the Chinese press was filled with the humble (and one cannot help but believe, in many cases, humiliating) confessions of the best-known Peking professors. These men, who had been the intellectual leaders of China, vied with each other in public expressions of intellectual submission to the Communist Party and repudiation of past beliefs. Typical of the confessions publicized was that made by the Dean of the College of Law of Peking University, who abjectly apologized for the "serious mistake of holding on to my own views."

The professors admitted to, and resolved to rid themselves of, such a plethora of sins that it is difficult even to list them all. Individualism, reformism, objectivism, dogmatism, sectarianism, opportunism, feudal thoughts, "compradorism," a "pro-America, worship-America, fear-America" mentality, reactionary capitalist thoughts, bourgeois and petty-bourgeois ideology, liberalism, a non-political standpoint, the "mistaken pedagogical philosophy of 'freedom of thought,' 'freedom of study,'" and others.

The basic aims of the campaign were succinctly summarized by Vice-Minister of Education Ch'ien Chun-jui when he said: "In the course of this study movement, we should adopt the Marxist standpoint, approach, and method, fall back upon revolutionary patriotism, internationalism, and collectivism, and follow the working class's basic viewpoint of union of theory and practice, to eliminate with determination the . . . influences of the Anglo-American reactionary capitalist class and overcome the erroneous trends of individualism, objectivism, sectarianism, and dogmatism."

Actually, however one interprets these complicated labels and "isms," it is clear that the government's basic objectives are to obtain complete acceptance of the Party's collective will, to suppress intellectual independence and freedom, and to force the professors into the accepted ideological mold. From their statements, the Communist leaders appear to believe not only that this is necessary and desirable per se, but also that it is dialectically necessary to facilitate implementation of their new educational policies, which emphasize technical and political training and call for the conversion of "old-fashioned universities into new people's universities."

On October 1, 1951, after the Ideological Reform campaign had started, the Government Administration Council (GAC), highest administrative organ in the Peking Government, promulgated a decree entitled "Decision on the Reformation of the Educational System." The new educational system outlined by this decision places primary emphasis upon development of elementary education, education of political workers and cadres, and technical education. At the university level, technical education is particularly emphasized, and it is clear that the Communists reject the accepted "old-fashioned" idea of universities as centers for independent scholarship and thought. Ma Yin-ch'u, President of Peking National University, for many years regarded as the leading university in China, stated in a speech shortly after promulgation of the GAC decree: "The aim of higher educational institutions is to train advanced technical personnel and principal cadres for national construction." Ministry of Education officials have asserted that in the next five to six years institutions of higher learning in China should train 150,000 to 200,000 "senior construction cadres" for industrial, agricultural, communications, transport, medical, and similar technical work. (Middle-school-level technical institutions are called upon to train 500,000 "junior cadres" in the same period.) This is the fundamental task that the universities are now being reorganized to carry out.

It is not surprising that many Chinese professors, brought up on the traditions of liberal education, resent both ideological thought control, which demands that they "gradually turn themselves into Marxists," and the trend toward mass production of university graduates who at best will have little more than a minimum of knowledge and skill in some specialized technical field. The Communists themselves now admit the existence of passive opposition to their educational reorganization. Professor Wang says that in the two universities where he taught, the opposition to current educational trends is widespread and deep among professors, but that it cannot be anything more than passive because of the police controls which effectively enmesh the universities as well as all other institutions in China under Communist rule. This is undoubtedly one explanation for the fact that the Ideological Reform campaign in Peking, which was originally slated to last only four months, did not end on schedule but was merged with a new and even more intensive movement, the Three-Anti campaign.

Since early 1952, when this merger took place, all normal university classes and activities have been virtually suspended. The professors, with the "assistance" of their students and university employees, have been caught up in a full-time process of denunciation and confession which seems designed to wipe out the last traces of independence and intellectual integrity that may have remained after the first stage of Ideological Reform.

At the start, the Three-Anti campaign was not primarily ideological in its aims. Originated in August, 1951, in northeast China as part of a local Increase Production and Economy drive, it developed in December into a national campaign to rid the government and Party of corruption, waste, and bureaucratism, and to combat the "corrosive" influence of the bourgeoisie, alleged to be the main cause of these evils. In January of this year, its scope was expanded again, and attention was focused on the bourgeoisie—especially merchants and other commercial interests—in a companion Five-Anti campaign against "five poisons": bribery, tax evasion, stealing of state property, cheating on government contracts, and stealing of "state economic intelligence." These two campaigns have undoubtedly affected more people, and have had more far-reaching effects, than any others centered on urban areas to date. It was natural and logical that the Communists would apply this attack on the bourgeoisie to "bourgeois thought" in the universities, and in early 1952 Ideological Reform in the Peking universities continued with renewed vigor under the Three-Anti slogans. As in the case of the original ideological campaign, this new one did not begin elsewhere in the country until somewhat later, and consequently it is still in full swing in many Chinese universities.

The Three-Anti campaign in Peking's universities was led by the Cultural-Educational Subcommittee of the Economy Checkup Committee, established to supervise the over-all movement, and in all the universities Economy Checkup Subcommittees were established. The campaign was described as a "grave and acute class struggle" against the "bourgeois mentality"; in fact, it developed into a complicated and very real struggle between various groups of professors, between professors and junior teaching personnel (instructors and assistants), and between the teaching staff and students. It is standard Communist practice to intensify and manipulate group conflicts of this sort to achieve the desired end; such tactics had already been used in the universities, but never to a comparable extent. The official Communist papers described the role of the students in the campaign with what, to any outside observer, seems to be grim humor. "The students," reported one paper, "organized themselves into groups to interview the teachers, mobilize them, hold heart-to-heart talks with them, help them do away with their doubts, and sincerely assist them in their ideological reform."

The campaign reached its climax in bitter denunciation meetings of backward elements—meetings such as those in which Lu and his colleagues were denounced—and, according to recent arrivals from Peking, by the time the campaign was over almost everyone in the universities from presidents to gatekeepers had publicly humbled themselves, or been humbled, before the power of the regime.

During the campaign, token attention was given at the beginning to the anti-corruption, anti-waste, and anti-bureaucratism slogans under which the struggle was being waged, and exhibitions of the "vast waste" in the universities were held. ("Even the garbage in the institutes of higher education is found to be full of the blood and sweat of the people.") But the central idea was the "demarcation of the ideological line between the bourgeoisie and the working class," between "foe and friend." The "evidence of bourgeois mentality" cited in attacks on the professors included examples of everything that the Communists have disliked about professors' attitudes. The list of sins varied in different universities. In one, for example, it included: obstruction to the organization of "universities of a new type," reluctance to give up "American standards," rating research above teaching, unwillingness to sacrifice academic standards for the benefit of students active in political work, general indifference to politics, and "individualism." The president of another university complained that the professors "turn up their noses at the laboring masses," "think themselves above class distinctions and politics," "think that . . . they represent labor," "hold that technique has nothing to do with politics," "pay little attention to the practical requirements of the country's new industrial and agricultural construction," "are still incapable of fostering a hatred for America," "cling to old methods," "give no encouragement to the students' political study," and are guilty of irresponsibility, departmentalism, and a tendency to observe old school ties. These are merely examples; many others could be cited. Obviously, the aim was to attack all evidence of nonconformity with the ideology and policies of the new regime.

It is impossible from a distance to judge the extent to which the apparent submissiveness of the professors is real and sincere, or the extent to which there has been passive resistance that has led Communists increasingly to use force and intimidation to keep the intellectuals in line. Some of the public "confessions" sound phony, but others have the ring of authenticity. In this connection, however, the remarks made by Professor Wang to me are of some interest. He does not think that more than a small proportion of the professors in China's universities sincerely support the regime

now. "One of the first things one learns under the Communists,"
he says, "is that one cannot disagree. I think most of the professors
in Peking are simply playing a role. They can't help it. I know
something about that, because I 'confessed,' too. As a matter of
fact, the Communists liked my confession; it was considered the
second-best confession in my university. If I could get away with
it, I am sure the professors in Peking are able to do so, too. There
isn't anything else they can do." It would be a mistake, therefore,
to assume that the professors are completely converted or wholly
intimidated after their "ideological reform," or that China's universities have completely changed their character as a result of the
government's new educational policies.

A standard technique employed by the Chinese Communists in
their "campaigns" is to apply extreme pressure for a short period
of time and then to relax the pressure, boasting of their magnanimity, while they consolidate gains made—which are always
short of the extreme goals and maximum aims defined in the campaigns. This is the stage that is now being reached in the campaign
to reform China's intellectuals ideologically. It may be some time,
therefore, before the Communists complete the process of converting "old-fashioned universities into new people's universities." But
the aim has now been defined, and in their Ideological Reform
campaign they have made a big step in that direction.

THE "FIVE-ANTI" CAMPAIGN

July–August, 1952

Origins of the Nationwide Campaign

Most mass campaigns in China—the movements that have kept the country in a state of almost constant upheaval since 1949— are closely directed and orchestrated affairs, involving the mobilization of millions of people to "struggle" against designated "enemies" of the regime and to carry out certain specific policy aims of the government. They are controlled mob actions and disciplined emotional binges on a massive scale, and they illustrate the successful application of mass psychology to politics, which is fundamental in the pattern of Chinese Communist rule.

Agrarian Reform, the Campaign Against Counterrevolutionaries, and the Resist America and Aid Korea movement were the most massive organized efforts in China between 1949 and 1951, but there were many others of lesser importance. The Communists rarely, in fact, try to carry out any important domestic policy without organizing a mass campaign to support it. In recent months, several campaigns have been in progress, including one—the Five-Anti campaign—that is of special importance. To understand either the character of Chinese Communist rule or the process of revolution now going on in China, it is necessary to have some knowledge of these tremendous spectacles of organized mass action directed by the Party.

The chapters on China in future histories of the Far East will probably devote most of their space for the year 1952 to the Korean War, but it is certain that millions of people in China's cities will remember the first half of 1952 primarily as the period of the Five-Anti campaign. This campaign was summed up as follows by a Shanghai newspaper in June, when the struggle was drawing to a close there: "Though numerous mass movements have been staged in Shanghai before this, not one of them can approach the present one in scope, extensiveness, organization, discipline, influence, and effect."

During the past few months, people in Hong Kong have watched the progress of the Five-Anti campaign with worried fascination. Hong Kong is a commercial city, and thousands of businessmen here have realized that only a delicate political border has exempted them from direct involvement in the frenzied activities directed against businessmen on the mainland. Indirectly, Hong Kong has been affected in many ways. Private trade and commercial activities in China's large cities came to almost a complete halt during the peak of the campaign, and as a consequence Hong Kong's trade with the mainland dropped from HK$148 million* in December, 1951, to HK$68 million in March, before it began a gradual recovery. Commercial travel between Hong Kong and the mainland almost ceased; key personnel in private enterprises in China were forbidden to move while the campaign was in progress, and most Hong Kong businessmen decided that they would not voluntarily enter the lion's den. Many Hong Kong branches of mainland business establishments lost contact with their home offices. One company I know merely received terse communications from its home office signed with an impersonal, official "chop" and ominously lacking the manager's own seal; nobody in Hong Kong knew the fate of the manager. Other Hong Kong branches received frantic messages requesting money. The head of one Hong Kong factory received a phone call from the manager of his Shanghai home office; "Send a million Hong Kong dollars, or I will be put in prison," the manager pleaded. The money was not sent because the factory head, like many businessmen here, decided that complying with extortion demands would probably not help the people in Shanghai in the long run. Quite a few companies did comply with such requests, however. For example, one Hong Kong establishment which had kept several hundred thousand Hong Kong dollars in a trust fund for a small group of mainlanders since 1949 sent the entire sum to the mainland in response to urgent requests from the persons involved. This kind of thing made Hong Kong businessmen rather bitter; many who for opportunistic reasons had recently maintained a sympathetic, or at least noncommittal, attitude toward the Peking Government decided that they did not like the Communists and did not care who knew it. One of the leading pro-Communist businessmen in Hong Kong, for example, changed his stand completely and began

---

* Approximately U.S.$25 million. HK$6 is the equivalent of slightly more than U.S.$1.

talking about the Communists' "banditry" after he had been asked to send HK$50,000 ransom money to a brother who was managing a factory of his on the mainland.

Although it was possible to see directly many of the effects of the campaign upon the fortunes and attitudes of Hong Kong businessmen, it was extremely difficult to obtain a clear picture of what was going on in China's cities while the campaign was in progress, because of the blackout of direct news and the severance of many normal links with the mainland. A few weeks ago, however, after the mainland ban on travel was lifted, a trickle of Chinese businessmen again began coming to Hong Kong. From them and from their friends (many of them are extremely wary, however, about describing their experiences immediately after they come out), it is possible to fill out the picture of what took place during the Five-Anti campaign and what the results of the campaign have been.

At present, the major cities of China, still groggy, are experiencing a sort of "morning after" daze following the intense intoxication and strain of class warfare, public denunciation, and self-confession involved in the Five-Anti campaign. They are gradually pulling themselves together, however, after a long period during which normal economic life and activity have been greatly disrupted. Now the business class—the main component of the "bourgeoisie," who were the target of the campaign—is trying to reassess the new situation in which it finds itself.

To discover the genesis of the Five-Anti campaign, one must go back to the fall of last year and to another mass movement, the Three-Anti campaign, which began on August 31, 1951, in Manchuria (in present-day China, this area is in some respects a kind of political and economic laboratory where many plans and policies are tested before being applied on a nationwide basis). During the fall of 1951, the campaign progressed with relatively little fanfare, and although it was reported in the Peking press and elsewhere it did not spread to the rest of the nation until later. Slowly, however, reports about corruption began appearing in other parts of the country, and the campaign became national in scope.

Apparently, it was in December, 1951, that a top-level Party decision was made to transform the Three-Anti campaign into a nationwide drive "with fanfare," and Po Yi-p'o, head of the North China Bureau of the CCP Central Committee, was appointed chairman of a Central Government Economy Inspection Committee. On December 10, the campaign began in a serious fashion in

Central Government organizations in Peking, and before the month was over it was well under way in all government, Party, army, and Party-affiliated organizations above the *Hsien* level all over the country.

The actual extent of the corruption the campaign was intended to eliminate is difficult to determine, but there is no doubt that since the Communists moved into the cities in 1949 corruption has grown sufficiently to be a source of real worry to top Chinese leaders. The Communist press early this year was filled with reports of individual corruption cases, and Communist leaders freely admitted the seriousness of the problem. One month after the campaign started in Peking, Po Yi-p'o reported that 1,670 cases of corruption had been uncovered in 27 Central Government bodies, and a month later it was officially reported that several thousand cases had been exposed in Peking. Similar situations were revealed all over the country. For example, in Canton, Party officials announced in early February that they had already rooted out 70 to 80 "tigers" (big corruption cases involving graft of about JMP$200 million*) and that they expected to discover in Canton alone 400 to 500 more big cases and 4,000 to 5,000 medium and small ones.

Party branches and cells all over the country devoted themselves during this period to "tiger hunts," inspections, self-assessment, and confession; and checkup teams were sent out by higher Party organs to investigate. The aim, it soon became clear, was not only to reduce corruption, waste, and bureaucratism, but also to cleanse the Party and the entire bureaucracy of "rightist" deviations and "bourgeois" thought. The campaign extended through the spring of this year, and the national Party authorities outlined detailed rules for judging cases and meting out punishments, and for setting up special People's Tribunals for the duration of the campaign. By the time the climax had been reached, a large number of Party members, including some of middle and higher rank (but none at the very top level), had been purged and punished.

While the campaign was in progress, observers in Hong Kong speculated and debated about whether this house cleaning was an indication of weakness or strength on the part of the regime. By the time it was all over, I believe the consensus was that it was a sign of self-confidence on the Communists' part that they could openly and successfully attack deviations, corruption, and other

* JMP stands for "People's Currency." For rough conversion purposes, JMP$1 million can be considered to be the equivalent of about U.S.$40–50.

weaknesses in their own ranks, and the net effect of the campaign, in the short run at least, was to increase organizational discipline.

Long before the Three-Anti campaign had run its course, however, the attention of the government and Party began to shift toward the bourgeoisie. It was apparent that the greatest corruption took place in government and Party agencies that dealt with economic matters and had closest contacts with commercial and industrial circles, and as time went on more and more blame was shifted to the bourgeoisie.

In January, 1952, a direct attack on the bourgeoisie was initiated in speeches made in Peking by Premier Chou En-lai and Po Yi-p'o. At first, these attacks were based on the Three-Anti slogans, but they later were expanded and developed into the new Five-Anti campaign. The bourgeois class was severely chastised for having cheated and stolen huge sums of money "from the government and from the people," and the guilty were ordered to confess and make restitution.

From January through May, the Five-Anti campaign was vigorously promoted in all the important cities of China. The Communists went to great lengths to arouse the masses against the bourgeoisie, and during the course of the campaign class warfare between employees and employers was at times bitter and intense as a result of the general mobilization of workers and shop assistants in the struggle against the business class. The struggle, however, was one carried out under the close control and direction of the Party.

Although a considerable number of businessmen were arrested during the campaign, it was by and large a struggle without physical violence. The mood, however, was one of fear and tension, and in this respect the campaign was a successor to the Campaign Against Counterrevolutionaries, which took place in the cities last year. It involved less actual violence, but affected many more people. Some observers have called the Five-Anti campaign the urban counterpart of the Agrarian Reform movement. In one sense it was; like its rural counterpart, it was a general attack on a leading economic class. But there were also important differences. Agrarian Reform aimed at liquidation of the landlord class and complete reorganization of rural productive relations by redistribution of the landlord's land holdings, whereas the Five-Anti campaign had the more limited aim of undermining the influence of the bourgeois class in the cities without actually liquidating it or completely eliminating its functions. Businessmen were thoroughly terrorized while the campaign was in progress, however, by the kind of treatment they received. The manager of one large company was kept locked in his office for seventeen days, while he was being interrogated and threatened; he confessed all his real and imagined sins several times, but his confessions were repeatedly rejected as unsatisfactory and incomplete. Another businessman was questioned continuously for three days and nights; the weather in Shanghai at the time was still wet and cold, and this man was clad only in his underwear for the whole period. Managerial personnel in another large company were handcuffed in their office for a long time before the Communists decided that they were telling the truth when they denied that they were concealing large amounts of money. This type of humiliating and terrifying treatment was meted out to thousands of Chinese businessmen to force them to confess their "illegal earnings" and to make repayment for them to the government. It was all-out psychological warfare.

The Five-Anti campaign was carefully organized on a national scale, and detailed rules and regulations were promulgated by the Central Government.

The general principles for treatment of businessmen were defined as follows: (1) leniency for past mistakes, but severity for new mistakes; (2) leniency for the majority, but severity for the minority; (3) leniency for those who made frank confessions, but severity for those who resisted; (4) leniency for industrialists, but severity for merchants; and (5) leniency for ordinary merchants, but severity for speculators. As it worked out, almost all businessmen suffered financially, roughly according to their ability to pay, but the harshness of the treatment they received did, in general, follow these five principles. Speculative merchants, of whom China has had a tremendous number, were treated most severely, while many industrialists were spared the worst because the Communists were concerned about keeping up production.

On March 8 of this year, the Government Administration Council in Peking approved detailed measures for classifying and treating all businessmen according to the amount of money they were found to have made by "evading laws" or by making "illegal profits." These "Standards and Measures for Dealing with Industrial and Commercial Establishments Classified into Various Categories in the Five-Anti Campaign" defined five categories of businesses:

(1) Law-abiding establishments—those which committed no acts against the law.

(2) Basically law-abiding establishments—those which obtained benefits as a result of law violations of less than JMP$2 million, and certain ones whose "illegal earnings" exceeded this amount but whose cases were not too serious and whose confessions were satisfactory. (The regulations required all "illegal earnings" over JMP$2 million to be restored to the government.)

(3) Semi law-abiding establishments—those which made "illegal earnings" of over JMP$2 million, but whose cases did not constitute a "serious danger to the state"; this category included a few fairly "serious" cases in which the persons involved performed "meritorious service" by denouncing other business establishments. The regulations required restoration of all "illegal earnings" by these people to the government. (The majority of small businesses fell into the second and third categories; they had to make payments to the government, but received no further punishment.)

(4) Serious law-breaking establishments—those which made fairly large "illegal earnings" and were either a "serious danger to the state" or refused to confess. According to the regulations, companies in this category not only had to restore their "illegal earnings" to the state, but also had to pay "appropriate fines." The fines were almost always determined on the basis of what the traffic would bear.

(5) Completely law-breaking establishments—those which committed the most "serious crimes," resulting in "grave danger" to the state or causing "serious loss by the state and the people." Business establishments in this category, according to the regulations, not only had to make repayments and pay fines but also were subject to partial or complete confiscation of assets; the men involved could be sentenced to prison, forced labor, or death.

The classification of business establishments and determination of their crimes and penalties were not a legal process. They took place in mass meetings, committee meetings, and private interrogations, all directed by the Five-Anti committees set up in the cities, the teams of political workers under their control, and the activists mobilized from among the workers. The money and other assets taken from the businessmen were handled by the top campaign committees, together with the People's Courts, public security organs, and other government agencies. (Their distribution and use have not been revealed.)

The "most serious cases" were turned over to special revolutionary People's Tribunals (*ad hoc* bodies, different from the People's Courts) established for the duration of the Five-Anti campaign. These tribunals, each organized with a presiding judge (usually the head of the local People's Court), two deputies, and several judges, assisted by "representatives of the people," were empowered to make arrests and to pass sentences, which could include specification of sums of money to be repaid to the government, fines, confiscation of property, "surveillance," "reform through labor," prison terms, and death. Any death sentence, or prison sentences over ten years, required higher approval, however.

Great emphasis was placed during the campaign on the need for public denunciation and confession. The government guaranteed full protection to anyone making a denunciation, and the treatment accorded to businessmen depended to some degree upon their willingness to confess. Frank confession could lead to a one-grade reduction of criminal status, while refusal to confess automatically resulted in raising the classification of the case by one or more grades. Special consideration was given to persons who performed the "meritorious service" of denouncing others.

It is not easy to summarize the many results the Five-Anti campaign had achieved by the time it drew to a close in May and June, but some of its principal effects are clear.

There is no doubt that the business class in China's cities has been terrorized and intimidated to such an extent that the "five poisons" will be much rarer in the future than in the past, particularly since the Communists now warn that they will not be so "magnanimous" again. This means that tax evasion will probably be greatly reduced, that attempts to bribe government or Party personnel will not be undertaken lightly because of the risks involved, that businessmen will probably hesitate before attempting to obtain any information about government economic plans and activities that might be of particular use to them, and that in contracts with government agencies private businessmen will have to be extremely careful about satisfying the government's requirements. In general, businessmen will have to lean over backwards to observe the government's laws, regulations, instructions, and policies, in order to stay out of trouble.

Having said this much, however, one has only started to suggest the scope of the real results of the Five-Anti campaign, which are of much wider and more fundamental significance. Here is a brief listing of some of the more general results:

The campaign undermined the position of the urban bourgeoisie in China, greatly reduced its wealth and assets, ostracized it as being dangerous and subversive, and probably eliminated any possibility of significant political influence on its part.

It intensified class conflicts in the cities, isolated the business class, separated businessmen from their employees, and encouraged conflicts among businessmen themselves.

It produced large revenues for the government, which was important to state finance, and removed most of the remaining fluid capital in China from private hands.

It resulted in the collection of considerable amounts of much-needed foreign exchange that had previously been successfully concealed from the government, thereby increasing state control over China's limited foreign-exchange resources.

It made a large contribution to the government's unceasing fight against inflation in China and actually brought about at least a temporary reduction in the price level.

At the same time, however, the campaign severely disrupted normal commercial activity and adversely affected normal production. Commercial markets stagnated, and industrial production dropped during the campaign. The production loss may have amounted to close to the equivalent of two months' output in China's urban economy; this is a loss that can never really be made up.

The campaign greatly increased government control over, and direction of, the remaining private sector of the Chinese urban economy. This was one of its most important results. Many private enterprises are now private in name only, and all private enterprises are subject to innumerable controls. In fact, now the government probably has effective enough control over private industry and trade as a whole to apply state planning in various degrees and forms to the entire economy. This has been accomplished on the eve of a great campaign of national construction to increase production, a campaign initiated in June, immediately after the Five-Anti campaign.

In the process of increasing state controls, the Five-Anti campaign also helped to discourage private initiative, and it excluded from national life (or at least from key roles in the economy) a small but important number of skilled business leaders who in the past have made a significant contribution to China's economic development.

It also demoralized to a certain extent Party and government personnel who deal with private businessmen and with economic matters. The Communists now admit a tendency on the part of many bureaucrats to avoid economic and financial responsibilities, because of the risks and possible penalties involved.

What does all of this add up to? It is difficult to give an easy answer. One thing is certain, however. The Five-Anti campaign gave urban society and the urban economy of China its most severe shake-up since the Communists came to power, and although China is still, in a formal sense, going through a New Democratic stage in which the bourgeoisie and private enterprise are tolerated, the Communists have actually advanced one further step along the road toward socialization.

The Campaign in Shanghai

"I consider this city's Five-Anti struggle to be the key to success or failure of the nation's Five-Anti campaign," Mayor Ch'en Yi of Shanghai said on March 25 of this year, when he announced the official beginning of the great mass campaign against businessmen. The campaign against the bourgeoisie had to be successful in Shanghai, he said, because "Shanghai is China's bourgeois center." The development of the campaign in the sprawling metropolis on the Whangpoo River is therefore of particular interest. Other big cities in China went through a similar process, but it was in Shanghai that the Communists attacked the real stronghold of China's bourgeoisie and business class. The attack was successful and encountered only light resistance.

Preparations for the Five-Anti campaign in Shanghai began about three months before Ch'en Yi's speech. As early as December, 1951, the Shanghai municipal government, in response to statements made by national leaders, called meetings of leading businessmen to explain to them the drive against corruption, waste, and bureaucratism, and to urge them to confess their complicity in these crimes. From December 19 to 26, the Shanghai Federation of Industry and Commerce called meetings of the chairmen and vice-chairmen of all local business and trade associations, to which heads of private enterprises without exception must now belong, and began to extract confessions of bribery, tax evasion, and similar sins from them.

In January of this year, after the speeches by Chou En-lai and Po Yi-p'o which opened the direct nationwide propaganda attack against the bourgeois class, the Shanghai Increase Production and Economy Committee, which was to lead and direct the campaign, issued a public call to the masses to denounce law-breaking merchants and industrialists. The committee requested that denunciations and information be sent to them, and it guaranteed government protection for the denouncers and informers. At the same time, the committee called upon businessmen themselves voluntarily to confess their sins of bribery, tax evasion, cheating the government, and so on.

By late January, an extensive propaganda drive was under way. Teams of propagandists toured the city and mobilized workers and shop assistants to help them. They plastered the city with posters, written slogans, banners, and "wall newspapers." Some of the teams in local districts consisted of up to 200 members; they went into factories and stores and demanded confessions from the owners and managers. Loudspeakers set up outside shops and at important street corners blared questions and accusations at businessmen: "Hey, boss, have you confessed yet?" Workers, and even casual passersby, were encouraged to shout at businessmen through these public loudspeakers.

Preparations for the campaign progressed rapidly during January and February, and by the end of February "several tens of thousands" of denunciations containing data on businessmen had been received by the Increase Production and Economy Committee. This material was sorted, analyzed, and carefully studied, together with all other known information about individual business establishments. Then, even before the campaign was officially started, the committee, on the basis of these data, attempted to classify Shanghai's 163,400 business establishments (excluding the 110,000 hawkers). According to their classification, 15 per cent were "law-abiding," 50 per cent were "basically law-abiding" (including many companies that had "cheated the government" of considerable sums of money but were willing to confess and perform "meritorious service" by denouncing others), 30 per cent were "semi law-abiding," and 5 per cent were given the ominous labels of "serious law-breaking" and "completely law-breaking" establishments. In short, the committee decided that almost 140,000 business establishments in Shanghai would have to make payments to the government, that more than 57,000 would be squeezed hard, and that about 8,000 would receive the harshest treatment.

While this "research" was going on, organization and training for the campaign were intensified. The Municipal Increase Production and Economy Committee established branches in each city district. Special training classes were organized, and 10,000 workers and shop assistants were indoctrinated in the campaign's aims and policies. Then, in mid-March, a large number of cadres were transferred and placed under the direction of the committee; they came from government organs, the army, and experienced Three-Anti work groups. These cadres were organized into Five-Anti Investigating Teams, which studied the lists of private enterprises, and the available data about them, went over the denunciations already made, established liaison with workers and shop assistants, decided upon "key points" or targets where they would work first to gain experience, and finally carried out "combat maneuvers."

From March 21 to 24, seventy-four of these teams fanned out over the city and carried out experimental "key point" work in selected private enterprises. To facilitate the progress of the campaign, the government issued orders forbidding managers, vice-managers, and key personnel to leave the city; the orders warned against any destruction or alteration of business records, forbade closures, and required continued payment of wages and provisions of meals to employees, even if business operations temporarily ceased.

Finally, on March 25, Mayor Ch'en Yi formally opened the campaign with his speech to the political workers. He described the government's policies ("stern" but "flexible") and once again issued a call to businessmen to confess the "five poisons" and to contribute "meritorious service." At the same time, he tried to reassure the frightened businessmen somewhat by telling them that this campaign was different from the campaign against landlords; the businessman, he said, were not to be eliminated as a class, as the landlords had been. He emphasized that production should be maintained as much as possible during the campaign, and stated that the government would help private enterprises in difficulty by giving them processing orders, contracting to buy their goods, and extending loans if necessary.

The business class in Shanghai was already living under a reign of terror, however. Businessmen's private and professional lives were being exposed in detail to their employees and to the public. Their books were being minutely examined. They were under constant pressure to confess, although many of them were never clear what it was that they were supposed to confess. If they did confess, the first confession was almost always turned down as incomplete and inadequate, and it had to be followed by one or two more. They were also being urged to denounce their friends and colleagues. And by this time most of them saw the writing on the wall and realized that their fluid business assets and capital were soon to disappear. Yet the terror to which they were subjected was largely psychological; there was very little physical violence in this campaign. In essence, what the businessmen were required to do was to admit that they were sinners, guilty of the "five poisons," that they had "cheated the government" and "stolen from the people," and that they deserved punishment. But some held out against doing this, and they were bitterly denounced. For many, the psychological pressure was too great to stand, and a wave of suicides began to sweep over Shanghai. In all, there were probably several thousand suicides during this period, and a number of well-known leading businessmen were among them.

The government made every effort to stir up the working people of Shanghai against their employers, but at the same time it kept the situation under tight control. It issued a stern "eight-point discipline" defining who could do what; the masses were not allowed to punish their employers or to take the payments they made—this was the prerogative of the government authorities. The mob was incited to action, but it was kept under discipline. It was class warfare "by the numbers," with strict rules.

After the campaign was formally under way, a three-step procedure was outlined for all business establishments. After the owners and managers had filled out lengthy questionnaires and submitted them to the Increase Production and Economy Committees, they were to perform "self-reporting for public assessment" (public confession and denunciation). The next step was examination and consideration of each case by workers and shop assistants collaborating with the political cadres. The final step was ratification of their decision by district committees and the municipal committee. When this process was completed, the businessmen had to pay what was required, and if there was any further punishment it was then carried out.

Business in Shanghai had already been seriously disrupted before March, but at the peak of the campaign, in March and April, commercial activity came to an almost complete stop. The doors of business establishments remained open, because official decrees required it, and payrolls had to be kept up, but few business transactions took place. Shanghai had the appearance of a dead city. Factories and productive concerns went on producing to a certain extent, but they were adversely affected, too. Government factories were least affected, but no operations could continue normally. Raw materials were hard to get. Buyers were not buying. Goods coming off production lines piled up in the form of unsold stocks. Government agencies responsible for economic activities were barely functioning because of the combined effects of their internal Three-Anti campaign and the more general Five-Anti campaign. In short, economic life was almost completely disrupted for a period of about two months and considerably disrupted for a much longer period.

After March 25, the campaign developed in four distinct phases. First, from March 25 to 31, the seventy-four Investigating Teams worked over their lists of stores, factories, and companies, and fully mobilized the workers and shop assistants. Five-Anti committees and work teams were organized in all trades and in important factories and stores. Workers' Representative Conferences were called to stimulate greater activity. Capitalists' Representative Conferences were convened, and trade associations were used to apply direct pressure on businessmen.

The second phase lasted from April 1 to 12. More than 1,000 committees and 2,540 work teams, with 35,000 members, were organized by the Municipal Increase Production and Economy Committee, and 25,000 local union cadres and activists were given special campaign training. This "army" of campaign workers was dispatched, district by district and trade by trade, to organize workers and shop assistants, hold meetings, obtain confessions, and teach the "art of struggle." They held meetings of managerial personnel and of workers and staff members; they helped the workers examine the "evidence" on their employers and then called mass meetings to announce their decisions and force public confessions from the employers. If satisfactory confessions were not forthcoming, a district committee meeting was held to put on pressure. If this did not work, the municipal committee sent one of its elite Five-Anti Investigating Teams to apply psychological third-degree methods. These teams often kept businessmen locked in their offices for days, under continuous interrogation. If this treatment failed to produce results, the incorrigibles were hauled off to jail. There had to be a confession. In each case, the verdicts were made by the political cadres, with the assistance of the workers and shop employees, and on the basis of information provided by the workers, employees, and businessmen themselves; but it was essential that the businessmen confirm and accept the verdicts by their confessions.

A new twist was given to the tactics of the campaign during this phase when Five-Anti Merit Achieving Teams were organized; these consisted of businessmen who had already confessed, and they were used to denounce and obtain confessions from other businessmen.

By April 12, the authorities in Shanghai announced that they had won a basic "victory without a fight" in the campaign, but instead of slackening their efforts they increased them. The third phase began; it lasted from April 20 to 30. More than 600,000 workers and shop assistants took an active part in this phase, according to the Communists' own claims, and the cases of more than two-thirds of Shanghai's business establishments—mainly small ones that had been classified as "basically law-abiding"— were disposed of.

There was still no letup in organizational activity, and the incessant meetings continued. Trade Union Cadre Conferences, Workers' Representative Conferences, Conferences of Senior Staff Members of business establishments, and Capitalists' and Managers' Conferences were held, all with the purpose of determining the sins of businessmen and ensuring that they confessed to having committed them. More than 1,600 businessmen who had confessed were mobilized to work on their colleagues. Businessmen's families were also utilized to put pressure on the family breadwinners, and in many districts there were actually Conferences of Capitalists' Families convened for this purpose. District committees also called meetings of representatives of larger industries and organized the persons who attended into "mutual aid" and reporting groups to work on each other.

This endless activity to obtain confessions may be somewhat mystifying to a person unfamiliar with Chinese Communist political techniques, but it is an essential element in these mass campaigns. The demand for confessions has both practical and deep psychological motives. In this case, one of the practical aims was to extract every possible scrap of information from businessmen about their past, their business activities, and their assets. It was on the basis of this information that the cadres could determine the financial levies to be imposed and attempt to justify them. Psychologically, a complete confession seemed to be necessary in Communist eyes as a symbol of absolute submission to the regime, and there is no doubt that the process of extracting confessions put a damper on any latent sparks of open resistance. Furthermore, the process itself, involving bitter recrimination and denunciation, broke down former patterns of relationships and associations and greatly weakened the position of the businessmen involved.

The specific sins the businessmen had to confess were endless. Chinese businessmen for many years have operated in a relatively amoral atmosphere in which laws, rules, and regulations have been viewed mainly as obstacles to be evaded; and tax evasion, bribery, use of official connections, and sharp dealings have been common, if not standard, practice. It is true, therefore, that many businessmen have contravened known laws, and the Communists were able to determine actual law violations on the part of almost everyone. Stated Communist policy was to collect evaded taxes and "illegal earnings" on government contracts only since 1951, and other illegal earnings only since October, 1949, but this was not strictly adhered to; early violations—during the pre-1949 period, when enforcement of laws was lax—were also punished. Furthermore, many of the "crimes" of the businessmen, as defined by the Communists, had less to do with laws than with vague moral judgments proclaimed by the Communists. For persons who proceed from the premise that making a profit is exploitation, and therefore immoral, it is logical to conclude that "large" profits are "illegal" because they involve "stealing from the people." One Shanghai businessman who has come to Hong Kong since the end of the Five-Anti campaign summarizes it this way: "In fact, if you made a decent profit, this meant, by definition, that you had done something illegal in the eyes of the Communists. You revealed the ways in which you made the profit, and these were your crimes. You then confessed your crimes, and the Communists took away your 'illegal profits' and returned them to the people—or rather to the People's Government—whom you were supposed to have cheated when you made the profit."

The climax of the Five-Anti campaign in Shanghai came early in May. The cases of most business establishments were cleaned up by this time. A few "serious cases" were still unsolved, but these were turned over to the People's Tribunals. By now, the overwhelming majority of people in Shanghai had been drawn into the struggle. The Communists estimated that 80 per cent of the workers and shop assistants in the city had taken part in mass denunciations.

When it was all over, a small number of businessmen languished in jail, but by and large, despite the intensity of the campaign, the same people were still around. Although the businessmen had not been "eliminated as a class," they had been stripped of their wealth and capital, as well as their dignity and self-respect.

In the epilogue to the campaign, in conformance with the practice that has become standard in most of the Chinese Communists' campaigns, great publicity was given to the regime's claims of magnanimity. Stressing leniency, the government offered to give businessmen in trouble low-interest loans, processing contracts, and purchase orders, failing to mention, however, that a great many of the businessmen in trouble would have been in reasonably good shape had it not been for the Five-Anti campaign and other Communist policies which victimized, persecuted, and impoverished them.

"Shanghai is now like a malaria patient who has just gone through a racking fever," one recent arrival from that city reports. "The temperature is approaching normal again, but the patient feels weak. And he wonders when the next attack will come."

There is little doubt that Shanghai will suffer another attack, although it may come in a somewhat different form, because mass campaigns have followed each other in rapid succession since the Communists' takeover and are now an established method of carrying out their policies.

The Five-Anti campaign had many unique characteristics, but it also had certain important features common to most past campaigns (and probably to future ones as well):

It was initiated by the top Communist leaders in the nation's capital, who defined the aims as well as the general principles to be applied over the whole country.

It was preceded by intense propaganda and mass psychological mobilization.

It was symbolized by a few specific but flexible slogans, and concentrated on a well-defined enemy.

It was highly organized at the local level and involved the mobilization of huge numbers of people who were induced to take an active part in meetings and organizations.

It stimulated mass action, but kept the activities of the masses under tight discipline and control.

It was led by professionals working in small groups and committees, which directed the activities of larger organized groups.

It not only encouraged but insisted upon class warfare, and it shrewdly utilized and manipulated group conflicts and tensions to achieve its purposes.

It operated according to a plan, starting with careful preliminary preparation, proceeding to "key point" experimentation, going through definite phases, and finally reaching a climax.

It required both mass denunciations of the enemy under attack and public confessions by the enemy.

It built up to a peak of intensity and then ended on a theme of magnanimity and leniency.

These, in general, are the characteristics of mass campaigns in China today. China in 1952 is not a relaxed place in which to live; the keynote of life is struggle.

The Campaign's Impact on the Bourgeoisie

One result of the Five-Anti campaign has been a fundamental change of position in Chinese national life of an entire class, the bourgeoisie. Despite protestations to the contrary, the Communists have, in effect, labeled the bourgeoisie as a class enemy of the regime, allowed to exist only on sufferance. This fact puts a new light upon the "coalition of four classes" which the Communists assert is the basis of New Democracy in China.

The Chinese Communists view social change as a process of revolution by stages, in which Communism can be achieved only after several distinct preliminary stages have been completed. According to this view, as developed by the Chinese Communists in the years before they came to power, the destruction of "semi-feudalism and semicolonialism" in China must be followed by a period of New Democracy before the final steps can be taken toward socialism and Communism. During the period of New Democracy, according to this theory, the regime is supposed to be built upon the foundation of a four-class coalition of workers, peasants, petty bourgeoisie, and national bourgeoisie.

The preamble of the Common Program reads as follows: "The Chinese People's Democratic Dictatorship is the state power of the People's Democratic United Front, composed of the Chinese working class, peasantry, petty bourgeoisie, national bourgeoisie, and other patriotic democratic elements, based on the alliance of workers and peasants and led by the working class."

There has never been any question about the Communists' intention eventually to eliminate the bourgeoisie, an "exploiting class," but they have maintained that during the period of New Democracy—vaguely described as being a fairly long period—the bourgeoisie would have an essential contribution to make and therefore must be included in the class coalition of the regime.

All of this is not quite so theoretical as it might appear on the surface. It means that the Communists have conceded their dependence in many respects upon the skills of China's industrialists and businessmen during the preliminary period of economic development and industrialization that must precede future socialization. They have recognized that today the country's economic skills are still concentrated in the hands of the bourgeoisie and that for this reason the bourgeoisie will be difficult to dispense with completely until the bureaucracy of the People's Democratic Dictatorship is capable of taking over their functions.

At the time of their assumption of power, the Communists made many reassuring statements to dispel the anxieties of China's industrial and business leaders and to obtain their acquiescence and cooperation. In July, 1949, for example, Mao Tse-tung asserted in "On People's Democratic Dictatorship": "The national bourgeoisie is of great importance during the present stage. . . . We must unite the national bourgeoisie into the common struggle. Our current policy is to control capitalism, not to eliminate it." He added, however: "But the national bourgeoisie cannot serve as a leader of the revolution and should not occupy a major position in the state administration. This is because the social and economic status of the national bourgeoisie has determined its weak character, its lack of foresight and of sufficient courage."

At the same time, while recognizing the need for obtaining the cooperation of China's industrial and commercial classes, top Communist leaders were worried about the possible influence of these classes upon the revolution, as it transferred its "center" from rural China to the cities, and Mao himself, in March, 1949, warned the CCP's Central Committee to beware of an attack from the "sugarcoated bullets" of the bourgeoisie.

The early conciliatory statements and initially mild policies of the Communists had a reassuring effect upon many Chinese businessmen, however, and in the period of Communist takeover the majority of China's bourgeoisie attempted to make an adjustment to the new regime.

Developments since the beginning of this year have given these people a rude awakening, however. They had been prepared partially by the fact that between 1949 and 1952 the Communists had steadily become tougher in their treatment of the bourgeoisie, but the abrupt change in the tone of Communist statements early this year came as a shock. It was in January that the Communists began a direct propaganda attack on the bourgeoisie. It started in connection with the Three-Anti campaign, designed to purify the ranks of the bureaucracy by combating the "corrosion" of the bourgeoisie, but once it developed into the Five-Anti campaign, the ideological front was characterized by direct and bitter denunciations of the bourgeoisie as a class.

One can only speculate about the real motives for this open ideological warfare against the bourgeoisie. Probably there was genuine concern among Communist leaders about increasing corruption and slackening discipline in the regime's bureaucracy, through the corrupting influence of "bourgeois thought." It is also possible that Communist leaders decided it was now the time to check any possible growth of political power or influence on the part of the bourgeoisie. Of the groups or classes that under the old regime had exercised significant political influence, the bourgeoisie was the only one which prior to 1952 had escaped direct attack by the Communists. And although there was every indication that the bourgeoisie was for the most part passive and submissive under the Chinese Communist regime, it was nevertheless true that it maintained a certain amount of economic power and did not really accept the new state ideology, which aimed at its ultimate liquidation. Consequently, the bourgeoisie's very existence has presented the theoretical possibility of political opposition to the regime. There is no doubt that the ideological attack made on them as part of the Five-Anti campaign has had the effect of ostracizing members of the bourgeois class, discrediting their ideas, discouraging friendly relations between them and Party or government personnel, and reducing the influence of "bourgeois thought" upon the regime. The Five-Anti campaign has now greatly weakened the economic basis of the businessmen, and at the same time, in ideological terms, has labeled their ideas as dangerous and subversive, thereby greatly reducing the possibility of any future political opposition being inspired or led by them.

The opening shot of this ideological attack was fired by Premier Chou En-lai in the speech he made on January 5 of this year to the Standing Committee of the People's Political Consultative Conference. It was mild in comparison to the barrage that followed, but it started things off. NCNA reported:

Chou stated that the national bourgeoisie has its active progressive side—that is, having been oppressed by imperialism, feudalism, and bureaucratic capitalism, part of them participated in and sympathized with the people's liberation struggle during a certain period, and to a certain extent, after liberation, gradually participated in the construction of People's China and played a certain active role under state leadership. But the national bourgeoisie of China also has its dark and decadent side—that is, having many ties with the imperialist, feudal, bureaucratic, and compradore economy and at the same time, like the bourgeoisie of all countries in the world, having the nature of seeking only profit, benefiting at the expense of others, and speculating, a number of them after liberation . . . often stole state assets, endangered the people's interests, and attempted to corrupt public functionaries through the practice of bribery, were guilty of swindling, profiteering, smuggling, and tax evasion, in pursuit of the private interests of a few individuals.

Po Yi-p'o made the point more clearly in a speech five days later. "The campaign against corruption, waste, and bureaucracy," he said, "is . . . a struggle against the decadent thoughts of the bourgeoisie and also a determined counteroffensive against the attack of the bourgeois class against the working class and the Communist Party for the past three years."

These statements were followed by a huge volume of similar ones that swelled into a flood of propaganda against the bourgeoisie, and as the Five-Anti campaign developed, the tone became increasingly denunciatory. Ch'en Yi in Shanghai said: "This is a fight against the enemy, a fierce counterattack against the trap of corruption prepared by the enemy." Yeh Chien-ying in south China said: "After thirty years of hard struggle, we defeated our enemy, but one more enemy still remains and that is bourgeois class thought."

Among the bitterest statements were those in the periodical *Hsueh Hsi*. An article in the February 10 issue spoke of the "fierce attack on the Chinese working class and the Chinese Communist Party" and "the reactionary, dark, and deteriorated phases of operation of the bourgeois class." It concluded by stating that although bourgeois thought is "not restrained by law" at present, it "is not permitted to be spread about freely or to undermine or weaken the leadership of the working-class ideology." The March 1 issue contained an article which said: "The lust for gold has led them [the members of the bourgeoisie] to sink to such depths that they are more poisonous than snakes, more ferocious than tigers and wolves." Their only salvation, the article maintained, was to "confess their guilt in time. . . . Especially, they should denounce others so as to prove that they themselves have returned to the people's standpoint."

The peak was reached in the March 16 issue, in an article by Ai Ssu-ch'i, one of the best-known Chinese Communist writers of popularized Marxist philosophy, who some months previously had written an article maintaining that the bourgeoisie had a progressive as well as a reactionary side, a thesis he now completely repudiated:

> The movement against corruption, against waste, and against bureaucratism is a determined counteroffensive against the ferocious attack of the bourgeois class, a fierce battle between the ideology of the working class and the ideology of the bourgeois class. This struggle has fully bared the true face of the ideology of the bourgeois class and has enabled us to understand clearly the extent of the reactionary, rotten, and ugly nature of the ideology of the bourgeois class. It does not possess any progressive and active elements, and it definitely cannot constitute a force for the promotion of the development of the revolutionary enterprise of the Chinese people. On the other hand, it actually produces the serious effect of erosion and disintegration of the revolutionary forces. . . . The bourgeois class is an exploiting class. The exploitation of the toiling masses on the basis of the system of private ownership under capitalism, and the making of profits, constitute the material living condition on which the bourgeois class exists. The bourgeois class must undermine the material interests of the working class and other toiling masses for its own existence and development. The class status of the bourgeois class is antithetical to the interests of the toiling masses.

Toward the end of the Five-Anti campaign, these attacks moderated in tone. Communist leaders began making assurances to the bourgeoisie that the campaign was not designed to wipe them out, and started calling upon them again to cooperate "under the leadership of the state." The Party would be "magnanimous" for the present, the leaders said, but they also warned that in the future, even though during the period of New Democracy the "bourgeois class is allowed a rational existence," there would be less tolerance of corrosive influences. Finally, they asserted that despite all the denunciations, the bourgeoisie still belonged to the class coalition of the regime.

The Communists claim, therefore, that nothing has been changed, that the bourgeoisie can still exist, and that the revolution will march forward under the banner of a class coalition that still includes them. Actually, however, a cloud of distrust and suspicion now hangs over the bourgeoisie, and this has greatly influenced their treatment as well as their attitudes toward the regime.

It is quite certain that China's business class, and others lumped under the classification of bourgeoisie, will never again be given the same latitude or be treated with the same degree of relative mildness as they were prior to the Five-Anti campaign.

The members of the bourgeoisie themselves now realize that in effect they are on parole, for as long as the Communists consider them to be useful economically and harmless politically. The overwhelming evidence presented by people now coming to Hong Kong from the mainland indicates that the Five-Anti campaign destroyed whatever remaining hopes and illusions businessmen had about their long-range future, and that for the first time most of them are completely cowed and passively hostile to the Communist regime. They have the feeling that they are living on borrowed time. This means that the bourgeois class in China can be expected to drag its feet in the future, even more than it has in the past. The Communists can force them to work for the regime, but performance under duress is likely to be less efficient than when there was at least some reason for hope.

The Campaign's Importance to National Finance

Among the important results of the Five-Anti campaign was the fact that it produced a large amount of revenue for Communist China's state treasury. In effect, the campaign imposed an extraordinary and discriminatory tax levy upon the bourgeoisie of the country, and this levy has been an essential element in the government's general fiscal policy.

Many Chinese businessmen bluntly assert that the Communists' main aim in the campaign was to "shake down" private enterprise in order to obtain needed revenue, and they dismiss all other aspects of the campaign as ideological window-dressing. Their opinions are not unprejudiced, of course, but there is no doubt that financial motives were extremely important in the campaign.

The Communists now operate with an enormous (for China) national budget which in the past two years has expanded rapidly with increasing military expenditures resulting from the Korean War, a great enlargement of the bureaucracy and government payroll, and an extension of government activities into all spheres of national economic life. In the opinion of financial experts in Hong Kong, government revenues have not increased at the same rate as expenditures, and budget deficits have crept upward. The Five-Anti campaign, and similar mass campaigns during the past three years, have made possible disguised, special tax levies to supplement regular state revenue.

In 1950, the Communists carried out a "Victory Bond" campaign that probably netted the equivalent of nearly U.S.$140 million. During this campaign, the main burden of which fell upon urban businessmen, many forms of coercion and intimidation were employed to force "voluntary" subscriptions, and quotas were assigned to businessmen and other urban groups. This forced loan is still being serviced by the government, but it provided much-needed revenue when it was collected. In 1951, the government promoted a nationwide "Arms Donation" campaign to obtain funds for the purchase of airplanes and heavy military equipment. (No explanation was given of how local-currency donations were to be converted into foreign exchange to purchase these arms.) According to summary figures released in June of this year, this campaign was expected to net the equivalent of about U.S.$250 million. Although people of all strata throughout the country were pressured to give donations, the main burden again fell on the urban population, and on businessmen in particular. The East China Region contributed 38.3 per cent of the total donations from all over the country, and Shanghai alone gave 15.3 per cent. This year, the Five-Anti campaign required thousands of people to make payments to the government for back taxes, "illegal profits," and fines; the target was exclusively the business class, and it is estimated by some that the government's receipts from the campaign were more than double those of last year's donations campaign, reaching the equivalent of over U.S.$500 million.

The financial importance of these special tax levies can only be evaluated in relation to the general financial situation of the government in China at present. This is difficult to do because of the lack of trustworthy data; facts about China's government budget and national income have always been vague and incomplete, and this is particularly true now due to the secrecy surrounding Communist policies. (Budget figures are currently classified as "state secrets.") It is possible, however, to make "educated guesses."

There are reasons to believe that there was a significant deficit in China's national budget in 1951 and that the deficit will be even larger in 1952. Consequently, the Communists face the problem of extracting larger and larger sums of money from those sectors of the economy which have some capital left. The Five-Anti campaign provided a part of the answer to the problem. The consensus of several leading Chinese banking sources in Hong Kong is that the U.S.$500 million figure is a conservative estimate of receipts from the campaign. One expert believes that the government took in closer to U.S.$800 million in the form of cash, foreign exchange, gold, silver, merchandise, and materials, and an additional amount in the form of fixed capital taken over from private enterprises. Although the Peking Government has not made public the details of how such receipts are handled, it is certain that they enter the balance sheet of the national budget in some way; if they are handled in the same way as receipts derived earlier from the Three-Anti campaign, the fluid assets are probably treated as "state income" and the fixed capital as "state investments." In any case, it is possible that the Five-Anti campaign contributed close to 10 per cent of the total national budget for the current year.

The Chinese Communists are doubtless worried, however, about the future. In the years since they came to power, they have tapped most of China's accumulated savings and fluid capital resources, and there is not much left now to draw upon. At first, they depended heavily upon the income derived by confiscating accumulated grain holdings in rural China (one of the main forms of savings and wealth in China before the Communists takeover), but these have now been siphoned off not only through confiscation but also through taxation. Then they turned to the cities, and through their successive campaigns they have now squeezed most of the savings and fluid capital from the urban economy. Some Chinese businessmen who have come to Hong Kong from the mainland believe that perhaps the Communists can put the squeeze on the urban population once more, and obtain the last hidden savings and capital of the business class, but that thereafter there will be nothing left to squeeze. In short, by a process one can describe either as confiscation or as discriminatory taxation, the Communists have taken over most of the previously existing private savings and capital stocks in China, and in the future they will have to depend primarily for tax revenue upon the slice they can obtain from current production. This will mean higher tax rates, which could create serious problems even in a country controlled to the degree China is today.

Increased revenue was not the sole financial aim of the Five-Anti campaign; control of inflation was important, too. The Com-

munists fully recognize the threat of inflation, and they realize
that it was one of the principal factors undermining the Nationalist regime. Consequently, they have made great efforts to prevent
price inflation. But—as one might expect in a wartime period—
their efforts have not been completely successful; for example, the
wholesale commodity price index in Shanghai rose by 17.39 per
cent between January, 1950, and February, 1952. Nevertheless,
they have had considerable success, and in general prices have
been kept under control by drastic deflationary tactics. They have
tried, on the one hand, to sponge up paper money and decrease
purchasing power in every possible way; the Five-Anti campaign,
together with regular taxation, has accomplished this quite successfully. They have also reduced the rate of money circulation.
They have tried—by severely punishing speculators, sterilizing
bank savings, and so on—to accomplish this on a continuing
basis, but the Five-Anti campaign made a large contribution on
this score, too. Commerce almost stopped. Persons who had
capital were afraid to use it. And direct government control of
prices, as well as indirect control through state buying and selling,
were greatly increased during the period of the campaign. As a
result, the lid has been kept on prices, despite budget deficits.

While the Five-Anti campaign was in progress, the government
was actually able to bring about a drop in the prices of many commodities. In April, at the height of the campaign, state-operated
consumer-goods stores lowered their prices on 10,000 goods in
Shanghai, 4,000 in Peking, 3,000 in Wuhan and the central south,
900 in the northwest, and 600 in the northeast. The average price
reduction was 8 per cent, and in some cases it was as much as 40
per cent. Since private enterprises had to follow the trend in gov-
ernment-established prices, the general price level dropped at least
temporarily.

Improvement of the tax-collection system was another important
result of the Five-Anti campaign. It was not without significance
that collection of the 1952 business income tax came at the peak
of the campaign, when businessmen were terrorized and were
concerned more about their safety than about their money. Furthermore, by giving a clear indication that tax evasion was futile,
because the government would catch up with the offenders in the
end, the campaign undoubtedly did a good deal to undermine the
traditional Chinese propensity for tax evasion. During the past two
and a half years, despite the institution of increasingly strict controls, the Communists have not been able to overcome completely

the effects of such long-standing Chinese traditions. They state, for example, that from 1949 through 1951 they uncovered 155,856 cases of tax evasion in Shanghai alone. However, as a result of the Five-Anti campaign, there will probably be far fewer attempts at evasion in the future; there is not much point in evading taxes if the government is likely to make you confess, and pay up, a year or two later.

The Five-Anti campaign also enabled the government to increase its control over foreign-exchange resources, both at home and abroad. Many Chinese merchants and industrialists—as well as ordinary citizens who had converted their savings to hard currencies—were able to conceal part of their holdings until the beginning of this year, but under the psychological strain of the Five-Anti campaign they broke down, and their holdings were flushed out. In the cases of some large holders, exchange holdings could not be extracted because they were frozen in accounts in the U.S., but the government got its hands on much foreign exchange that had been concealed, not only in China but in places such as Hong Kong. "Cheating the government" of foreign exchange was considered to be one of the very serious offenses, and the penalties imposed were often severe.

All these financial aspects of the Five-Anti campaign—particularly the increased revenue obtained for the government budget—have been extremely important to the fiscal position of the regime in 1952. In a sense, however, the Five-Anti campaign has been one of the last phases of a revolutionary period in which the regime has been able to support itself at least partially on the accumulated fat of the Chinese economy. This period is now approaching an end. The hidden savings in both the rural and the urban economies appear to have been, for the most part, uncovered, collected, and used up by the government. There may be, as some people believe, a thin layer of fat still remaining, but that will be gone in another campaign or two. Then the government will be financially dependent on taxation imposed upon current agricultural and private industrial production and profits extracted from the socialized sectors of the economy to balance the largest national budgets, support the largest nonproductive government payrolls, and finance the most ambitious economic development plans in the history of China. There will no longer be special groups in the country able to bear a disproportionate share of the financial burden, as has been the case during the past three years.

The Campaign's Effects on Socialization

The growth of government control over private enterprise has been a continuous process in China since 1949, and the process has been speeded up this year. One of the most significant results of the Five-Anti campaign has been what might be called the indirect or disguised socialization of private enterprise. Very few businesses or industries were actually nationalized during the campaign, but the government increased its controls to such an extent that at present many so-called private enterprises have become, in reality, appendages of the state. In many cases, although private ownership continues, it means very little; the fiction of private enterprise continues after socialized control, in disguised forms, has been firmly established.

The Communists' ultimate aim, of course, is to socialize the entire economy, and they have already nationalized a great many important economic enterprises. Transportation, utilities, virtually all heavy industry, and the majority of large-scale consumer-goods industries are already state-owned or state-operated. Foreign trade is, for all practical purposes, a state monopoly; private companies still in business in this field operate on a commission basis for government organizations. The purchase and sale of major agricultural products such as wheat and cotton are handled in large part by government companies; the same is true of most important industrial raw materials. Almost all wholesale trade in the larger cities is monopolized by the state. And the government has already gone into retail trade in a big way; it has established extensive chains of specialized stores dealing in foodstuffs and other necessities, as well as state consumer-goods stores selling general products.

Despite the expansion of state enterprises, however, the Communists continue to assert that private enterprise is to play a significant role in the economy during the period of New Democracy. But this assertion is always qualified in many ways. For example, Premier Chou En-lai in his speech on January 5 of this year stated that private enterprise must accept the "guidance of the state economy" and the "leadership of the working class," that there must be a "general plan of production" for the entire economy, and that "only legitimate profit is permissible [for private enterprise] within the limit set by the state or the price fixed by the state." Ever since 1949, Chinese businessmen have speculated on what phrases of this sort would really mean in practical terms, and they have hoped for the best. As a result of the Five-Anti campaign, however, many have come to expect the worst. They have concluded that the "significant role" for private enterprises will for many amount to nothing more than being subcontractors, agents, or employees of the state.

During recent months, the distinctions between state and private enterprises have become blurred. One Chinese businessman who recently came out of Shanghai puts it this way: "It is useless to try to draw a clear line between government and private enterprise in China today. Actually, there are very few differences between the two. Owners and managers of so-called private enterprises are for all practical purposes in the employ of the state. The government makes their important decisions for them. The only reason the government doesn't take over all private enterprise completely is that it doesn't have the trained personnel yet." This description of the situation is undoubtedly an exaggeration, but it accurately indicates the current trend in China. It appears that during the New Democratic period, when the Communists are laying the groundwork and preparing for general nationalization at a future date, more and more private enterprises in China will move into a sort of twilight zone in which they will be neither state-owned nor "private" in any real sense.

This trend accelerated greatly during the Five-Anti campaign. Private enterprise lost most of its fluid capital, and therefore its real independence, during the campaign. Under the guise of obtaining "illegal profits," back taxes, and so on, the government even took from many thousands of enterprises—probably the majority, if one can judge from reports received in Hong Kong—the capital needed for current operations; it then turned around and loaned them what they needed to keep going. In other cases, the Five-Anti fines and assessments were obviously more than could be paid, and the government accepted IOU's which created an indebtedness to, and consequent dependence upon, the government. To cite a specific example, I know of one business establishment in Hankow that was assessed for an amount equivalent to U.S.$100,000 during the campaign, which was 30 per cent more than the total net income of the establishment since the Communist takeover. After considerable haggling, the firm managed to get the amount slightly reduced; it paid what it could and gave an IOU for the rest. Private enterprises that have been forced in this fashion into a position of indebtedness to the government could be taken over by the government at any time, but there is no indication that this is the Communists' intention at present. Instead, the government still seems to prefer indirect control. But the granting of loans during the Five-Anti campaign was used as a wedge for direct infiltration of many private enterprises; for example, often when the People's Bank gave a loan to a company it also sent its own representatives to take over key watchdog positions, such as those of assistant manager, accountant, and personnel chief.

The assessments and fines imposed during the campaign were not the only factors that undermined the financial independence of private enterprises. A process of natural attrition also took place as a result of the campaign. While business stagnated, private companies were required to continue supporting their full payrolls. Government companies lowered prices, and private businesses that had sizable stocks on hand took large losses. Industrial companies that were able to continue production piled up unsold stocks, and the government "helped them out" by buying their products at low prices. Other industrial establishments had difficulty selling, even to the government, because the functioning of government agencies was also disrupted during the campaign. Still others had difficulties keeping up production—partly because they encountered serious problems in obtaining raw materials, largely monopolized by the government; yet they, too, had to maintain their payrolls and keep paying fixed costs. Then, on top of everything, the business income tax came due at the peak of the Five-Anti campaign, and many businessmen had to obtain loans from the People's Bank to pay their taxes.

The combination of Five-Anti levies, taxes, and the attrition caused by depressed markets was a one-two-three blow from which private enterprise in China is unlikely really to recover as long as the Communists are in power. The government was remarkably solicitous as the campaign drew to a close—loans were extended at very reasonable rates, and payments on both Five-Anti levies and taxes were sometimes postponed or reduced—but this did not alter the basic fact that thousands of private enterprises had lost all financial independence as a result of the campaign.

During the campaign, the government increased its control over private enterprise in a wide variety of ways. One of the most successful methods was the organization of "joint public-private" companies. Businessmen from Shanghai report that the number of such companies increased significantly during the campaign, and there is some indication that as this pattern can be applied more generally it may become standard for the larger and more important private enterprises in China during the transitional period of New Democracy. From the government's point of view, this pattern is both simple and effective; a so-called "joint" board of directors is established, but then the government representatives on the board make all the important decisions. Sometimes a number of private companies in the same line of business are grouped together as a combine under a joint board. One specific case that I know about involves a group of more than ten private companies in Shanghai. Each of these companies still retains its managerial staff and board of directors, but in fact they have lost all their power. Superimposed on them is a central office of several hundred persons, controlled by government functionaries, and a joint board of directors, with government representatives as well as representatives of each member company. The government men on the board and in the joint office determine all important policies and make all the vital decisions. The capital, personnel, and accounts of the member companies are pooled and can be interchanged. There is very little substance, actually, to the idea that the member companies are still in existence at all as individual private enterprises. Almost the only "private" characteristic they have now is the fact that if any dividends are issued the original stockowners will receive them. Managerial control is completely in the hands of the government, and the "private" companies act as branches of the government agency controlling them. The advantage of this scheme, from the government's point of view, is that the personnel of the private companies can be fully utilized. Even on this score, however, the government is selective; at least two of the managers of individual companies in this joint enterprise were arrested during the Five-Anti campaign.

Another method employed to establish firm government control over private enterprises without resorting to nationalization was instigation by Communist cadres of internal takeover by the staff members and workers of an enterprise. The case of a large retail store in Shanghai can be cited as an example. The staff and workers of this store were encouraged to denounce the owner-manager and subsequently to announce their assumption of control. The owner-manager was informed that henceforth he would not be permitted to exercise managerial functions or to withdraw profits from the store. He was granted, in lieu of his profits, a monthly allowance.

In other cases, the government established control of private enterprises by purchasing blocks of shares. I know of one company in Shanghai, for example, in which the government bought a 30 per cent share of the stocks and then took over approximately one-third of the positions on the board of directors. Since then, the Communist board members have been in control. In theory, of course, the non-Communist members of the board can still outvote the government men, but if you ask a businessman from Shanghai whether this actually happens he will laugh in your face. Fear intimidates the majority, and any dissent or opposition to the decisions of the Communist minority involves the possibility of psychological persecution or worse.

It is not really necessary for the government to have representatives in a company or on its board of directors in order to control it, but such representatives obviously facilitate control. They are able to integrate private enterprises into the state's economic plans at least to some extent, ensure implementation of government policies, and prevent evasion of government regulations. Because the process of government infiltration is far from completed, however, the government still finds it necessary to exercise much of its control over private enterprises by less direct methods. Remote control in itself can be very effective, however, and in many ways it extends even to Hong Kong, where the branches of mainland companies are in many instances closely supervised by Communist representatives. Hong Kong branches of mainland "private" banks, for example, no longer can make their own decisions on how they will use their capital; they receive instructions from a Chinese Communist representative, resident in the colony.

Private enterprises in China no longer have any prerogative of privacy. The investigations carried out during the Five-Anti campaign were very thorough, and the details of business methods, organization, costs, prices, and profits are now known to both the government and the employees of private companies. If exclusive information or techniques formerly had anything to do with a company's competitive position relative to other private enterprises, or its bargaining position in dealing with the government on contracts and purchase orders, they no longer do.

Another result of the campaign was the emergence of both employers' associations and labor unions as more effective instruments of government control over private enterprises. This was not a new development, but the economic-control functions of these organizations were significantly expanded during the campaign.

All private enterprises in China today must belong to a trade association, and in every city these associations are organized into a general Federation of Industry and Commerce. In theory, these are private bodies, but actually they serve as government-controlled front organizations. The owner of a Shanghai factory, who himself was an executive of one of these associations, described to me how this works. His association was made up of representatives of all Shanghai companies in his line of business, and it held a general meeting about once every two weeks and executive meetings several times a week. At each meeting, whether general or executive, a man sent by the municipal Federation of Industry and Commerce attended and, in a quiet way, played the leading role. This man, although not a Party member, was a political worker for the Party and received his instructions from the Party. Every night, he, and similar political workers who controlled about eight other associations, met with a Party member who outlined current policies to them. The genuine businessmen who made up the membership of the trade association knew that they did not really control it; the quiet little man who attended their meetings was recognized as being in charge.

These organizations were greatly strengthened during the Five-Anti campaign and were a major instrument used by the authorities to put pressure on businessmen. At the conclusion of the campaign, steps were taken to bring them into a more effective nationwide organization. An All-China Federation of Industry and Commerce Preparatory Conference, attended by 160 leading businessmen from various parts of China, was held in Peking in late June, and it adopted a constitution for a permanent organization.

Already some of these associations, in consultation with government agencies and companies, have begun to set maximum prices and minimum standards for their members, and it is likely that in the future they will be utilized to obtain from private businessmen all sorts of "voluntary" pledges to implement government policies. This development was suggested by an article in the February 10, 1952, issue of *Hsueh Hsi:* "After the conclusion of the [Five-Anti] movement, the Federations of Industry and Commerce should call upon and organize industrialists and merchants for the conclusion of new patriotic pacts, with opposition to the five vices as their contents, and undertake regular inspection and supervision over the faithful implementation of such compacts."

Labor unions have also developed into an increasingly important instrument of government control over private enterprises.

During the Five-Anti campaign, they were used, in accordance with the basic principles of class warfare, as one of the principal means of applying pressure on businessmen and extracting information and confessions from them. They were not only strengthened organizationally during the campaign, but their economic-control functions were also substantially increased.

The *Workers Daily*, organ of the All-China Federation of Labor in Peking, defined the responsibilities of unions as follows, in an article published on May Day this year: "Under the leadership of the Economy Checkup Committee, trade unions should organize the working masses to supervise the capitalists so that they may be restrained from repeating acts of the 'five poisons.' This is the main task confronting employees and workers in private enterprises." Their main responsibility, in short, is to help the government control private enterprises rather than to concern themselves with problems of more direct concern to workers.

In some cities in China, all contracts between state agencies and private enterprises must now be signed by union representatives, who together with representatives of the enterprises' senior staff members sit in on the contract negotiations, review contracts, and help to determine "legitimate profits." Because of the detailed knowledge of operations that union members now possess, they are called upon particularly to review cost estimates made by the managers of private enterprises.

Unions have also been given a share of responsibility for internal plant management in private factories, which they exercise through Labor-Management Consultative Committees. The line separating management and union responsibilities in this respect is sometimes rather vague, and there have been cases in which the Communists have reprimanded unions for going too far in encroaching upon management functions, reminding them that their job is merely to supervise and that the managers of private enterprises do still have basic responsibility for managerial functions.

As a result of all these developments during the Five-Anti campaign, the organizational mechanism now exists in Communist China for the government to make decisions of many sorts affecting private enterprises—decisions regarding production plans, specifications, costs, production rates, and profits—and to ensure that they are implemented. This means that, to some degree, the Communists can now include the remaining private sector of the economy in their attempts at over-all state planning. The integration of private enterprises into their economic planning may be somewhat less than perfect, but at least the government is now in a position to try to fit them into over-all plans.

During the course of the campaign, another important trend was the expansion of activities on the part of state enterprises. As a result, the already dominant position of state enterprise in the urban economy increased in importance, and this in itself reduced the independence of private enterprises.

"The government is the only buyer in China's cities today." This statement made to me by a Chinese businessman who came to Hong Kong from Shanghai recently is an exaggeration, but it nevertheless contains an element of truth. There is a clear trend toward narrowing and limiting the free market, and this trend was accelerated during the Five-Anti campaign.

More and more private enterprises in the production field are finding themselves in the position of working for the government on a contract basis. In some cases, the government buys the produce of private enterprises, setting the price and profit margin when the goods are put on the market. In others, the government moves in at an earlier stage and places "processing orders"; when it does this, it is able to set specifications and delivery time as well as prices and profits. The scale of government buying is already so large that many private producers cannot find non-government buyers.

Even when government buying does not completely dominate the market, and significant private outlets for sales do remain, government purchases are often large enough to establish prices. This is true now even in the consumer-goods field in big cities. In Shanghai, for example, if the state consumer-goods stores reduce the price of soap, private sellers are forced to reduce their price, too. This is often very hard on private enterprises because their costs and overhead are usually higher. (Two different wage scales prevail, and the one in state enterprises is lower.) By dumping or buying, and manipulating their prices, government companies are now able to exercise a high degree of regulation over the market.

During the Five-Anti campaign, the government greatly increased its buying and selling, and consequently its influence on the urban economy as a whole. Because the free market stagnated, the government was able to move in and take over. It bought stocks that were not being sold. It placed orders with producers who had no markets. And it sold at prices that were difficult for private business to match. As a result, the government established itself as the undisputed leading buyer and seller in the free market.

The campaign not only resulted in an increase in the volume of government contracts with private enterprises, it also strengthened the controls the government exercises over establishments under contract. Cheating on government contracts was one of the specific vices publicized in the slogans of the campaign, and great emphasis was placed upon the need to investigate cost estimates and profits, with a view to reducing both. Private enterprises were severely penalized for past sins in this regard: overstatement of costs, production of substandard goods, late deliveries, "unreasonable profits," and so on. It was decided that in the future both costs and profits would be more carefully supervised, and that costs would be determined on the basis of "average conditions obtaining in factories managed properly and reasonably." And on June 24, Ch'en Yun, head of the Committee on Finance and Economics in the Peking Government, outlined a national policy of restricting profits on contracts with private enterprises to 10, 20, or (in exceptional cases) 30 per cent.

One important psychological factor must also be mentioned in any assessment of the increase of government control over private enterprises that took place as a result of the Five-Anti campaign. Many private companies were penalized for "illegal profits" and other "crimes" on the basis of comparisons with the prices, costs, and quality of products of state enterprises. In short, the practices of state enterprises were used as a standard for judging private enterprises. As a consequence, many private businessmen decided that to avoid future trouble they would have to follow the lead of state enterprises as closely as possible. One Shanghai businessman I know tells me that he is now selling his products at a price that entails a considerable loss, "just to stay out of trouble"; the price is that charged by competitive state enterprises.

The results of the Five-Anti campaign as it affected private enterprises in China's major cities can be summarized, therefore, as a great decrease in the independence of private enterprises and a great increase in government control. The state is becoming the real entrepreneur for the economy as a whole in China, and private businessmen find the scope for independent decisions on their part steadily decreasing. In short, the campaign made it possible for the government to speed up the process of socialization without resorting to nationalization except in a relatively few cases.

Now the Peking Government has embarked on a great program

to increase production and develop industry. Top leaders maintain that the Five-Anti campaign has laid the groundwork for this new campaign. In one sense, it undoubtedly has. Tight government control over private enterprises will make it possible to try to formulate plans for the economy as a whole. However, one cannot help but speculate about the possible effects of reduced incentives and loss of initiative on the part of private entrepreneurs. Chinese businessmen have already lost so much, and have so little to gain, even if the new campaign is successful, that they can be expected to show little enthusiasm for the efforts they are being called upon to make.

COLLECTIVIZATION

October, 1952

The Chinese Communists have started on the long, hard road to agricultural collectivization, even though their current land-redistribution program is not scheduled for completion in some major areas of China until next spring.

The Agrarian Reform policies pursued by the Communists to attract peasant support during their struggle for power, and to consolidate power since 1949, have been based upon redistribution of land and "liquidation of the landlords as a class." But it is now clear that this program is merely a first step, preliminary to collectivization.

The general outline of the process of future collectivization in China has taken shape this year. It calls for a transitional period, lasting several years, in which peasants will be organized first into mutual-aid teams and then into agricultural producers' cooperatives, in preparation for ultimate collectivization of a more complete sort. At the same time, state farms, machine tractor stations, centers supplying improved tools, and experimental collective farms are to be organized to point the way toward the final goal.

It is obvious that the Communists, in planning for collectivization, are following the road already traveled by the Soviet Union, but it also appears that they are capitalizing on the experience of the Russians in an attempt to avoid some of the pitfalls previously encountered by them.

On June 30 of this year, on the second anniversary of the promulgation of the 1950 Agrarian Reform Law, Peking announced that "agrarian reform has been completed in the overwhelmingly great part of China." More specifically, it was claimed that except for areas inhabited by racial minorities (where implementation of the program has been postponed), agrarian reform has been wholly completed in northeast China, Inner Mongolia, and north China, 85 per cent completed (in terms of total farm population) in northwest China, 90 per cent completed in east

China, and 81 per cent completed in both the central-south and southwest regions of China. With the exception of minority areas, the remaining districts—Sinkiang Province and parts of Tsinghai, Kansu, Yunnan, Kweichow, Kwangtung, and Kwangsi—are scheduled to have completed agrarian reform by either this winter or the spring of 1953. The Communists' claims about the progress of land redistribution may be an exaggeration, since reports in mainland publications indicate that they are encountering serious problems in carrying out agrarian reform in south China, and that the struggle against landlords, "bandits," "despots," and "counterrevolutionaries" continues in many areas where in theory these elements have already been liquidated. But it does appear to be true that by the spring of next year the Agrarian Reform Law will have been implemented in all major regions of the country.

The general situation in areas where the law has been thoroughly implemented might be described briefly as follows: A segment of the rural population, classified by the Communists or their revolutionary People's Tribunals as "counterrevolutionaries," "bandits," and "despots," has been physically liquidated. The landlords, who under the old regime were the community leaders in most rural areas, have been "liquidated as a class"; their land and most of their capital have been confiscated and distributed to landless and poor peasants. In the process of class warfare against the landlords, the middle, poor, and landless peasants have been organized into Peasants' Associations under Communist control, and the activists among them have emerged to join with Party members and the leaders of new Communist-organized mass organizations of various sorts to form a new rural elite and bureaucracy. The landlords' holdings, distributed by the Peasants' Associations, have become the private property of the persons to whom they were distributed. Although the amount of land held by so-called middle peasants has been the standard for general equalization of land ownership, there are still variations in the acreage owned by peasants. This is due partly to the fact that, according to current Chinese Communist policy, the "rich peasant economy" is temporarily preserved. Rich peasants are allowed to retain the land they cultivate, either alone or with hired hands, and many are permitted to keep ownership of some land they rent out. But, although they are generally the most efficient producers in any region, rich peasants are not given official encouragement; on the contrary, they are supposed to be politically "neutralized." The temporary policy of tolerating them is dictated by the Communists' desire to keep up agricultural production as much as possible while carrying out their rural revolution.

The essence of the Communists' agrarian reform, therefore, has been confiscation of landlords' holdings (small portions are allotted to the landlords themselves if they can cultivate them) and redistribution of the land to small, individual peasant-proprietors. Until recently, this was regarded by a great many people in China, including the poor and landless peasants who have received land, as the final aim of Communist policy. The Communists formerly did not attempt to disabuse people of this misconception. Although there have been, in the past, a few direct and many oblique references to future collectivization, the Communists have played down the fact that land redistribution is merely a tactical stage on the road to collectivization. Now, however, when completion of agrarian reform is in sight, individual peasant proprietorship, which constituted the declared aim of agrarian reform, is already being labeled as "backward."

At the end of last year, Wu Chueh-nung, Vice-Minister of Agriculture, outlined three separate stages in the development of Chinese agriculture under Communist rule: (1) agrarian reform; (2) the reorganization of agricultural production through mutual-aid teams and agricultural producers' cooperatives; and (3) "collectivization of agriculture on a nationwide scale on the pattern of collective farming in the Soviet Union." The Communists are now completing the first step and embarking upon the second. The immediate task was briefly outlined in an editorial on January 1 of this year in the official Peking *People's Daily*: "In the sphere of agriculture," it said, "we should organize peasants into organizations of mutual aid, producers' cooperatives, and supply and marketing cooperatives in a more planned manner."

There are a number of theoretical and ideological factors that impel the Chinese Communists to push forward toward collectivization as rapidly as possible. In discussing agricultural problems, they frequently quote Lenin's statement that "small-scale production gives birth to capitalism and the bourgeoisie constantly, daily, hourly, with elemental force, and in vast proportions." Individual peasants, with their "petty bourgeois" mentality, are considered to be a constant potential threat to the country. In surveys of selected areas where agrarian reform was completed some time ago, the Communists have noted, with alarm, a resurgence of capitalist features such as usury and renting of land,

and a strengthening of the "rich peasant economy" with a trend toward reconcentration of land. This undoubtedly lends considerable urgency, in their minds, to the need for preliminary steps toward collectivization.

Furthermore, the Communists' general economic program calls for industrialization of the country, and this requires an agricultural economy that can produce a surplus. They firmly believe that large-scale collective methods, with or without mechanization, will increase agricultural production. A recent article in *People's Daily* stated, for example: "Chairman Mao has pointed out that land reform is a revolution, and organization a revolution. Both of these revolutions can bolster the productive forces and augment production." Developments in the Soviet Union cast doubt on the proposition that large-scale collective enterprise in agriculture, even if accompanied by mechanization, necessarily results in increased production, but this does not seem to shake the Chinese Communists' faith that it will.

There are other practical justifications for rapidly introducing collective forms of agricultural organization. The experience of the Soviet Union indicates that collectives provide effective means for imposing government controls on the rural population and for guaranteeing delivery to the state of the grain required to support an enlarged bureaucracy and the agricultural raw materials required for state-controlled industry. It is possible to achieve these objectives through organization, whether or not collectivization leads to increased production—or even if it results in lowered production.

The transitional period leading to collectivization in China may be a long one, however. Peasant resistance can be anticipated from the start, and it may become violent as the process develops. But the Chinese Communists, benefiting from Soviet experience, are apparently planning a gradual process, to minimize the opposition that could be expected from abrupt, radical changes.

In 1949, Mao Tse-tung wrote in "On People's Democratic Dictatorship": "The education of the peasantry presents a serious problem. The peasant economy is dispersed. According to the Soviet Union's experience, it takes a long time and much painstaking work before agriculture can be socialized." More recently, Kao Kang, top Chinese Communist leader in Manchuria, said that the correct policy for China is one of "gradually leading the peasants toward collectivization through examples set by state farms and agricultural producers' cooperatives."

This emphasis on the need for a planned, orderly process, leading step by step toward collectivization, contrasts with the experience of the Soviet Union. There, after several sudden advances and retreats, collectivization finally took place during a frenzied four-year period (1928–32) in which perhaps 5 million kulaks were dispossessed and the mass of peasants were forced into collectives.

The Chinese approach seems to be more calculated, with every stage preparing the way for, and minimizing possible opposition to, the next one, in a sort of dialectical process. This applies even to the first stage, the land redistribution now being completed; despite the violence and passion involved in agrarian reform, the Communists seem able to keep the process under control to a large degree.

The first step in agrarian reform is liquidation of armed opposition. Next comes mass organization and indoctrination, then (in most areas) rent reduction and repayment of peasants' deposits by the landlords. There is then careful preparation for the climax: land classification, class demarcation, and elimination of any possibility of resistance from the landlords and other opponents of the program. Finally, redistribution of the land is carried out.

With very little time lag, steps toward collectivization are now being started. Peasants are first organized into mutual-aid teams, which are later to be converted into agricultural producers' cooperatives; finally, collective farms will be organized. It is this step-by-step process that is distinctive about Chinese plans. The goals, including collective farms, state farms, and machine tractor stations (or equivalent centers for mechanical improvements of a more simple nature), are adapted from Soviet models, but the process of achieving them involves a more gradual succession of stages.

In August of this year, the Peking Ministry of Agriculture issued a statement claiming that 35 million peasant families, representing 40 per cent of all peasant families in the country, have already been organized and belong to one of the 6 million mutual-aid teams or 3,000 agricultural producers' cooperatives now said to be operating in China. This claim may be high, but there is no doubt that strong pressures, intensive "education," and the preferential treatment given to organized peasants are effectively supporting the accelerated drive to get peasants into the first simple forms of collective production units.

Furthermore, the 60 per cent of the peasants who have not yet joined any sort of collective production units are not exempted from organization. Except for the rich peasants—who are excluded from almost all organizations—most others belong to Peasants' Associations, which, under Party leadership, exercise a considerable degree of control over their members. No over-all statistics on Peasants' Association membership are available, but figures for specific regions—40 million members in central-south China, 33 million in southwest China—indicate that virtually all those classified as middle peasants or lower belong to the associations.

In addition, a high percentage of China's peasants now belong to rural supply and marketing cooperatives, which regulate the sales of agricultural produce and the purchases of industrial and consumer goods. Although in theory these cooperatives are a special element in the economy, distinct from both state enterprise and private enterprise, they are in fact government-run and controlled. Increasingly, they are dominating the markets for agricultural goods, and they therefore indirectly exert a strong influence on production. Recent official figures reveal that the cooperatives' membership in China now totals 106 million, mostly in rural supply and marketing cooperatives.

There are many gradations and variations of mutual-aid teams, the first step in the organization of collective production units. In their simplest form, they consist of a small group of families—usually fewer than half a dozen—who agree to help each other by working jointly and using each other's tools and animals. This type of mutual aid has historical precedents in China, where it occasionally developed among the poorest peasants, particularly in times of natural calamity. Simple teams of this sort were usually temporary and seasonal, disbanding after accomplishment of the specific tasks they were organized to perform. This was mutual aid of an informal and spontaneous nature, but the Chinese Communists are now putting it on an organized basis.

One of the first moves required to regularize and develop more highly organized mutual-aid teams is to convert them into permanent, year-round units. Such teams require a systematized division of labor, and during slack seasons the team members can work together in collective tasks other than cultivation, such as subsidiary, nonagricultural production. Once this stage has been reached, organized management is required. The Communists now state that 20 per cent of the 6 million mutual-aid teams already established are permanent, nonseasonal units of this sort.

One of the characteristics of simple mutual-aid teams, as contrasted with more developed forms of collective agricultural organization, is the fact that in them the peasants not only retain title to their land but also receive, as private income, the produce from their own plot of land. The Communists admit that this is the cause of many conflicts and frictions among the members of the team; each one is primarily interested in his own land, and therefore wants the team as a whole to work his portion in the best way and under the most favorable conditions. Every member, for example, wants his own land to be weeded early, to be sown at the best possible time, and to be harvested after maximum ripening. He also wants the team to work long hours on his land and shorter hours elsewhere.

The Communists seem to believe, however, that these conflicts within the mutual-aid teams help to prepare the way for "higher forms" of organization, and facilitate adoption of a system of further division of labor and distribution of produce on a more centralized basis. There are several types of organizations which they still refer to as mutual-aid teams, but which are actually transitional forms already possessing some of the characteristics of agricultural producers' cooperatives. When several of these teams are merged into larger units, it is relatively easy to convert them into producers' cooperatives.

One large "model mutual-aid team" in north Anhwei Province is described in Communist publications as follows: A total of 22 families, including 136 villagers, make up the team. Under the direction of a 9-man central committee, 89 full-time workers and 12 half-time workers, divided into 3 agricultural production groups, cultivate about 73 acres of land. They share the use of the 20 oxen and donkeys, 5 carts, and 27 plows owned by members. However, 3 families are detached from agricultural work and spend their time on subsidiary enterprises, including the making of vegetable oils, malt, sugar, and bean curd. Because of this division of labor, there is a need for dividing the joint produce on some basis other than every man taking the produce of his own land. The work of both men and animals is classified, therefore, and distribution is made on the basis of "equal pay for equal work."

Membership in mutual-aid teams is "voluntary," but the Communists have evolved effective means of applying pressure to force "voluntary" action. Initiative is taken by Party members and village political workers. They enlist the assistance of peasant activists (particularly those who have encountered production difficulties) and model peasants and start organizing a few families; from then on the process relies on a snowball effect. Once it is under way it is given added impetus by provincial and *Hsien* model workers' conferences, mutual-aid teams' representatives conferences, and training classes for chiefs of mutual-aid teams.

The Communists claim that the mutual-aid teams increase production by overcoming shortages of tools and animals, result in a more efficient use of labor, make possible collective efforts to improve irrigation and combat pests, and facilitate organization of surplus farm labor for secondary production. There is some logic to all of these claims, but whether or not the goals are achieved depends on many factors that are difficult to evaluate, such as methods of team management, rates of agricultural taxation, and other factors affecting peasant attitudes and incentives.

The value of the teams from the state's point of view is unquestionable, however. For example, they play a leading role in the "patriotic production-increase emulation" drives by which efforts are made to stimulate harder work and to guarantee deliveries to the state of agricultural products. The government is now attempting to obtain production pledges from peasants in the form of "patriotic compacts," and organized units are much more convenient to deal with than individual peasants. More than 1 million of the 6 million existing mutual-aid teams are said to have taken part as organized units in such production drives this year.

Another way in which the teams are invaluable from the government's point of view is to facilitate collection of agricultural products by state agencies. If official claims are to be accepted, the Communists have made surprising progress in bringing the distribution of major agricultural products under the control of monopolistic state trading companies. These companies deal to the maximum degree through rural supply and marketing cooperatives, and the latter encourage the formation of mutual-aid teams and producers' cooperatives with which they can deal. The pattern that is emerging is as follows: A state trading company that handles one special product will make a contract with supply and marketing cooperatives (this often takes place at a provincial level, and the provincial cooperative organization divides the contract among its lowest village-level subsidiaries), which then make contracts for future deliveries with organized peasant units. Frequently, state marketing companies are brought in, and "linked" contracts or barter arrangements are made. At the village level, this might mean that a mutual-aid team would agree to furnish the local supply and marketing cooperative with a specified amount of rice in return for a certain amount of fertilizer and cloth. This system gives the government great control over internal trade, and because of its monopolistic nature it facilitates regulation of prices and, indirectly, determination of what will be produced.

The degree to which this system enables the government to monopolize trade in agricultural products can be illustrated by a few official figures. This year, 70 per cent of the total amount of wheat marketed in China is to be bought by the state, and in most provinces 50 per cent of state buying is being done through cooperatives. All state purchases of cotton are being carried out through cooperatives this year, and by July contracts with cooperatives covered 40 per cent of the year's total cotton crop. In Hunan, one of China's major grain-producing provinces, over 90 per cent of the new rice reaching the market this year is to be purchased by the state through cooperatives; the situation is undoubtedly similar in other provinces, for which figures are unavailable. Cooperatives are referred to as the "foundation for the state to control industrial raw materials and export goods," and it might be added that mutual-aid teams and agricultural producers' cooperatives appear to be the foundation for efficient operation of supply and marketing cooperatives.

To help develop mutual-aid teams and agricultural producers' cooperatives, the government is now giving all sorts of "economic and technical help and preferential treatment" to them; this assistance gives them an advantage over their individual peasant competitors. According to one recent official press report:

> This year the state has extended farming loans to the amount of more than JMP$3,000 billion [roughly U.S.$135 million], principally to mutual-aid teams and agricultural producers' cooperatives. New farming implements, improved seeds, and agricultural chemicals and apparatus have also been introduced principally through mutual-aid and cooperative organizations. The state farms are gradually strengthening their technical help to mutual-aid teams and producers' cooperatives, and the state banks in some districts are beginning to sign "credit contracts" with mutual-aid teams and producers' cooperatives. The supply and marketing cooperatives of various districts also sign "linking contracts" with mutual-aid teams and agricultural producers' cooperatives.

"All this," the report concludes, with fine understatement, "plays a great part in helping the development of cooperatives and mutual-aid organizations."

It appears that the establishment of agricultural producers' cooperatives, the second stage on the road to collectivization, generally will be accomplished by merging several well-developed mutual-aid teams and reorganizing them into cooperatives. A succinct definition of agricultural producers' cooperatives was given in a recent issue of a Chinese Communist periodical:

> An agricultural producers' cooperative is an economic organization of unified management and collective labor, based on private ownership of land. It is a higher form than the mutual-aid teams, which are quite common in China at the present time. It is, however, a lower form in comparison with the socialist collective form, and is therefore a transitional form between the two. Its main characteristic is that members invest their land in the common enterprise, being credited with the corresponding number of shares. Its other features are a combination of agriculture with subsidiary occupations, a certain degree of production planning and division of labor, and a certain amount of common property—including modern agricultural implements.

One of the 3,000-odd producers' cooperatives of this type claimed to be organized already in China is located in Chuanti village, Shensi. It was established in the spring of 1951, nine years after completion of land reform in the area (under Communist control during the Sino-Japanese War) and eight years after the first mutual-aid team was set up. The cooperative was established by merging two of the ten mutual-aid teams existing in the village in 1951. These two teams had seventy-six members, including sixteen women, from eighteen households, and they cultivated about eighteen acres of land. Establishment of the cooperative, in which local Communist Party members took the lead, was claimed to be necessary because "the scattered nature of peasant holdings . . . became a more and more obvious obstacle to economical production," because it "became necessary to find a planned way to use the manpower which the mutual-aid teams had freed," and because the mutual-aid teams "could not accumulate enough capital."

Each member of the Chuanti cooperative, according to Communist sources, retains a small plot of land for private use, and the rest, even though theoretically still privately owned, is collectively farmed. About 7.5 acres, out of a present total of 24 acres, are retained for private use. Cultivation of the remaining 16.5 acres is under centralized management by a committee chosen by the cooperative, and the produce, after taxes, is divided between public savings reinvested in the cooperative and private income distributed to members. It is reported that in 1951, of the net profits (i.e., after costs of production were deducted), 8 per cent was retained as public savings, 40 per cent was distributed to members as dividends on the land they invested, and 52 per cent was distributed as wages. The savings were reinvested, 60 per cent for production and 40 per cent for welfare, education, medical service, and recreation. Land dividends were distributed according to a value given each private share on the basis of its previous yield, and wages were computed on the basis of "work points," every ten points representing a "work day" defined as a "day's ordinary labor at average efficiency." Various types of labor were rated either more or less than ten points, and there was a daily checking, and a tabulation every ten days, of the value of the work done by members.

Many management problems arise in running these producers' cooperatives. The consolidated assignment of labor, the planning of land use for crops, decisions on joint or individual use of tools, remuneration for the use of private tools and animals, assessment of labor, direction and leadership of work teams, accounting and finance, and similar problems must be solved. Probably the thorniest problems involve distribution of the produce. Several alternative methods are used. Sometimes land and labor are both treated as stock. In other cases, a fixed rent is paid on the land, and the remainder is distributed on the basis of work. Occasionally, distribution is based entirely on labor. The Chinese Communists show a definite preference for remuneration based to a large degree upon labor, in order to stimulate hard work, but it is difficult to ignore the right to remuneration for land, since the land is still theoretically private property.

The Communists claim that all sorts of advantages result from organization of producers' cooperatives, but since the claims are made to advance their program, it is difficult to evaluate them. They claim, for example, that in the cooperative at Chuanti land utilization was improved by consolidation of plots, that acreage was increased (very slightly) by removal of boundaries, that labor productivity was increased by 22 per cent as a result of collective effort and planning, that the entire labor of eight persons was diverted to subsidiary occupations, that agricultural techniques were improved, that collective effort made possible the purchase of better equipment and the setting aside of small plots for experiments and seed selection, that crop yields in 1951 were raised by 32.7 per cent over 1950, and that the conflicts of personal interests which had existed in the original mutual-aid teams disappeared. This is a very bright picture—so favorable that one is inclined to believe it may represent the theory rather than facts typical of the cooperatives.

At the final stage in the collectivization process, the transformation of agricultural producers' cooperatives into collective farms, private ownership gives way to joint ownership of the consolidated farmland.

Although collective farms are not to be widely organized for some years, according to current Communist plans, experimental models have already been set up, principally in Manchuria and Sinkiang. The "first successful collective farm in China," called "Spark," was organized near the south bank of the Sungari River in Manchuria last year. The experience gained there does not have applicability to most other parts of China, since the farm was established on virgin soil, with a heavy investment of government capital and with unusual advantages such as the existence of a rare tractor station nearby, but it, and other experiments like it, are intended to serve as examples of the final goal and as the basis for propaganda in favor of collectivization. The farm did go through the step-by-step process leading from mutual-aid teams to agricultural producers' cooperative to collective farm, but the process was compressed into the relatively short period of four years.

The Communists now proclaim that this farm has "proved the possibility of organizing farming as an industry." They admit that "the age-old desire to own land individually is so deep that for these peasants to have been able to pass beyond that stage and put as much interest into the collective as into their individual property is indeed a tremendous step forward." But they add: "It shows that the road to larger-scale and better standards of agriculture is not quite so difficult as some people might have imagined."

According to articles in Chinese Communist publications, Spark has twenty-six families cultivating about 250 acres of land. It is a full-fledged collective, in which the land and capital are jointly owned, and it is run by a control committee elected by a meeting of the general farm members. It has a considerably more complex management than existing producers' cooperatives. Its officers include a chairman, a vice-chairman, and a committee member in charge of finance and food, all three of whom do not take part in agricultural production. The control committee also has under it a production section (which manages thirty-four men and twelve women engaged in actual farming), a horticulture section, a dairy section, a rice mill, and a work shop.

The net produce of the farm was reported to be distributed as follows in 1951: 27.3 per cent to the state in the form of taxation, 10 per cent retained by the collective (to be increased this year to 12 or 15 per cent), 6 per cent to the state in the form of "donations and contributions," and 56 per cent to peasant members. The amount given to members was divided according to a system of assessing labor by "points." Every specific job was rated, and actual crediting of points was based upon efficiency and quality of work, with occasional bonuses for "encouragement." Male labor was divided into seven grades, ranging from eight to eleven points, and female labor was classified into 3 grades, from six to seven points. The farm is now considering adoption of a system of "fixed quotas," however, with bonuses and penalties based on actual performance as compared with the quotas.

This is the type of farming that is the main goal of Chinese Communist policies. In addition, however, the Communists are planning to develop several kinds of state agricultural enterprises modeled, as in the case of collectives, on their prototypes in the Soviet Union. "In order to set an example to the peasants and to enable the state to control some important farming products," Peking *People's Daily* stated on January 1 of this year, "we should during 1952 greatly develop state farms and strive to operate successfully state farms in every province, every administrative district, every *Hsien,* and every *Ch'u** (under conditions that land is available)." The larger state farms, run by the Farm Management Bureau of the Ministry of Agriculture, are to be set up on wasteland and are to range in size from 2,500 to 10,000 acres, which is tremendous for China. A small percentage of the larger state farms are to be fully mechanized, while the remainder are to have improved tools and equipment.

The actual development of state farms to date probably varies in different parts of the country, but by the middle of this year east China was reported in Communist publications to have 718 state farms cultivating a total of about 95,000 acres. Of these, 268 are run by *Ch'u* governments, 371 by *Hsien* governments, and 73 by governmental organs of a higher level. Six of the 718 are classified as really "large-scale" farms, having nearly 1,700 acres. Manchuria is the region where state farms are most widely developed, how-

* The next administrative level above the village.

ever; of the "major mechanized state farms" in China at present, 30 are in Manchuria, 10 in north China, 3 in east China, 1 in the central-south, and 1 in the northwest.

One of the larger state farms, about 8,250 acres, is located at Lutai, in north China. Organized in 1949, on wasteland, by 275 cadres and workers sent by the Ministry of Agriculture, this farm now is said to have almost 1,300 workers who are experimenting with Soviet techniques, such as machine sowing of rice and close planting of cotton. It is highly mechanized and has a tractor brigade, repair shop, and smithy. The workers, who are paid flat wages, are organized into a trade union, and the farm is managed by an administration committee which provides services of various sorts to the workers. Production is regulated by a five-year plan.

State farms of this sort, whose workers "have become members of the rural proletariat of a socialist nature," are intended "to demonstrate to New China's emancipated peasants the superiority of scientific, mechanized farming and collective labor." Their two main specific functions are to "educate the peasants" and to provide technical aid to mutual-aid teams, agricultural producers' cooperatives, and the "peasant masses."

Mechanization of agriculture is also an important aim of the Communists, even though they believe that organization alone can accomplish some of their aims and realize that mechanization is a rather distant goal. "Our organization," a recent *People's Daily* editorial stated, "is still geared to the basis of existing production tools, or slightly improved tools, and not machinery," but the Communists are nevertheless proceeding with experiments in mechanization. "In every administrative region, province, and administrative district, we should establish state factories or repair shops to supply the countryside with modern farming implements," *People's Daily* said on January 1 of this year. There has been very little publicity about such factories and shops, but undoubtedly some have been established. In addition, a few machine tractor stations, modeled after the ones that played a very important role in collectivization in the Soviet Union, have been organized. The first station of this type, with six Soviet tractors, was established in Manchuria this spring. This station makes plowing contracts with nearby peasants and uses collective farms, agricultural producers' cooperatives, and "good" mutual-aid teams as "key points to carry out services." It also, in theory at least, "enables organizations of cooperation and mutual aid to develop and improve" because "in using tractors, plots of land must be linked up."

Although the pattern of collectivization in China has become fairly clear, the schedule that Communist leaders hope to follow is more difficult to determine. A few indications of the pace of development currently planned have been given, however. The northeast (Manchuria) can be taken as an example, although it is the most "advanced" of all regions in China and is ahead of the schedule of socialization elsewhere. The Communists claim that at present 80 per cent of the peasants in the northeast are organized, and that a large percentage of the mutual-aid teams there are permanent, year-round ones. The goal for agricultural producers' cooperatives in the northeast this year is one or two per *Hsien*. Several hundred state farms have already been established, and the goal for this year is at least one in every *Ch'u*. And a few experimental collectives and tractor stations have been organized. A top Communist leader in the northeast states: "With the development of industry, the rural villages will be provided with modern farming tools in five to six years, the agricultural cooperatives will be the main form of organization for agricultural production, and collective farms and state farms will also move one step forward." He adds, "In five to six years, it is expected that modern horse-drawn agricultural machinery will be employed in the greater part of the northeast . . ." The northeast, of course, is much more richly endowed and technologically advanced than any other region of China, so its timetable is undoubtedly ahead of that for the country as a whole.

The program of agricultural collectivization the Chinese Communists propose to follow raises a number of basic problems and questions.

One of the main problems the leaders will have to face eventually is how to deal with the rich peasants. Generally the most efficient agricultural producers in any region, the rich peasants are also a bulwark of individual capitalist agriculture and a major obstacle to collectivization. They were eliminated in the Soviet Union only after a costly and violent anti-kulak campaign.

The Chinese Communists are frank in admitting that their current policy of tolerating the rich peasants is temporary (at certain periods in the past rich peasants were liquidated along with landlords), but it appears that they hope to cope with the problem by less disruptive means than those used in the Soviet Union. The present policy seems to be one of isolating the rich peasants and undermining their position by discriminatory treatment. Rich peasants are not only excluded from mutual-aid teams and producers' cooperatives; they are also barred from Peasants' Associations—more serious since these associations perform many governmental functions. The Communists' progressive land tax places a heavy burden on them, and they are also discriminated against in government loan and assistance policies. This may indicate a policy of slowly squeezing them until they gradually are undermined and lose their economic independence—a policy that has been successfully applied to private enterprise in China's cities. In any case, one can be sure that they will eventually be "liquidated as a class," although if they are sufficiently weakened the harsh methods used against Chinese landlords may not be required.

The problem of general peasant resistance is certain to increase as the collectivization program develops, because it is not only the rich peasants who favor private ownership of land. Regardless of propaganda in favor of collectives, the Chinese peasant is likely to retain his deep-rooted desire to own his own piece of land, and it is difficult to believe that collectivization can be achieved in China except by strongly coercive measures.

The probability of strong peasant resistance, even if it is confined by police-state methods to passive resistance, is one of the factors that makes the Communists' belief that collectivization will lead to increased agricultural production very much open to question. Despite certain obvious technical advantages which collectivization in theory can bring, such as consolidated use of land (the fragmentation of individual holdings is a serious problem in China), the productivity of land cannot be divorced from the incentives and attitudes of those cultivating it. This has been illustrated in the Soviet Union by the wide discrepancy between the output of collective land and that of private plots retained by members of collective farms. (The latter are more productive because the peasants devote more and better care to them.) It may be even more true in China, where farming has traditionally been so intensive (with consequent high per-acre yields) that it has often been described as "gardening"; less enthusiasm could cause a considerable drop in production.

The nature of Chinese agriculture has, in fact, raised many questions in the minds of non-Marxist observers as to the applicability, even in theory, of collectivist conceptions of state-run "large-scale mechanized farming" to China. The ratio of labor to land is very high in China. Methods of cultivation are extremely intensive. Mechanization of wet farming (which prevails over much of China) is certainly very difficult, and the prospects of China's producing enough farm machinery to mechanize even dry farming regions are remote. And it is difficult to foresee rapid industrialization in China, which would be necessary to absorb agricultural labor displaced by mechanization.

There is no doubt, however, that collectivization, to the extent that it can be carried out in China, will tighten the government's control over the rural population and over the produce of the agricultural economy. This, in fact, is undoubtedly the main motive and justification for it. There are many reasons to believe that the peasants do not want it, but the state requires it to proceed with its plans for socialization.

THE "GENERAL LINE OF THE STATE"

January, 1954

Dialectical materialism, according to Emile Burns in his book *What Is Marxism?*, is the view which holds "that [reality] is not static, but in motion, developing and dying away; that this development is gradual up to a point, when there is a sharp break and something new appears; that the development takes place because of internal conflict, and the sharp break is the victory of the rising factor over the dying factor."

Reality is certainly not static in Communist China today. The dialectic of social, political, and economic revolution continues to unfold, as Chinese society goes through the process of "developing and dying away."

In the economic sphere, the steady development of a state-controlled "socialist" economy continues, and as a result of the internal conflicts involved in this process, the private economy is slowly but surely dying, especially in urban areas. And the vestiges of the private economy are undergoing a basic transformation.

The Communists have recently proclaimed a new "general line of the state during the period of transition" to socialism, which marks another phase of their program to socialize industry and commerce in China. Under the slogan of "Encouraging private capital to develop toward state capitalism," this new definition of economic policy outlines the process by which private enterprise in China is to be changed and liquidated, step by step, "over a considerably long period of time."

Although the Communists have always maintained that they would socialize China's economy as soon as it became feasible, and have frankly stated that the present coexistence of state and private enterprise is temporary and tactical, a substantial change has taken place in the treatment of private sectors of the economy during the past four years.

In 1949, the Common Program made clear that state-owned enterprises would be the "leading force of the entire social economy," but also stated that the "People's Government shall encourage the active operation of all private economic enterprises beneficial to the national welfare and to the people's livelihood and shall assist in their development." Many, if not most, Chinese businessmen interpreted this to mean that if their private factories and shops were not liquidated or nationalized, they would be able to continue to function, for an undetermined but fairly long period of time, as private enterprises. Despite the steady increase of government controls over the entire economy, the optimism of some businessmen continued until 1952. Then, suddenly, private enterprise was subjected to severe attack in the Five-Anti campaign, which intimidated the business class, took away much of its capital, and greatly increased government control over private enterprise. By the end of the campaign, in the summer of 1952, the independence of private businessmen had been undermined to such an extent that in many cases a process of partial socialization had taken place without actual nationalization. Chinese businessmen woke up to the fact that the immediate alternatives facing them were not clear-cut—that they did not, in fact, face a choice of private enterprise or complete socialization. They realized that like tadpoles they might go through a steady metamorphosis and end up being frogs without quite knowing what had happened.

This metamorphosis has actually been going on for some time, but neither the Communist leaders in China nor their business victims have been clear about the stages involved in the process, which to date has been rather haphazard. Now, the newly proclaimed "general line of the state during the period of transition" outlines several distinct stages by which the Communists plan to socialize what remains of private enterprise in the Chinese economy.

This clarification, needless to say, has not pleased China's businessmen. Recent arrivals from Shanghai report that despite general austerity, food shortages, and rationing of grain, the night clubs and expensive restaurants in that metropolis are experiencing a peculiar boom as businessmen, with an "eat, drink, and be merry" attitude, spend the money they have left. The prospect of losing their "tadpolehood" and turning into "frogs" through several stages of "state capitalism" is uninspiring for Chinese businessmen, to say the least.

The *People's Daily*, explaining the new "general line of the state" on November 11, said:

State capitalism is the economic alliance between socialist elements and capitalist elements under the direct leadership of the socialist economy. State capitalist enterprises are those capitalist enterprises which, under the control of the People's Government and employing various forms, link themselves and cooperate with the state-owned socialist economy, and accept the supervision of the working class. State capitalist economy is still not socialist economy, but it is no longer private capitalist economy in its general sense, and is an economy of a transitional nature.

On the previous day, Li Wei-han, a leading Party member who is Vice-Chairman of the Peking regime's Committee on Financial and Economic Affairs, had made a major speech outlining the "general line of the state" to the first National Congress of the All-China Federation of Industry and Commerce. The two main economic tasks at present in China, Li stated, are the development of the socialist sectors of the economy and "reform of the non-socialist sectors." The government's policy toward private industry and commerce, he said, is one of "utilization, restriction, and reform"—reform meaning the "leading of different enterprises, in accordance with their different conditions, on to the path of state capitalism, so as to facilitate the final realization, when the conditions exist, for their socialist reform."

Li Wei-han's November 10 speech to the organized "representatives" of Chinese industry and commerce will undoubtedly remain a landmark in the development of one important phase of Chinese Communist economic policy. He began by stating that the first stage of China's two-stage revolution (first "New Democratic revolution" and then "socialist revolution") actually ended with the founding of the Peking regime in 1949, and that China is now in a transitional period leading to socialist industrialization. He went on to say that in this transition both agriculture and private industry and commerce must be "reformed." The prescribed stages for the metamorphosis of agriculture—mutual-aid teams, agricultural producers' cooperatives, and finally collectives—are not new, and in this field Li's statement merely marked a decision to proceed according to plan. (After a rapid start in the direction of collectivization in 1952, the Communists slowed down considerably on this program in 1953; now they can be expected to speed up the process again.) Li's definition of several stages for the transformation of private industry and commerce into socialized enterprise is new, however, and throws additional light on the road to socialization in China.

All private enterprise, Li implied, must pass through stages of "state capitalism" in preparation for ultimate socialization. There are several different forms of "state capitalism," he said. First of all, there are the "lower forms," in which the state merely purchases the products of private industry, acts as selling agents for industry, or deals with private merchants who must sell at official retail prices. More advanced "intermediate forms" include those in which the state in dealing with private industry places orders for processing jobs, orders all of an industry's production of finished goods, or underwrites the marketing of an industry's entire output. In commerce, the "intermediate form" is one in which merchants become purchasing or marketing agents for government organizations. The "highest form" of "state capitalism" in both industry and commerce is the "joint state-private enterprise."

These various forms of "state capitalism" ("new forms may yet be created," Li said) represent, of course, merely different degrees of direct control by state economic organizations and agencies. In "joint state-private enterprises," government representatives actually take part in management and themselves make all important decisions. But even the "lower" forms involve a high degree of government control. The *People's Daily*, in an editorial on November 14, stated:

> We know that private enterprises, once they have accepted orders from the state for processing jobs and finished products, cease to be private capitalist enterprises in the general sense, and become a kind of state capitalist enterprise. Such enterprises carry not only a moral obligation, but also a legal responsibility, for the fulfillment of the state's plans. Furthermore, the relationship arising out of placing of orders for processing jobs and finished products is not the general relationship between buyer and seller, nor is it merely a relationship bound by a contract, but rather it is the relationship between a leadership party and the party led. Accordingly, such acts as the undermining of orders placed for processing jobs and finished goods in the attempt to create disturbances and hold sway in the small world provided by the free market are obviously not tolerable to the government and the people.

If private businessmen resist, the editorial warned, "they will be heading on the road of destruction of their own volition."

The function of private enterprise during this transition period, according to the Communists, is simply "to supply finished products to the state" (i.e., produce on contract to government organizations), assist in the "interflow of supplies" (i.e., take part in domestic trade under the control of state trading agencies), "accumulate capital for the state" (i.e., turn over surpluses and profits to the state, through taxation and other levies), and "train technical and management cadres for industry" (i.e., pass on their knowledge and skills to government workers who will eventually supersede private entrepreneurs). Profits are to be strictly regulated —as are all other aspects of business operations—and the net income of private enterprises is to be divided among the state income tax, the operating reserves of the enterprises themselves, and welfare bonuses to employees, with the remainder, which cannot exceed a fixed per cent of the total, going to managers and owners. Businessmen remain under a pall of suspicion in which their potential subversiveness is constantly emphasized. Li Wei-han stated: "The basic nature of the bourgeois class that seeks solely its own profits will inevitably produce an undermining influence against the state and the people's livelihood . . . if there are no appropriate restrictions, or if the restrictions are not adequate, the evil nature of the bourgeois class in seeking only profit will assert itself."

To those not familiar with Communist jargon, many of the recent statements on the "general line of the state" sound like gobbledygook. Why are there so many fine distinctions between different "higher" and "lower" forms? Why do the Communists not nationalize all economic enterprises completely and get it over with? The answer is that they would like to, but recognize that they still are not capable of taking over direct control of the entire economy. Economic planning is in the most rudimentary stage in China. Even as far as state-owned enterprises are concerned, it is evident that although the Communists have completed the first year of their Five-Year Plan, they still do not have any effective over-all plan or planning mechanism. Yet the Peking regime believes that it is essential to subject private enterprise to their plans and controls as much as possible. Perhaps most important, the Communists still have a long way to go before they can train the bureaucrats who can take over all the managerial functions of private businessmen, so they are trying, by various means, to convert as many businessmen as possible into partial or complete employees of the state in the various forms of "state capitalism." Under "state capitalism," the entrepreneurial functions of businessmen slowly disappear, but they continue to manage enterprises under government control and direction. The problem of relations between the government and the business class in China is certainly one of the most complicated ones the regime faces in the present period, because the government desires both to use private businessmen and to destroy them, and the program for various stages of "state capitalism" is the means by which it hopes to achieve these two aims.

The increase of state ownership and control over the Chinese economy has proceeded steadily, without halt, during the past four years. By the end of 1952 (there are no summary figures yet available for 1953), 70–80 per cent of heavy industry and 40 per cent of light industry in China were state-owned. Of the total industrial output of large-scale industrial enterprises, 60 per cent came from state-owned enterprises, 6 per cent from "joint state-private enterprises," 3 per cent from state-controlled cooperatives, and only 31 per cent from private industries. In short, less than one-third of China's industry remained in private hands. The situation was not very different in commerce. During 1952, state trading agencies and cooperatives handled over 50 per cent of the total business turnover in domestic markets in China; in the wholesale field, the figure was close to 100 per cent for many commodities, and in the retail field it was roughly 30 per cent in China's major cities. In short, the private sector of the economy—the sector subject to the forms and controls envisaged in the current program to develop "state capitalism"—has steadily shrunk.

At the same time, "state capitalist" relations between government agencies and remaining private enterprise have rapidly increased. By the end of the third quarter of 1953, state trading agencies (which employed 400,000 workers and had established 13 specialized companies with branches all over the country) monopolized 65 per cent of all wholesale trade in China and purchased most of the products of private industry. For example, in Tientsin, principal industrial center of north China, three-quarters of the output of private industries in this period was purchased by state companies. In Canton, largest economic center in south China, 64 per cent of private industry's output in the last quarter of 1953 was produced on government contract, while in Peking over one-half the production of private industry in the first two quarters of 1953 was sold to state agencies. "Joint state-private enterprises," which are considered the "highest form" of "state capitalism," have progressed farthest in Shanghai, where more than sixty large factories have already undergone this transformation. As these figures indicate, "state capitalist" forms of government control over private enterprise had developed considerably even before the new "general line of the state" was proclaimed last November. This process is now to be accelerated and applied to all private enterprise in a regularized step-by-step program.

The way in which this program for furthering "state capitalism" was announced last November is typical of the means by which the Communists use representatives of victimized groups in China to sponsor onerous policies. The first exposition of the new "general line of the state" was made not by a Communist official but by a businessman at the opening session of the first National Congress of the All-China Federation of Industry and Commerce, on October 23. It was Ch'en Shu-t'ung, seventy-eight-year-old founder of the Commercial Press (formerly one of the leading business organizations in China) and now a mouthpiece for Communist policy, who proclaimed that "we industrialists and merchants have . . . changed our features," and "only by sincerely accepting the leadership of the state-owned economy and supervision of the working masses may private industrialists and merchants manifest their positive role." The most important speech, of course, was that by Li Wei-han, who laid down the Party line. But the Congress closed on November 12 with a speech by Li Chu-chen, manager of a leading Chinese salt company (also over seventy years old), who said: "We shall say here first that we private industrialists and merchants will joyously and enthusiastically support the general line of the state during the period of transition and are prepared to accomplish, through state capitalism, our reform from capitalism to socialism. . . . At the same time, we must also exercise serious vigilance, and refrain from repetition of the 'five poisons.' " His audience was composed largely of representatives of private enterprise from all over China. In short, the ultimate death knell of private enterprise in China was tolled by businessmen, speaking to businessmen. But the strings were really pulled from behind the scenes by the Communists themselves.

From the summer of 1952 until the announcement of the new "general line," the Communists had been relatively quiet regarding their policy toward private enterprise. The Five-Anti campaign shook business to its foundation, and recovery was slow. Furthermore, the shakeup of the campaign had to be followed by organizational consolidation. Since 1952, therefore, local Federations of Industry and Commerce have been organized throughout China as important instruments of direct control over businessmen. These federations include not only representatives of organized business groups, but also representatives of state enterprises, cooperatives, and "joint state-private enterprises." At the city and *Hsien* level, the federations organize the businessmen under them into guilds or trade committees; they set up branches in the *Ch'u;* and in the districts even handicraftsmen, stall merchants, and traveling merchants are organized into associations under the federations. A provincial and national hierarchy is superimposed above these local organizations. The entire network, which is an effective channel for transmitting Communist directives and implementing government controls over businessmen, has been thoroughly organized during the past year, and the first National Congress, in October–November, merely symbolized the successful completion of this process. It was an appropriate place and time for the Communists, through their unofficial private agents for dealing with China's businessmen, to announce their new policy decisions.

Although the new "general line of the state" represents an acceleration in Communist China of government attempts to control the vestiges of private enterprise, the liquidation of industry and commerce will undoubtedly still take some time. Li Wei-han stated:

> The stage of transition calls for the passing of a considerably long period of time. The actual length will depend on the efforts and accomplishments of the people of the whole country in socialist industrialization and socialist reform. Gradual transition means advancing steadily. It calls neither for stagnation nor for hasty advance.

The dialectic of revolution has not yet reached the point of the final sharp break heralding the "victory" of socialism over capitalism in China, therefore, but the metamorphosis of private enterprise goes on, and the economy is definitely "in motion, developing and dying away."

PART V

ECONOMIC DEVELOPMENT

PUBLIC WORKS

October, 1952

The dynamics of Communist revolution in China are both destructive and constructive. On the one hand, the Chinese Communists are attempting to destroy the old pattern of society. On the other, however, the energies released by the revolution are at the same time being directed into constructive channels.

Under Communist rule, for example, China has undertaken the development of many public-works projects involving the mobilization, organization, and regimentation of literally millions of workers. These projects, the largest of which are in the fields of water conservancy and transportation, have been dramatically publicized by the regime. They have made a deeper impression on some people, including non-Communist visitors from other parts of Asia, than the police-state, totalitarian aspects of the regime.

I recently had a long talk with a man who worked on one of these projects, the Chungking-Chengtu railway in the southwest China province of Szechwan. Mr. Wu, who arrived in Hong Kong less than two months ago, was in charge of a construction group on one section of the Chungking-Chengtu line.

Mr. Wu is a quiet, soft-spoken man who, like a great many Chinese, appears to be basically nonpolitical in his outlook, despite the fact that he has been caught in the whirlpool of politics in China throughout his life. Under the Nationalist regime, he worked as an officer in a railway engineering unit of the Nationalist Army, but he was never involved, he says, in Kuomintang politics. Although he is a northerner, from Manchuria, the revolutionary sweep of the Communist armies overtook him in southwest China in 1949. For a short while after the Communist takeover, he was unemployed. Eventually, however, the authorities got around to registering him and suggested that he go to Szechwan to work on the Chungking-Chengtu line. He was not actually forced to go, he says, but he had no alternative and accepted without either any particular objections to or enthusiasm about the job. At the same time, in other parts of the country, hundreds of men with technical qualifications of various sorts were similarly recruited and sent to Szechwan to take part in railway construction.

Work on the Chungking-Chengtu line had been started many years earlier, and some progress was made by the Chinese Nationalists. When I visited Szechwan in 1948 and traveled by road along a route paralleling the projected railway, part of the roadbed had been laid and a few bridges were standing, but no work was currently going on. Construction was in a state of suspension because of a shortage of rails, lack of adequate finance, poor organization, and the general apathy and inertia which characterized the last days of Kuomintang rule on the mainland.

Soon after the Communists took Szechwan, however, work on the railway was quickly started again. Thousands of workers were organized. Technicians were collected from all over the country. And needed equipment and supplies were rushed into the province.

Between June 15, 1950, and the summer of this year, work was pushed at a rapid pace, and on July 1 service on the line was officially inaugurated with great fanfare. The Communists hailed this event as an important symbol of their drive toward national construction, stating that "in a little over two and a half years after the liberation of all Szechwan Province, the People's Government has completed a task which past regimes failed to accomplish in decades."

More than 100,000 civilian laborers eventually took part in the work on the Chungking-Chengtu railway, but construction was first started in June, 1950, with a nucleus group of 25,000 soldiers from the Chinese Communist Army. This has often been the case in large-scale public works initiated in China during the past three years. Noncombat troops provide a large reservoir of organized labor available for work on state projects. As a matter of fact, government plans in 1950, before the Korean War, called for diversion of a significant portion of inactive military personnel into productive activity, including agriculture as well as public works. The Korean War, with its heavy drain upon Chinese military manpower, has changed the situation, but army personnel are still used on many projects, particularly during the first stages when a civilian labor force is being locally conscripted and organized.

In time, the soldiers who started the work on the Chungking-Chengtu railway were replaced by civilian laborers requisitioned from the countryside through which the line passes. According to Communist propagandists, "100,000 emancipated peasants answered the government's call to work on the construction of their own railway." Actually, these peasants were drafted from the villages of Szechwan and organized into semimilitary work groups.

Mr. Wu describes the over-all organization of the main civilian labor force on the railway as follows: Apart from the regular Railway Bureau, responsible for general administration of railway affairs, a special Railway Construction Commission was established in Chungking, directly under the Southwest Military and Administrative Committee, the supreme local government body ruling southwest China. Subordinate to this commission, a People's Labor Supervisory Department, responsible for organizing the railway construction force, was set up.

Under the People's Labor Supervisory Department, four subsidiary supervisory departments were organized, each with jurisdiction over one of the four administrative districts into which the Communists divided the large province of Szechwan. In north Szechwan, to which Mr. Wu was assigned, there were five large working groups under the local supervisory department. Subdivisions of these groups corresponded roughly to military units, from regimental to platoon levels. These units comprised the general labor force. Technical personnel were organized separately and were assigned to certain segments of roadbed. The entire 330-mile length of the Chungking-Chengtu line was divided into several general sections, and each of these was subdivided into three sections, which were in turn split up into three or four branch sections.

The usual method of distributing the labor force along the line was to assign a work unit equivalent to a regiment to a branch section for a certain period of time, and then to move it on elsewhere.

Mr. Wu was in charge of one of the branch sections of the railway—a 1.25-mile stretch near the western end of the line. Theoretically, his branch section should have had three engineers and three surveyors, but when Mr. Wu took over, one of the engineers had just been sent to a penal Labor Reform group, and the other fell sick; because of the shortage of technical personnel, Mr. Wu then assumed full responsibility, despite his lack of university training in engineering. The work unit assigned to his section consisted of about 1,000 men, divided into various sub-units along military lines. Over-all leadership was exercised by a commander, a vice-commander, and a political officer, and the headquarters included an educational-cultural officer who was a woman. Some of the group leaders at various levels, according to Mr. Wu, were military personnel, while others were handpicked local civilians, who accompanied the workers from their home districts. The commander was a member of the *Hsien* government in a nearby district, while the vice-commander and political officer were professional military men.

Recruitment of the 1,000 men in this unit, according to Mr. Wu, was accomplished as follows: Orders, sent under the authority of the Southwest Military and Administrative Committee, went out to all the *Hsien* governments in the region assigning quotas of workers they were required to produce. The *Hsien* governments then set about the job of obtaining the specified number of "volunteers." This was not too difficult. The Communists are skillful at manipulating public meetings in which men are indirectly forced to "volunteer" for all sorts of activities and duties; the process is really one of disguised conscription. In this case, furthermore, the drafting of workers was facilitated by the fact that economic conditions in many villages in the region were poor, and the prospect of work and food was enough to attract some men without a great deal of government pressure.

After selection, the men were organized into small groups in their home districts, and they then walked, some of them from 25 to 35 miles, to an organization point along the rail line, where they were grouped into regular units. The workers brought with them their own personal effects and simple tools, including bamboo carrying-poles and small pickaxes. Larger tools, such as hammers to break stones, were provided by the authorities, although the workers were responsible for any damage or deterioration.

Most of the work on this section of the railway consisted of simple manual labor—namely, excavating earth and depositing it on the roadbed. The workers were paid according to the amount of work done, and the pay per day was usually just sufficient to maintain a single person. Payments were made periodically, by groups. For example, earth-moving was paid for according to a standard of so-much per 2.5 cubic meters of earth; this was estimated to be what an average worker could move in a day, and compensation was set on the basis of what the authorities calculated was required for one man to support himself for a day. Once a month, the engineer estimated the amount of earth moved by a particular group, by measuring the size of the pit from which the earth had been taken, and a lump-sum payment was made to the group. At first the workers were paid in rice; the daily payment, based on work-day units computed in catties of rice, amounted to about JMP$9,000, but this was later changed to JMP$7,000 per unit, paid in paper currency (equivalent to roughly U.S.$0.25 a day).

From their pay, the workers had to purchase their own food and clothing, both of which they obtained from government sources. At first they were quartered in local houses, but later mat-shed barracks were built by the workers themselves, and they had to pay for the materials required for these sheds.

Mr. Wu says that, despite the low pay, some of the workers felt they were not too badly off; they ate rice regularly, which many would not have been able to do in their home villages. But two factors created a good deal of psychological dissatisfaction. In the first place, the pay did not provide any surplus to send home to their families. And secondly, the pace of work was considered unreasonable. The authorities were eager to rush the railway through to completion, and labor competition was constantly fostered to increase the volume of work accomplished. As a consequence, the red flowers given to model workers and the red flags presented to model units became the symbols of physical exhaustion rather than badges of merit.

As construction work on the railway progressed, the authorities picked out the healthiest and best workers and organized them into a permanent Railway Engineering Corps under the Railway Bureau. This group did much of the later work involving some technical skill, such as rail-laying and bridge construction. Mr. Wu believes they will also be used on future railway construction in Szechwan and probably elsewhere. Most of the other workers were sent back to their home villages when the job approached completion; many of them had been away from their families for over a year by the time they returned home.

In addition to this primary labor force of conscripted local peasants, two other sources of organized labor were tapped by the authorities for work on the railway. One consisted of the forced laborers in local Labor Reform groups.

Every *Hsien* in Szechwan, according to Mr. Wu, has a Labor Reform group, consisting of from 200 to 600 men sentenced to varying periods of penal labor, under the control of the local *Hsien* Public Security Bureau. Most of these men are former landlords or military and political officials of the old regime, and they work on many sorts of state projects. When there was a manpower shortage at a certain point in the Chungking-Chentu line, nearby *Hsien* governments were requested to provide groups of laborers for temporary duty. Mr. Wu says that although these men were generally given the same sort of treatment as workers in units under the People's Labor Supervisory Department, the work was much harder on them, since the majority were men who had not been accustomed to manual labor before the Communist takeover.

The other supplementary source of labor was provided by an organization called the Unemployed Workers Group, consisting largely of former members of the Nationalist military forces. Mr. Wu knows little about this organization, since he had no personal contact with it, but he says men from it were used principally during the early stages of work, along with Communist soldiers, and were later replaced by civilian groups.

The various types of conscript labor organized to work on the railway may not be the same as those used on many public-works projects elsewhere in China, and treatment of the workers in other places may be either better or worse; it is difficult to generalize about China today. But it is clear that the Communists are mobilizing conscript labor of many sorts on a scale that may be larger than anything seen in China since the imperial dynasties, which constructed such huge public works as the Great Wall and the Grand Canal. The Chinese lack equipment and supplies, but the Communists are maximizing the use of their primary resource— manpower.

In one sense, almost all this labor is "forced labor" but it would be a mistake to assume that all people in China have the same reaction to this term that contemporary Westerners would have. It is true that the widespread organization of political opponents of the regime into penal work units such as the Labor Reform groups is something new even in China, but there are numerous traditions for *corvée* labor of a less drastic or punitive sort in Chinese history. Drafting of workers has, in fact, been a standard method of obtaining labor for the construction and maintenance of public works, and even under the Nationalist regime a system of labor obligation to the state was in effect. Therefore, the reaction of most Chinese to the Communists' conscription of large labor groups can be expected to be based less on the principle of conscription itself than on the question of how the laborers are actually treated and how great a burden the system places upon the people (principally the peasantry) in practice.

Mr. Wu had some significant remarks to make about the quality of work on the railway, as well as about the labor force, and to the extent that the facts he describes are typical of public works elsewhere in China, they indicate that the speed of Communist accomplishments in the field of public works may be more impressive than their quality and durability.

"In five or six years," Mr. Wu estimates, "there will be a need for many major repairs on the Chungking-Chengtu line." In his opinion: "The quality of the work was very poor. Rigid time limits, and a system of holding all personnel responsible for arbitrary plans, forced everything to be sloppy. Speed of construction was the most important thing in the eyes of the authorities." "Repair work," he reiterates, "will be tremendous in the future."

Mr. Wu speculates: "The reason for the emphasis on speed is probably the fact that projects of this sort really impress many people. They are good propaganda." This is undoubtedly one explanation. It is true that huge public works, and all the propaganda fanfare accompanying them, do impress many people. It is also probably true, however, that the Communists attach considerable economic, strategic, and political importance to the Chungking-Chengtu line, and wanted to finish it rapidly for this reason. The line links the hinterland of one of China's largest and most productive provinces with cheap water transport on the Yangtze. The fact that Szechwan is a major rice-surplus area, one of the few in China, is also important.

Strategically, a railway in Szechwan greatly improves the area as a possible base in the event of war. The Communists undoubtedly have not forgotten that the Nationalist Government was able to hold out in Szechwan against the Japanese for seven long years; any Chinese government planning for the contingency of war and foreign invasion would regard Szechwan as an important potential rear base. Furthermore, Szechwan has long been an area with strong local feelings of regionalism, and it has often exercised considerable *de facto* autonomy. Improved transportation makes it easier for the central authorities to impose controls over this rich and remote province and to keep it under their unified administration.

Despite all possible explanations of the premium placed on speed in the construction of the railway, however, the poor quality of work may mean that the Communists will be plagued by rapid deterioration and will face the necessity for constant repairs in the not-too-distant future.

During the construction of the railway, the Communists paid their usual tributes to Soviet assistance, advice, and "advanced techniques." Soviet help on this project was negligible, however, in Mr. Wu's opinion. Although he heard that there were Soviet advisers attached to the Railway Bureau, he himself never saw one of them. Two construction techniques of reputed Soviet origin were used, but Mr. Wu does not believe they made any spectacular contribution to the building of the railway. The simplicity of these two techniques is interesting, however. The Soviet advisers are said to have made a study of Chinese stone bridges and then to have advised that, due to the shortage of steel, all small bridges on the line should be built of stone. The Soviets also taught the Chinese a new technique of earth filling and beating. This method involves building up the roadbed in 3-centimeter layers, which are then beaten down to 2 centimeters by workers using simple stone pounding blocks before the next layer is added. This technique allegedly results in a stronger roadbed and saves time over the old method of building the roadbed in its entirety and then letting it settle during a longer period of time. These new methods, like most of the reported Soviet technical advice to the Chinese, are concerned primarily with means for saving materials and time. No equipment was received from the Soviet Union; at least, Mr. Wu did not see any, and no claims were made to this effect even in the Chinese Communist press. The locomotives and rolling stock on the Chungking-Chengtu line were old ones collected from other parts of the country, and steel rails came from expanded production in Chungking itself, as well as from other industrial centers in China. The Soviet advisers, in short, merely passed on to the Chinese their own experiences in coping with the problems of an economy of scarcity.

China's main resource for the public works completed or initiated by the Communists during the past three years has been manpower, and the primary technical skill displayed has been in the field of social organization. Relatively little machinery or equipment is required for conservancy work in China, and even on projects such as railway lines the Communists have met the requirements, in part at least, by spreading and obtaining full use of existing equipment. Communist success in the public-works field does not necessarily imply, therefore, that the regime can achieve equal success in its plans for industrialization, because industrial development requires a certain minimum of capital equipment which may not be available. But there is no doubt that the Communists will be able to carry out significant development schemes in the public-works field with a maximum use of labor and a minimum use of equipment, and the schemes already completed or under way are fairly extensive in themselves.

In the field of railways, for example, by mid-1950 the Communists had almost completed rehabilitation of China's prewar lines, and they then proceeded with construction work on three major new lines: the 260-mile Laipin-Chennankwan line to the Indochina border and the 215-mile Tienshui-Lanchow line stretching into China's northwest, in addition to the Chungking-Chengtu link. The rate of progress on each of these lines averaged about five-eighths of a mile per day, and during 1951, many miles of new line were laid in China. By the end of 1951, the Laipin-Chennankwan line, of urgent strategic importance to the Chinese, was completed, and work on the other two lines, both of which have considerable economic and political as well as strategic importance, was finished this past summer. Altogether, a total of 780 miles of new rail lines had been completed by August of this year.

According to all reports—from objective observers as well as Communist propagandists—efficient management of the railway system as a whole is one of the most impressive things in China today. Furthermore, construction of new lines has not slowed down with the completion of the above-mentioned lines. Work on the Lanchow-Tihwa railway, which will link the capital of Chinese Turkestan with the rest of China (and ultimately will undoubtedly connect with the Turk-Sib line in Soviet Asia), and the Chengtu-Tienshui line, which will reach between southwest and northwest China, is already under way. Surveying is known to be in process along the Lanchow-Paotow route, and there are scattered reports, of uncertain reliability, about preliminary work on various other lines, mainly in remote interior provinces. Most of these railways have been included in Chinese development plans ever since Sun Yat-sen wrote his visionary book on railway construction, but during the years of war and civil strife in China actual building came to almost a complete halt, and many existing lines were destroyed or deteriorated. But the Communists are now pushing ahead on construction with full steam.

In terms of what can be accomplished with manpower alone, the Communists' conservancy schemes are perhaps even more impressive than their railway construction. For example, a nation-wide plan for river control was drawn up in late 1949, and in the ensuing three years, according to Communist claims, "the total volume of earthwork alone has reached 1.7 billion cubic meters, 10 times as much as was involved in building the Panama Canal, or 23 times what was involved in the Suez Canal." The number of peasants mobilized and organized for this work has been in the millions.

During 1950, the Communists first concentrated on restoring and strengthening about 26,100 miles of old river dikes ruined by the floods of 1949 and earlier years. Since then, they have embarked upon a number of mammoth new schemes. The largest is the Hwai River project, scheduled to be completed by 1955, which calls for construction of 13 storage reservoirs and 17 water detention basins, irrigation of over 8 million acres of land, and the erection of numerous locks. The whole project affects an area populated by more than 50 million people and watered by one of the most complex river systems in China. Another major project is going on at the Chinkiang section of the Yangtze River, where the Yangtze has periodically burst out of its gorges to flood the Hupeh plain. Other projects have involved improvement of the banks of the Yellow River ("China's Sorrow"), irrigation schemes in Ninghsia and Suiyuan, and control of the Yi and Shu rivers in southern Shantung and northern Kiangsu, to mention just a few.

As for results, the Communists claim that, using 1949 (a bad flood year) as an index base of 100, the area inundated by floods in China was reduced to 60 in 1950, 21 in 1951, and 8 up to September, 1952, and that during the same period over 8 million acres of land have been irrigated by new canals. These claims are impossible to check, but even if the true figures are lower there is no doubt that much has been accomplished.

Examples could also be cited in numerous other fields of public works—not only large national projects, but small-scale local ones. Almost every refugee from China, for example, reports that in towns and cities all over the country many projects of road building, construction of public buildings and housing, development of waterworks, and similar activities are going on.

As stated earlier, these accomplishments, and the revolutionary energy behind them, have made a deep impression on a considerable number of people. To the extent that one can judge Chinese "public opinion" from Hong Kong (a difficult task, at best), however, the majority of Chinese feel that the price paid for such accomplishments—ruthless disregard of the individual, thought control, regimentation of society, etc.—is too high. Mr. Wu, for example, believes that most people in Szechwan are bitterly dissatisfied with the Communists, despite the Chungking-Chengtu railway and other development projects now being carried out. He himself decided over two months ago that, although he occupied a fairly advantageous position as a technician under a regime that glorifies technicians, he did not want to continue living in the oppressive atmosphere the Communists have created. He decided to leave his country for the first—and conceivably the last—time, and he is now a "White Chinese" refugee in Hong Kong.

FINANCING DEVELOPMENT*

July, 1954

The Chinese Communists have embarked upon an ambitious program of economic development, concentrating on rapid industrialization. The first Five-Year Plan, started in 1953, is the main focus of current efforts. To pay for the program, the Communists have already, during the past four years, squeezed the country dry of savings; they are now forced to maintain the standard of living at a minimum level, in order to collect as much as possible of China's small economic surplus to invest in development projects. The course the Communists are following is a hard and austere one, promising improvement in the future, but demanding sacrifice today. The "small betterment of today must be subordinated to the big betterment of tomorrow," they proclaim, and they are systematically mobilizing the resources of the country—primarily by compulsory rather than voluntary methods —to make certain that the present generation of Chinese people sacrifice in the interest of industrialization and the future.

The task of acquiring investment capital is one of the most fundamental problems of economic development. It is particularly difficult in a poor country that has little economic surplus. It becomes doubly acute when a regime is determined, as the Chinese Communist regime is, to force the pace of development and to press for maximum speed. It is further complicated when

* The Chinese Communist and other statistics used in this and the next two chapters were the best ones available in 1954; those interested in more recent figures, even for this earlier period, should refer to any of several excellent studies of the Chinese Communist economy written by non-Communist economists in the past few years. When originally written, the reports that make up these three chapters contained rough estimates of what the Communists might achieve in production during the first Plan. These have been deleted, for the obvious reason that they are superseded by actual production figures for that period. It is worth noting, however, that the 1954 guesses were all underestimates. By the end of the first Plan period, in 1957, it was clear that Communist China had made fairly rapid progress in key sectors of the economy, especially heavy industry.

a country is cut off—or cuts itself off—to a large degree from the major sources of foreign investments and loans, as Communist China has done, and is attempting to rely primarily on its own limited resources.

In essence, the financial problem of developing modern industry in an underdeveloped country is one of forgoing current consumption, accumulating savings, and investing the savings in development projects. Both voluntary and compulsory methods can be used, in theory at least. People can be persuaded or encouraged to save and invest, or the state can take over the task of savings and investments for the society as a whole. It is the latter course that the Chinese Communists are following. Private initiative in savings and investments has been, for the most part, eliminated, and it is the state that is squeezing from the population the larger part of all the country's economic surplus above subsistence needs —both by direct taxation and by various means that are in reality forms of indirect taxation—and deciding how and where it will be invested.

The national budget is, therefore, one of the best keys to the process of capital accumulation and investment in Communist China. Unfortunately, however, budget information—like almost all economic data on contemporary China—is incomplete, distorted, and far from reliable. The obstacles to forming a clear picture of government finance in China are discouragingly numerous. In the first place, in 1951 and 1952 no specific budget figures were released by Peking: data for these years must be arrived at by applying the few percentage figures made public to specific data released in 1950 and 1953–54. Furthermore, figures on past budgets have been radically altered in subsequent years. The Communists' budget statements are clearly propaganda documents, in some respects, and every effort is made in them to disguise the real economic burden placed upon the population (especially the peasants and workers), to inflate the figures on investments in economic development, and to conceal the burden of military expenditures. Added to these and similar problems is the difficulty of converting Chinese figures into a more meaningful monetary unit: The official exchange rate between the Chinese Communists' People's Currency and the U.S. dollar is the most logical conversion rate to use, but it undoubtedly inflates the real value of the Chinese figures. Despite all these problems and difficulties, however, it is possible to obtain a general idea from available budget figures of the ways in which the Communists are mobilizing and using the resources of China in their program of development.

The most obvious and startling fact that the Communists' budget figures reveal is the rapid increase in state control over the national income of China. Budgets have steadily grown, and the state has extended its economic operations and controls to the point where a very large percentage of the product of the national economy is now collected and distributed by it. Before the Sino-Japanese War, the national budgets of China totaled approximately U.S.$500 million, which in terms of current dollar values might be somewhere near U.S.$1 billion. Since 1949, Chinese budgets have skyrocketed from roughly U.S.$3 billion in 1950 to approximately U.S.$10 billion this year.* (The official budget forecasts for 1954 call for expenditures of U.S.$10.5 billion and revenues of U.S.$9.8 billion.) These figures provide one index of the rapidly growing control of the Communist regime over China's entire economy. The state now collects and distributes an increasing percentage of the produce of China's peasants, it owns and manages a growing segment of the country's industry, it controls an ever larger share of domestic trade, and it has more and more people on the payroll of government agencies and government-owned enterprises.

It is difficult to convert these budget figures into a percentage of national income, because estimates of China's national income are so unreliable. Some prewar estimates of the country's national income were as low as U.S.$12–15 billion. At present, China's national income may be U.S.$20–30 billion. Even if, for purposes of rough guesswork, one tentatively accepts the highest estimate of U.S.$30 billion, this would mean that the regime's budget now totals approximately one-third of the total national income.

The high degree of state control over the national economy—which is constantly increasing—now makes it possible for the Communists to decide how a large proportion of the output of the economy will be used. In short, a high percentage of the capital accumulation and investment in China is being carried out by the state and is included in the national budget.

The way in which the Communists themselves analyze their "problem of capital accumulation" is of considerable interest.

---

* Here, and throughout this volume, Chinese yuan figures have been converted to dollar figures at the Chinese Communist official exchange rate. This is an artificial rate, but although it may exaggerate the international value of Chinese currency somewhat, the distortion may not be too great.

They start by emphasizing that they must rely primarily on internal capital resources rather than on foreign aid. Then they state that the major sources of internal capital accumulation, in order of importance, will be the following: (1) accumulation from state-owned industry; (2) accumulation from other sectors of the socialist economy, including trade and transport; (3) taxes of all sorts; and (4) bonds. It might appear on the surface that taxes are to be relatively unimportant, but this is highly deceiving. Apart from the bonds, which are a form of forced savings and are a very small element in the total picture, all the other categories can really be viewed as forms of either direct or indirect taxation.

"Profits from state enterprises," whether industrial or commercial, are really concealed deductions from the income of workers or disguised taxation imposed on consumers.

Some Chinese Communist writings state that Increase Production and Economy campaigns, especially in state economic enterprises, are the "main form" of accumulating capital for economic construction; these campaigns are essential in the Communists' program to increase the profits "from state enterprises." In essence, the campaigns to "increase production and economize" are efforts to get laborers to work longer, more efficiently, and more productively without commensurate increases in pay. The Communists also attempt to economize on materials, to reduce operating costs, and to increase efficiency, but it is in the ratio of labor productivity to wages that the main "economy" can be made. Workers are urged to work harder for rewards that are primarily psychological rather than financial. Ever since they took over, the Communists have pressed campaigns to achieve "increased production and economy," and a huge campaign with this label, launched in late 1952 on the eve of China's first Five-Year Plan, has become an important and seemingly permanent feature of the regime's economic policies. Discussions of the first Five-Year Plan, furthermore, frankly call for a greater increase in labor productivity than in wages.

Another major source of "profits from state enterprises"—and undoubtedly the most important one at present—is the mass of consumers in China, both rural and urban. The state owns and controls a large and increasing amount of industry and commerce in China. Last year, the Communists claimed that 50 per cent of all modern industry, accounting for 60 per cent of industrial production, was state-owned, and that 63 per cent of total domestic trade, including most wholesale trade and 32 per cent of retail trade, was handled by state agencies and affiliated cooperatives. Profits that formerly went to private entrepreneurs and owners are now being funneled into the state treasury. In short, the state now makes a profit—which might well be called a tax—on most economic transactions in China, and it is the mass of consumers who, in the last analysis, pay for this. Prices of basic necessities have been kept remarkably stable, through rigid controls, but the profits that formerly went into private incomes—some of which were consumed and some invested—are now channeled mostly to the state. Accompanying this basic change, there has been a drastic leveling of wealth and consumption in China, and there are now few, if any, large-scale concentrations of private savings that can be used for either private investment or above-average consumption.

The profits from state trade, as contrasted with state-owned industry, are not emphasized in Chinese Communist writings, but they are extremely important at present; the state has extended its control over trade very rapidly, and buying and selling constitute a large part of all economic transactions in the country. It is estimated that, on a nationwide basis, the profit margin on purchases and sales by state trading companies may be over 20 per cent. In Manchuria, according to official statements, state trade accounts for one-third of all "profits from state enterprises," and in other parts of the country, where there is less industry, the proportion may be close to one-half. It is probable, in fact, that state trading agencies provide one-fifth to one-sixth of the total receipts of the state treasury at present, if taxes on state trade and "depreciation funds," as well as their profits, are included.

By 1952, it was officially claimed that total sales of state trading companies were the equivalent of U.S.$4.5 billion and that retail sales of state-controlled cooperatives were U.S.$2.4 billion. It is possible that the state made nearly U.S.$1.5 billion in profit on these transactions.

The burden of these state profits on trade is distributed among all sectors of the population, but since China is basically an agricultural country, a particularly heavy burden is imposed upon the peasantry. The state is now attempting to buy the entire surplus grain crop in China, and it is making a profit on this operation at the expense of the peasants. Detailed information on prices paid to peasants by the state is difficult to obtain, but there is ample evidence that state prices are lower than those which merchants

—who are being driven out of the market—would be willing to pay.

The state makes a profit both on purchases of agricultural produce from the peasants and on sales of manufactured goods to them, and the ratio of agricultural and industrial prices is unfavorable to the peasants. A survey of Kwangtung Province in late 1952 indicated, for example, that in terms of grain, the prices peasants were forced to pay for industrial goods had risen greatly since 1949; plows, fertilizers, and cotton cloth had doubled in price, and the cost of necessities such as salt, kerosene, and vegetable oils had risen considerably. The price ratio in cities, about which more details are available, also shows that the state is making much of its profit at the expense of the rural population. To cite one example, in Shanghai at the end of 1952 it took 208.3 catties of medium-grade rice to purchase a bolt of cotton cloth, as against 162 catties in 1950 and 112 catties in 1936. A similar situation existed in other basic commodities and in other areas.

As industrialization develops in China, profits from state industry will become increasingly important as a source of income to the state. The Communists frankly say that light industries— which produce consumer goods—must be the source of most profits from state industry, and they assert, in fact, that "accumulation of capital" is one of the primary tasks of light industry. Heavy industry is devoted to producing equipment for new development projects; profits from these would merely increase the costs of the new projects, and would therefore be a transfer of funds from one pocket to another on the part of the state. The burden of profits from light industry, however, can be passed on to the mass of consumers.

"Depreciation funds" (amortization) are another significant source of "profits from state enterprises." Individual state enterprises, instead of building up private sinking funds, channel such funds into the treasury, and the state makes the decisions on where they will be invested or reinvested.

State enterprises are also taxed by the state, and income from this source provides a large and increasing share of total tax revenue. The burden of this taxation is for the most part also passed on to the mass of consumers.

Official figures show a steady rise in earnings from state enterprises, and this item is now claimed to be the second largest source of state revenue. From approximately U.S.$350 million in 1950, it has risen to U.S.$3.5 billion in the budget projected for 1954—

in short, a tenfold increase in four years. In terms of a percentage of all revenue, it has increased from slightly over 10 per cent to over 35 per cent of the total.

Despite the steady rise of income from state enterprises, the level of taxation has not been reduced since the Communist take-over in China. On the contrary, taxes have become heavier than before. Even in cases where tax rates have been lowered, improved and tougher methods of assessment and collections have increased tax yields.

The most important single tax in China is the grain tax, levied mostly in kind. The Communists have made strenuous efforts to tighten up and improve collection of the grain tax. In 1950, they established a unified system of collection and storage in granaries under the Ministry of Finance (later transferred to the Ministry of Food); local surtaxes were still allowed but were limited to 15 per cent of the Central Government's tax. Two years later, local surtaxes were abolished, and the entire system was completely centralized (although some special local levies for local projects are still allowed).

At present the Central Government collects and controls the entire tax. In general, the tax is levied in grain, although about 10 per cent is paid in other crops and about 10 per cent in cash in areas growing products such as cotton. Tax rates are now based on theoretical "norms"—i.e., what certain types of land "ought to produce" under normal conditions—and although detailed information is difficult to obtain, there are many reports that these norms are often set at unreasonably high levels. If production is above the norm, theoretically no tax is imposed on the surplus (this is designed to be an incentive to production); but if it is below the norm, no reduction of the tax is allowed except in special calamity situations.

Two different systems of levying the grain tax are still in use. In "old liberated areas," embracing a population of roughly 120 million people mainly in north China and Manchuria, taxes are levied as a set percentage of the crop or acreage. Rates vary for different provinces in Manchuria, ranging from 15 to 23 per cent of the main crops, with the average rate for the whole area over 20 per cent. In north China, a unique system is followed, based upon family units and acreage; the tax rate is 22 catties of grain per taxable mow (a mow equals one-sixth of an acre) of land; the number of taxable mow is determined by taking the total amount of land and deducting one mow per working member of the family.

In the rest of the country, the system used—which is expected to become universal eventually—is based on a progressive scale of rates and on total agricultural income. A peasant pays his tax in kind as a percentage of his entire income, the rate depending upon the level of his income. There are twenty-four different grades in the scale, varying from 7 per cent to 30 per cent.

Viewed superficially, these rates do not seem to be excessive, but there are many reports that, because of the methods of assessing land and setting "normal yields," the actual taxes paid are much higher than the rates would indicate; it is probable that the tax takes a large proportion of a peasant's surplus above minimum needs, and in some cases even cuts into his minimum subsistence requirements. (Whatever surplus is left, furthermore, is usually purchased by the state at low prices.) Therefore, although rents to landlords have been virtually eliminated as a result of the Communists' land-distribution program, the burden on the peasants is still extremely high, and in some places it may well have increased. The state has abolished private landlordism, but has replaced land rents with taxes and other levies. (It is significant that the Chinese Communists admit that more than 3,000 of their cadres were killed trying to collect the grain tax in the first year after their takeover.)

The amount of revenue obtained from the grain tax has increased steadily since 1949, but at a rate slower than that of other major forms of revenue; and the Communists have claimed that this indicates a decreasing burden on the peasants as related to other population groups. According to official claims, income from the grain tax increased from about U.S.$800 million in 1950 to slightly over U.S.$1 billion planned for this year (an increase of only 25 per cent). These figures represent a decrease of total revenue from 27 per cent to 13 per cent. Independent non-Communist estimates place the figure on revenue from the grain tax at a higher level, however—roughly U.S.$1.6 billion. Even if the official estimates are true, furthermore, they do not constitute "proof" of a lighter burden on the peasants. The state's grain purchasing program and its price policies on agricultural and industrial goods ensure the peasants' providing the largest share of the state's income; there is really no alternative, since China is an agricultural country.

There is no doubt, despite the onerous burden on the peasantry, that the heaviest direct taxation is imposed upon industry and commerce, both state and private. A good deal of this is passed on to consumers, rural as well as urban, but the one group that is hit hardest is private businessmen.

When the Communists came to power, urban taxation was chaotic and inefficient, and tax evasion was prevalent everywhere. All this was soon changed, however. At first the Communists simply cracked down on collection of taxes already on the books. Then, in 1950, they began to regularize and rationalize the tax system, simplifying and reducing the number of taxes. Finally, in 1952, the mammoth Five-Anti campaign clamped down on businessmen so ruthlessly that tax evasion, regardless of the unreasonableness of the taxes, was virtually eliminated for the foreseeable future. Since then, the process of simplification and rationalization has continued; the scope of urban taxation has been widened and collection has been improved. At present, everyone down to and including individual hawkers on the streets is subject to taxation.

At the end of 1952, a new tax, which in time will doubtless become the most important urban levy, was introduced. Called the commodity circulation tax, it is a single levy on a commodity from manufacturer to consumer. It is imposed on both state and private enterprises, and is passed on in large part to the consumer. At present, it is being applied on a trial basis to only twenty-two categories of commodities, but the plan is to extend it gradually. Rates, set as a percentage of state selling prices, are high, even on basic necessities. For example, the rate on cotton yarn is 22 per cent, on matches 21 per cent, and on wheat flour 10 per cent.

For most commodities not yet included under this new tax, the system is more complicated, and taxes are generally paid by the manufacturer, wholesaler, and retailer. There is a commodity tax, with rates comparable to those of the new commodity circulation tax. There is also a business tax paid by private wholesalers and retailers as a percentage of their total turnover, with surtaxes added. In addition, there is a business income tax paid by private industry and commerce on profits. Except for the business tax, most of the burden of these taxes is passed on to consumers, and the business income tax takes a large share of the small profits that remaining private businessmen in China are able to make.

These are the main producers of urban tax revenue, but there are many others, including stamp taxes, a tax on interest on deposits, a house tax, a tax on urban land, a tax on vehicles and vessels, a slaughter tax, and miscellaneous other levies such as feast and amusement taxes.

As in the case of rural taxation, the tax rates are not an accurate index of the real tax burden. One of the most prevalent ways of imposing taxation is a method called "democratic appraisal." Under this system, representatives of business groups are called into meetings with Communist participation, and the amounts of taxes to be paid are decided after prolonged discussion. This is a variation of an earlier method called "democratic assessment" in which the Communists arbitrarily set a sum to be paid by some organized group of businessmen—such as a guild or business association—and let the group decide how much individuals would pay.

Only a small percentage of taxes paid by private enterprises is levied on the basis of audited company accounts, partly because modern accounting is still undeveloped in China and partly because the authorities are suspicious (with reason) of doctored records. This method is used with some large modern companies, but the Communists carefully investigate before accepting a company's accounts.

Under a third system of assessment, used mainly for small shops and hawkers, the tax authorities investigate and then, on the basis of their own estimates, set fixed amounts of taxes to be paid at specified times.

Reports of refugee businessmen coming to Hong Kong from China indicate that these taxes add up to a tremendous total. Much of the tax burden is passed on to consumers, but without doubt private businessmen carry the heaviest burden of any single group in China. Although it constitutes only a very small percentage of the total society, private business provided—according to official claims—between one-fifth and one-fourth of all state revenue in 1953, and in the budget for this year one-sixth of the total revenue will come from it. It is being taxed out of existence (as well as being forced out of existence in other ways). As private enterprise has steadily declined, however, an increasing share of urban tax revenue has come from taxation of state enterprises, and almost all of this is passed on to consumers. As a result, whereas formerly a large percentage of tax income from this source was paid by the small business class in China, in the future almost all of it will of necessity be paid, in the final analysis, by the mass of the population, the peasants and workers.

Chinese Communist figures indicate that income from urban taxation, of which industrial and commercial taxes are most important, is now claimed to be the largest source of state revenue. From 1950 to 1954, it has increased 3.5 times, from U.S.$1.3

billion to U.S.$4.4 billion (planned figure). In terms of a percentage of total revenue, however, the figure has not changed very much; in 1950, urban taxation represented 43 per cent of total revenue, while in 1954 it is 45 per cent.

One of the most intriguing items in the Communist budget is the source of revenue called simply "other." From 1950 through 1953, this vague and undefined category accounted for over one-sixth of all revenue, and in 1952 it amounted to almost U.S.$1.9 billion!

A large portion of the income in this obscure catch-all category undoubtedly has come from several extraordinary financial levies the Communists have imposed upon the population. By these levies, the state has squeezed out of Chinese society a very large percentage of the private savings accumulated in the past and has dissipated most concentrations of private capital.

During the Korean War, the Communists conducted a huge "Arms Donations" campaign, from June, 1951, through May, 1952, in which the population was pressed to contribute money to buy war equipment. The campaign was carried out all over the country, but the squeeze was hardest on businessmen, particularly in Shanghai; almost 40 per cent of the donations came from east China and over 15 per cent from Shanghai alone. At the end of the campaign, the authorities announced that the campaign had netted the equivalent of U.S.$247 million.

Even before the Arms Donations campaign was formally completed, a new one had begun. From January through May, 1952, the Five-Anti campaign against the "five poisons" of the business class convulsed all of China's major cities. Under the guise of collecting "back taxes," "fines," and "ill-gotten money," the Communists extorted tremendous sums from businessmen. More than three-quarters of the business establishments in the principal cities —more specifically, 340,000 out of a total of 450,000 private enterprises of all sorts in nine leading cities—were forced to pay up. After the campaign was completed, the Communists officially stated that the equivalent of U.S.$1.7 billion had been collected; actually, the total may well have been even larger.

Confiscations of property have also provided sizable amounts of state income. When the Communists came to power, they acquired large warehouse stocks of commodities from state-owned enterprises taken over from the Nationalists, and also from confiscated enterprises of "bureaucratic capitalists." The proceeds from sale of these stocks were credited to the 1950 budget. During

Land Reform, which was carried out all over the country from 1950 through mid-1953, most of the property—including houses, grain, furniture—of about 20 million landlords was confiscated. The majority of this property was distributed among tenants, but some was taken over by the state. There are no official figures on what this netted the state, and it is not definitely known whether the receipts from this source appear in the budgets of the past four years; but unofficial estimates range as high as U.S.$2 billion, and it is possible that the budget figures do include some income from this source.

However, extraordinary levies of these kinds obviously cannot continue indefinitely. It is probable, in fact, that the ones already carried out have taken the fat out of the Chinese economy, and it is doubtful whether there is much left to be collected in the future. From now on, the Communists will have to rely almost wholly on what they can get from the current national income, and it is significant that the 1954 budget is the first one that does not have a very large slice of revenue labeled "other."

The only additional item of revenue that appears in budget statements is income from credit and insurance. The banking system in China is now completely centralized, and sizable state profits are made on interest charges on both rural and urban loans, paid by state as well as private enterprises. Compulsory insurance, administered by the Chinese People's Insurance Company and other institutions supervised by the People's Bank, also produces a significant amount of revenue. Budget statements indicate that state income from sources of this kind grew from U.S.$138 million in 1950 to U.S.$434 million last year.

Needless to say, after being subjected to all the taxes and levies already described, the average Chinese does not have very much surplus cash left over, but what there is the Communists efficiently collect or control.

Two sizable government bond campaigns have been conducted by the regime, in periods when no other special campaigns were under way. The first was in 1950. The original plan was to sell 200 million "units" of these bonds, but only the initial issue of 100 million, equivalent to over U.S.$100 million, was put out. Purchase quotas were established, and people all over the country were forced by various pressures to buy the bonds; as in the case of the campaigns already described, the heaviest burden fell on urban and business groups. These 1950 "Victory" Bonds were scheduled to be repaid in five years, but this was later revised, and redemption is still going on.

The second bond campaign is being carried out at present. The new "National Construction" Bonds, on which there is interest of 4 per cent a year, cannot be used as credit instruments, so they are an effective anti-inflation device. Urban areas have been assigned a purchase quota of 70 per cent of the total bonds, and businessmen must subscribe to over three-fourths of this. At the start of the campaign to sell these bonds, the announced target was about U.S.$250 million, but by June, 1954, it was officially announced that already over U.S.$340 million had been subscribed.

Apart from these bond campaigns, the Communists have exerted great efforts to develop "voluntary" individual savings. Savings have been accepted in terms of "parity units," pegged to the current value of basic commodities, to minimize any possible risks from inflation. Campaigns to induce people to open savings accounts have been conducted on a large scale. The People's Bank has established thousands of new branches, agencies, and "stations," reaching into local villages, factories, and urban areas, and the bank's personnel now totals more than 300,000, ten times the number of persons in government banking under the Nationalists. Slogans such as "Patriotic savings" are widely used, and their use implies that those who do not save are unpatriotic. And, as in the case of bonds, compulsory quotas (for minimum savings) are very often assigned to individuals or groups. The facts seem to indicate, however, that people do not have very much money they can save, and consequently private savings play a relatively unimportant role in the over-all financial picture.

Although state revenues in China have grown rapidly during the past four years, expenditures have also soared, and the government has been under severe financial strain. However, the Communists claim that since 1950 they have managed to balance their budgets. They admitted a 1950 deficit, which was partially met by issuing paper currency, but subsequent revisions have officially erased even this deficit on paper. Last year, the Communists claimed to have a sizable surplus, which they say is being applied to this year's budget.

The claims of budgetary surpluses are extremely dubious, however, and may well be the result of statistical legerdemain. Actually, despite the energetic collection of revenue from every conceivable source, the Communists have undoubtedly had sizable budget deficits.

It is remarkable, however, that the Communists have been able to stop currency inflation and to maintain stable prices for basic daily necessities. For almost a decade before they came to power, inflation had steadily spiraled upward in China, and by the time they took over, the currency and prices were in a shambles. Inflation continued during 1949 and 1950, but by the end of 1950 the Communists had checked it. The general price level rose almost 100 per cent during 1950; in the following year, the rise was only about 10 per cent; in 1952, the price level actually dropped; and since then it has been generally stable.

One of the main explanations for the regime's success with price stabilization, of course, is the fact that the heavy taxes and special levies it has imposed have been drastically deflationary and have sopped up a great deal of currency. Circulation of currency has also been reduced by other measures. The banking system is highly centralized and under complete government control. Control over cash is rigid. All state enterprises must deposit their receipts in the state bank within three days, and payments between state enterprises are made by account transfers in the bank. Private enterprises must use checks rather than cash for all transactions involving over JMP$300,000 (about U.S.$13). They must also maintain special accounts in the state banks for paying their taxes. And the state bank controls or supervises all credit and loans.

Since 1950, furthermore, state trading companies have dominated the wholesale markets and established the prices for all essential commodities. More recently, state trading has expanded rapidly into all fields, and the state now directly sets or controls the prices for innumerable goods.

Price stabilization has been achieved, therefore, by drastic measures, but there is no doubt that it has been a major accomplishment of the regime. And as the free market in China shrinks, the possibility of runaway price inflation in the future steadily decreases—even though the Communists may have continuing difficulty in financing their myriad government operations and their economic development program.

It is difficult to obtain reliable data on what has happened to the standard of living of the mass of ordinary Chinese since the Communists came to power, but it is possible to obtain a general idea.

The Communists assert that wages and the purchasing power of the masses have steadily risen. For example, they say that the average wage level in China rose 27 per cent in 1949, 12 per cent in 1950, and 15 per cent in 1951, and that by 1952 wages were 60 to 120 per cent above the 1949 level. (The target for 1954 is a 5 per cent increase.) At the same time, however, they admit that wages in 1952 were generally at the same level as before the Sino-Japanese War—a very low level to begin with. Regulations on wages give a clue as to how low wage levels actually are. In central-south China, for example, the minimum and maximum monthly wages of industrial workers were established, in late 1952, at the equivalent of about U.S.$14 and U.S.$53. Despite official claims to the contrary, general wage levels may well have declined in many places. For example, it is estimated that in Shanghai an average worker in 1949 received a monthly wage of about 160 "parity units" (pegged to commodities) and only 100 units (about U.S.$20) in 1952—a decline of approximately one-third.

Official claims of increases in "purchasing power" are also dubious. The claimed increases in the past have been as high as 30 per cent (in 1951), and this year the target is a 14 per cent increase. One indication that these claims are questionable, however, is the fact that the monetary value of "parity units," on which wages are based, has not risen as rapidly as general prices—which would indicate a decline in the real purchasing power of wages rather than a rise.

Refugees coming from Communist China report that although the wages of a small, especially favored group of industrial workers may have increased slightly since 1949, the general standard of living has probably declined. This seems likely, in the light of all that has taken place. It also seems inevitable, because the economic program which the Communists are attempting to carry out can only be financed out of the pockets of the mass of the population.

As *People's Daily* stated on October 30 of last year: "Workers' wages and amenities must be subordinated to the interests of national construction; the quantities and prices of agricultural products sold by the peasants must be subordinated to the interests of national construction; the demand of urban and rural people for betterment of life must also be subordinated to the interest of national construction."

The Communists' aim—and their justification for imposing a heavy financial burden upon the population—is the economic development and modernization of the country. The Chinese people must make sacrifices now, they say, so that as much of the nation's resources as possible can be devoted to economic development, particularly industrial projects. And it is true that large and increasing sums have been allotted annually to "investments in state enterprises" and "national construction."

But investments in new economic development are not the only explanation for the financial burden placed upon the mass of people by the state. The Communists have built up a huge Party and government bureaucracy; they maintain a tremendous military establishment; and they have fought one major war, in Korea, and contributed to another, in Indochina. The apparatus of power, both internal and international, is expensive. The military and administrative expenses of the present regime are in fact several times as large as total national budgets in China were before the Communists came to power.

Since 1950, "administrative expenses" in Chinese budgets have jumped from roughly U.S.$500 million to U.S.$1–2 billion. Until this year, this item has declined as a percentage of total expenditures—from almost 20 per cent in 1950 to about 10 per cent last year—but the absolute figures have risen greatly, nonetheless. A contributing factor in this rise has been the centralization of finance; since 1952, the financial autonomy of local governments in China has been eliminated, and the Central Government subsidies required to support local administrations now appear in the national budget. (Almost one-fourth of the 1954 budget consists of allocations to municipalities and provinces.)

Although the Communists are intentionally vague about what is included under various headings of their budget, undoubtedly the most important part of their administrative expenses consists of the salaries of the horde of government and Party employees in China. There is now a larger number of economically unproductive bureaucrats on the government payroll than ever before in Chinese history. Their salaries have been kept low, and corruption is reported to have been almost completely eliminated; but it costs huge sums of money to support millions of government functionaries, clerks, policemen, teachers, political cadres, and others, even if they are honest and live austere lives.

When the Communists came to power, they had already built up a large bureaucracy of their own, and they inherited—and continued to support—most of the bureaucrats from the previous regime. Since then, as the government and Party have extended their operations into every sphere of national life, the payroll has continued to grow. Furthermore, despite the Communists' periodic efforts to cut down the number of employees, and their dramatic campaigns against "bureaucratism" (such as the Three-Anti campaign, in 1952) people leaving mainland China paint a picture of an intensely bureaucratic state, with swarms of government employees everywhere. The totalitarian character of the regime has apparently created an unwillingness on the part of petty bureaucrats to assume responsibility, and there is great buck-passing, overlapping of jobs, and duplication of effort. There are no recent figures on the total number of employees paid by the state, but it may well be in the tens of millions. Three years ago, it was stated officially that there were 9 million people on the "supply system" alone (the system by which the needs of state and Party employees are directly provided by the state; salaries are minimal); the figure undoubtedly is much larger now. In 1950, as a matter of fact, Mao Tse-tung stated that one of the three primary economic tasks facing the regime was the job of cutting down the civilian and military payroll. This is one aim the Communists obviously have not achieved.

The burden of military expenditures is even greater than the costs of the civilian bureaucracy. Official statements admit this, and it is clear that the official figures are not an accurate key to real military expenses. Expenditures labeled either "military" or "national defense" in the budgets of China have risen from U.S.$1.2 billion in 1950 to over U.S.$2.2 billion forecast for 1954. As a percentage of total expenditures, these figures show a decrease, however, from approximately 40 per cent to about 20 per cent.

Although any estimate of real military expenditures must be based largely upon guesswork, it is probable that between one-third and one-half of China's total budget outlay is really devoted to building up and maintaining military power and that a large share of this item is disguised, and placed under different categories, in official budget statements. Military aims play a big role in China's current program of industrial development, and undoubtedly projects such as arms and munitions factories are classified as "construction" rather than as "defense."

China not only maintains a huge army, but has made great efforts to reorganize and re-equip its armed forces with modern matériel. Conservative estimates place the figure for China's regular army at 2.5 million; the actual figure may be considerably larger. These regular forces are backed by large numbers of Public Security troops, whose primary task is internal control. The cost of merely maintaining such large military forces is great. And the costs of fighting the Korean War were tremendous. The great financial strain of the war on China was a major reason for the Communists' willingness to negotiate a truce. It is probably significant, furthermore, that during 1951 and 1952 the Communists did not release any figures on their expenditures, and that in 1953 the Minister of Finance was fired. Top Chinese leaders have recently admitted that actual military expenditures during 1953 were higher than original budget estimates (they also admitted that less was spent on economic construction than was planned), and military costs are likely to continue to be a major burden on the Chinese economy.

For a poor country—relying mainly on its own resources—to attempt to support a huge totalitarian regime and to build up modern military power at the same time it embarks upon a large-scale economic development program is ambitious indeed. It is not surprising that the burden on the population is massive. There seems to be little prospect, furthermore, that either administrative or military costs can be reduced in the foreseeable future, and the cost of economic development will therefore be superimposed upon the economic burden of maintaining internal and international power.

The Communists' expenditures on cultural activities, education, and health have greatly expanded. In 1950, this item of the budget amounted to U.S.$319 million; the 1954 budget allots U.S.$1.5 billion to these purposes (including relief and pensions).

Great emphasis is placed upon "culture" and education in China because activities in these fields are essential to the political and economic aims of the regime. The Communists want to mold the minds of the new generation and to turn out thousands of technicians for modern economic development projects. Actually, it might be more accurate to label these expenditures "propaganda, indoctrination, and technical training." It is true, however, that the number of schools and students in China has grown tremendously. The Communists plan new enrollments of more than 90,000 students in institutions of higher learning and almost 1.5 million in middle schools (including technical and adult middle schools) during 1954. It is also true that public health and medicine, of a low-level sort, have been extended to an unprecedented extent. A majority of the *Hsien* in China now have "clinics" of one kind or another, and the Communists claim that in 1954 the number of hospital beds in China will increase to more than 200,000.

Even though accomplishments in these fields have been considerable, it is difficult to account for the huge sums of money allotted to them in the budgets if one examines the specific results. Consequently, non-Communist estimates of expenditures are lower than official claims; the actual figure may be nearer U.S.$500 million than U.S.$1.5 billion.

After taking into account all the expenditures already described, how much do the Communists have left for investments in economic development, and how, specifically, are they investing it? This is the key question if one is attempting to analyze the present development program in China and to arrive at some estimate of the resources being devoted to it.

From 1950 through 1952, investments in economic development appeared in Chinese budgets under the label "investments in state enterprises"; since 1953, they have appeared under a category called "national economic construction." Official budget statements show a tremendous rise in these expenditures, from U.S.$733 million in 1950 to a planned figure of U.S.$4.78 billion in 1954. These figures indicate an increase of over 650 per cent, and an increase as a percentage of annual budgets from 25 per cent to 45 per cent. The Communists now claim, in short, that they are devoting almost half of their total expenditures to economic development, and that these expenditures are by far the largest item in the budget.

These figures are not easy to evaluate. To what degree do they conceal expenditures that are clearly military? To what extent are operating costs, as contrasted with new investments, included? How much is merely for repair and maintenance of existing capital equipment rather than for new projects? These and other questions are difficult to answer on the basis of available data. Some non-Communist economists scale down the official estimates by as much as 50 per cent, but there is a lot of guesswork involved in any effort to interpret the official claim. This much is clear, however: The Communists are devoting very large sums of money to economic development projects, running into the equivalent of billions of U.S. dollars. There can be very little argument with the Communists' claim that they are investing a larger share of China's national income in modern economic development than any previous regime has done in Chinese history.

Until the end of 1952, most of the investments were, admittedly, devoted to restoration of the economy rather than to new projects. However, since 1953, when China's first Five-Year Plan was formally initiated, the Communists have claimed that they are investing increasing amounts in new projects. Their breakdown of expenditures on "economic construction" during the past two years is a revealing indication, therefore, of the general pattern of investment in their development program, even if the specific figures must be viewed with some skepticism.

Modern industry is the heart of the Communists' program, and consequently it is receiving the bulk of current investments. In 1953 and 1954, industry each year accounts for over U.S.$2 billion and 45–50 per cent of total expenditures on economic construction. Most of this, furthermore, is being devoted to heavy industries producing capital goods, rather than to light industries producing consumer goods. This year, for example, almost four-fifths of expenditures on industry are allotted to heavy industry and only one-fifth to light industry.

Transport and communications, which are vital to modern industrialization, receive second priority. About U.S.$500 million and U.S.$750 million, in 1953 and 1954 respectively, have been earmarked for investments in these fields. The largest single area of investments under this general category is railway construction.

By contrast, agriculture (including forestry and water conservancy) is receiving little new investment. It is true that investments in this field, which in many cases involve a great deal of cheap labor and not very much expensive equipment, may well be more productive per dollar invested than those in industry and transport; nevertheless, the low figures are rather startling in view of the fact that China is an agricultural country in which, at least for a long time, agriculture must provide most of the surplus for investment in economic development. In 1953 and 1954, about U.S.$500 million per year, or less than 10 per cent of total expenditures on economic construction, has been allotted to agriculture. In the 1954 budget, as a matter of fact, expenditures on agriculture are even lower than those earmarked for domestic and foreign commerce.

What this pattern of investment means is that although the peasants and the agricultural economy are the main supports of the Communists' development program, most of the investments are being made in modern industrialization in urban areas. The peasants are paying the greater part of the bill, but are receiving few immediate benefits. Another fact these figures reveal is that most of the current investments are being made in the kind of industries that will not create any sizable quick increase in the standard of living. The heavy industries on which the Communists are now concentrating are designed to turn out more equipment for new industries, which in turn can produce more equipment for still newer industries—until at some unknown date in the future the economic planners in the regime are satisfied that they have created a powerful industrial base. If a larger proportion of the investments were devoted to projects that had a more immediate impact upon the national economy and standard of living, the burden of squeezing the necessary "savings" for economic development out of the population might gradually become lighter. But this would be a slower process, and the Communists are determined to try to industrialize rapidly. The present burden on the population is not their primary concern; they have their eyes focused on the future.

To carry out their present industrial development program, the Communists face a difficult problem of acquiring foreign exchange as well as accumulating domestic capital. During the initial stages of industrialization, most of the capital equipment required for building new factories, expanding existing ones, and even maintaining old plants must be imported from abroad. China's machine industries are still undeveloped; the largest center of such industries in the past was Manchuria, and in 1945–46 Soviet troops removed (according to postwar surveys) 70 to 80 per cent of the capacity of Manchuria's metal-working industries.

Communist China's decision in 1949 to "lean to one side"—i.e., to align itself completely with the Soviet bloc—and its moves to challenge Western military power in Korea have accentuated the problem, because China thereby cut itself off from any possibility of Western loans and investments and brought upon itself a Western embargo on the type of industrial equipment most urgently needed for its development program. The pace of China's industrial development at present depends very directly, therefore, upon the ability and willingness of Soviet-bloc nations to export industrial equipment to China, and much of the equipment China needs belongs to categories that are still in short supply throughout the Soviet bloc.

The problem of paying for essential imports is also difficult because China is now receiving very little foreign assistance in the form of loans or grants, and it must therefore export to pay for almost all its imports—including those from the Soviet bloc. One of the most surprising aspects of Sino-Soviet relations is the failure of the Russians to give greater financial assistance to China. No free grants from the U.S.S.R. to Communist China have ever been revealed, and to date the only economic development loan made public has been the 1950 five-year loan of U.S.$300 million (U.S.$60 million a year), which has a low interest rate of 1 per cent annually but must be repaid in ten yearly installments, to be completed by 1963. It is possible that there has been some secret financial aid for military purposes, but it seems unlikely that additional aid for economic purposes would have remained concealed. The Soviet Union is sending equipment and technical advisers to China (much of the advice seems to be how to carry out projects with a minimum of equipment), but the Chinese apparently must pay for almost all of this Soviet assistance.

The problem of paying for essential imports can be better understood if it is realized that in the past China has always had a very unfavorable balance of trade, and a sizable percentage of its imports has been paid for with foreign exchange acquired from remittances from overseas Chinese and from foreign loans and investments. (Before the Sino-Japanese War, there was perhaps U.S.$3.2 billion of foreign capital invested in Chinese industry, which was a large percentage of the total capitalization of modern industry in China.) All these sources of foreign exchange have been cut off or reduced. Furthermore, at present, China's potential exports are largely agricultural commodities, specialized metals, and native products—none of which has unlimited possibilities of expansion.

China's present problem of paying for needed imports is further complicated by the fact that a radical reorientation of its foreign trade—a shift from the West to the Soviet bloc—has taken place. There is considerable evidence that increased costs of transport and unfavorable terms of barter exchange mean that China must pay very high prices for imports from the Soviet bloc. To the extent that this is true, it forces China to export even more than would otherwise be necessary to pay for the equipment needed for its industrial development.

As a result of these factors, the Communists have had to use every possible means to develop exports—mainly to the Soviet bloc, but also to some non-Communist countries—although this involves reducing the supplies of essential commodities available to the Chinese population. Even basic foodstuffs, such as grain, pork, and vegetable oils—now in very short supply within China—have been exported in sizable quantities for the first time in modern Chinese history, and Chinese consumers have been confronted with serious shortages and have been offered inferior qualities of these foodstuffs.

By tremendous efforts and rigid controls, the Communists have restored their foreign trade to prewar levels, despite the embargo restricting trade with the West. By 1952, China's imports and exports totaled U.S.$2–3 billion; 72 per cent of this total was accounted for in trade with the Soviet Union. In the first half of 1953, in trade with Western countries, China increased its imports and exports to U.S.$163 million and U.S.$205 million respectively —well above levels during the comparable period of 1952. By the end of 1953, China claimed that total foreign trade for the year was 36 per cent above 1952, and that 75 per cent of this trade was with the Soviet bloc. Efforts to push trade, particularly with Western countries, are continuing.

The percentage of total imports consisting of equipment and materials needed for industrialization has increased steadily. The Communists have restricted purchases of consumer goods to a bare minimum, and they claim that in 1953 "production materials" constituted 87 per cent of total imports. This means that to the maximum extent possible the Chinese are utilizing their limited resources of foreign exchange for imports related directly to their development program.

All these facts indicate that the Communists are doing everything possible to focus foreign trade policies on the task of supporting their program of industrialization, but it seems inevitable that they will face a continuing problem of obtaining and paying for needed capital equipment from abroad. In the immediate postwar period—before the Communist takeover—one American estimate indicated that in order to industrialize at the pace Japan had achieved during the early stages of its development, China would need foreign loans totaling over U.S.$13 billion in the first ten years. Now Communist China is attempting to accomplish the task largely on its own, with relatively little foreign financial assistance even from the Soviet bloc.

"Our country will industrialize itself and achieve socialism step by step," said *People's Daily* in an editorial not long ago. "This is the greatest cause, unprecedented in the history of China. It is the most glorious task of all patriotic people to struggle for this great cause. Everything for the building of the Fatherland—such is our patriotic slogan of today." It continued: "It is of course not easy to acquire the vast amount of funds required for industrialization." It concluded: "The small betterment of today must be subordinated to the big betterment of tomorrow."

"Promote the Spirit of Hard Struggle"—this was the title of the editorial, and it is the basic theme of Communist China's economic development program. The course the Communists have adopted is a hard one, and the present generation of Chinese is being forced to sacrifice for the future.

INDUSTRIALIZATION

July, 1954

The Chinese Communists have created for themselves a vision of China crowded with roaring steel machines, belching smokestacks, and blue-clad industrial workers. They aim to "transform China into a powerful, industrialized socialist state," and to create a "great socialist industrial country and one of the most advanced in the world." To them, modern industry is the symbol of complete independence, national power, and economic improvement.

Not only are the Communists determined to carry out the industrial revolution in the world's largest agricultural country; but they insist on trying to do it at a frantic pace, and the "socialist industrialization" of the U.S.S.R. is their model. They point to the Soviet Union, contrasting its industrialization in "ten to fifteen years" with the longer periods required for industrialization ("fifty to a hundred years") in Western countries, and they proclaim that China has decided to "travel the road of the Russians."

According to them, when their industrial revolution is completed, in a "comparatively short space of time," all modern industry in China will be socialized and will account for close to three-quarters of the combined product of industry and agriculture. In their impatience to reach this goal, they have already begun to inflate the importance of industry in China. When they first came to power, the Communists said that modern industry produced 10 per cent of total industrial and agricultural output; by 1952, they used the figure of 28 per cent; by 1953, the official claim had risen to 31.6 per cent. Now they assert that in ten to fifteen years modern industry will provide 30 to 40 per cent of all industrial and agricultural production in China and that ultimately it will account for 70 per cent.

At the present stage of their development, the Chinese Communists are hypnotized by heavy industries—particularly iron, steel, and machines—and these are receiving their greatest attention. They say that China's eventual goal is for heavy industry to constitute 60 per cent of all modern industry in the country.

Publications in China are full of discussions of these grandiose goals. They are also full of glowing accounts of rapid progress allegedly being made toward achieving them. A superficial reading of Communist propaganda statements could lead one to believe that China is currently making almost fantastic strides toward industrialization. Travelers from China report that work is proceeding on many projects, and these reports often contribute to the widely accepted image of a China industrializing at a very rapid pace.

The facts of the situation are fairly difficult to determine, however, since from the start the Communists have maintained great secrecy about statistics. Most economic data are classified as "state secrets," and the penalty for revealing such secrets is severe. Since the generalized data made public are usually presented in the form of percentage figures giving rises in production, there is much guesswork involved in trying to determine what these percentages mean (the base year or figure is rarely specified) and how they can be translated into real figures. There is also a great deal of confusion, in reports of industrial development in China, between new construction and restoration, replacement, or reconstruction of old plants. Further confusion arises from the fact that the Communists often fail to distinguish between projects completed, begun, or merely planned. Therefore, the task of judging real developments is extremely complicated, involving a great deal of economic jigsaw-puzzle work—the sorting out and fitting together of innumerable fragmentary reports on specific situations and facts.

Despite these difficulties, and the sizable margin for error in any estimates, an analysis of the incomplete information available can give some indication of China's actual plans and accomplishments in industrialization. On the basis of any careful study, it is clear that the Communists are devoting a great deal of China's energy, skills, and resources to industrialization, and as a consequence are making progress, but the pace is less spectacular than general propaganda claims would indicate.

When the Communists came to power, the small amount of modern industry already existing was badly disrupted and run down. Even before the Sino-Japanese War, China had less industry than any other important large nation. The attrition of over a decade of political chaos and war, plus the disruption of China's main industrial base in Manchuria by postwar Soviet removals and Chinese looting, meant that even existing industry was in bad shape. Therefore, the immediate task facing the Communists was one of restoring existing industry, in itself a tremendous job. For over four years, they have worked hard to get industry back into operation and to increase its productivity, and in this effort they have had considerable success. Many industries in China still do not have as much plant and equipment as before the war, but the Peking regime has provided needed raw materials and labor, opened up markets (to a considerable extent by state purchasing), pressed for greater utilization of existing equipment, and, where possible, expanded industrial plant.

By the end of 1952, the Communists announced that the "period of restoration" was completed; they claimed that all major industries except coal had surpassed the "pre-liberation peaks" of production. With the first Five-Year Plan, starting in 1953, they said, China would inaugurate a period of new construction and development.

Actually, much "restoration" is still under way and probably will continue for some time, but it is true that by 1952 China had made great progress in its efforts to get existing industry back into production. In view of all the difficulties encountered, the magnitude of this accomplishment should not be underestimated.

The Chinese Communists say that in terms of past production peaks, industrial output in 1949 was down to 10–20 per cent in iron and steel, under 50 per cent in coal, roughly 75 per cent in electricity, about 30 per cent in cement, and 70–90 per cent in most key consumer goods. By 1952, they claim, general industrial production of thirty-three major products had risen to 26 per cent above previous record levels (16 per cent in capital goods, and 32 per cent in consumer goods). More specifically, they claim that iron production in 1952 was 2 per cent above past peak levels, processed steel 48 per cent, petroleum 19 per cent, electricity 43 per cent, cotton yarn 41 per cent, and cotton cloth 67 per cent. (The only industry officially admitted to be producing below previous record levels was coal, which they said was 5 per cent below past peaks.) On the basis of the best detailed data available, almost all these claims are exaggerated. However, what is true is that industrial production in China by the end of 1952 was approaching past "normal" levels in many key industries.

In the three years of "restoration," fastest progress in raising low production levels was made in iron and steel. Starting at a level of 10–20 per cent of past peaks, iron and steel production in 1952 was, according to official claims, seven to nine times that in 1949. In the same period, coal, cotton yarn, and cloth production was doubled, while large increases were claimed in other industries. But, it should be remembered, most of these increases merely indicate restoration of industries that were badly disrupted in 1949 and were small and underdeveloped to begin with.

Toward the end of 1952, the Communists began to prepare for the start of their first Five-Year Plan of industrial development. In the fall of that year, a significant government reorganization took place; several important new economic ministries were established, a State Planning Commission was set up, and central control over regional administrations in China was tightened. At the same time, a series of Chinese delegations, including top government leaders and heads of key economic organs, made pilgrimages to Moscow to discuss with Soviet leaders the kind of equipment and assistance that could be obtained from the U.S.S.R. Members of these missions were in Russia from August, 1952, through June, 1953. There are many indications that hard bargaining went on between the Chinese and the Russians. Obviously, the Chinese did not obtain promises for as much equipment as they had hoped for, but agreements were made on a specified number of projects for which the Soviet Union would provide machines and technical advisers. On October 1, 1952, the first hint that a Chinese Five-Year Plan would soon begin appeared in the Soviet press; then, on December 24, Premier Chou En-lai announced that China's first Five-Year Plan would start in 1953.

In the year and a half since this announcement, the general aims of the Plan have been made very clear: to develop modern industry and to concentrate upon heavy industries, including metals, fuels, power, "machine-building," and chemical industries. But to date no detailed comprehensive plan has been revealed. As a matter of fact, there are many reasons to believe that no such comprehensive plan yet exists. Apparently, the Five-Year Plan at this stage consists primarily of annual goals for production increases in key industries and plans for a number of specific projects to expand old plants and construct some new ones.

By the end of the current Soviet aid program (1959 or thereafter), China hopes that production of coal will be 160 per cent, electric power 200 per cent, rolled steel 250 per cent, and steel ingots 400 per cent over 1952 levels.

Somewhat more specific has been the revelation that the "core" of the present Five-Year Plan consists of 141 major projects that are receiving Soviet "aid" (for which the Chinese are paying) Apparently, these projects were chosen during the Moscow Sino

Soviet discussions of 1952–53. Undoubtedly, the Soviet Union, which has a key bargaining position as virtually the only source from which China can now obtain needed equipment, played a large role in determining what these projects should be. Of the 141 projects, some merely involve renovation or expansion of old plants, so the actual number of new industries called for is unknown. Furthermore, the program really extends over a ten-year period; of the total, 50 projects were started during 1949–52, prior to the official announcement of the program, while present plans call for the start of work on all 141 by 1959—or halfway through China's second Five-Year Plan.

Although China now has a Five-Year Plan, it is uncertain how much real planning the Communists have been able to introduce into the economy. It is true that the state has extended various types of economic controls to all sectors of the economy, but China nevertheless is, and will for some time remain, a "mixed economy," with a complicated combination of state enterprises (under the control of both the central and local governments), private enterprises, cooperatives, and "state capitalist" enterprises. At best, it would be difficult to apply detailed planning techniques in such an economy. China, furthermore, has very few trained economic planners—or even economists for that matter—and although Soviet advisers, who are numerous, help fill this gap at top levels, they cannot possibly make up for all of China's deficiencies in skills.

The complete inadequacy of statistical data creates another major obstacle to planned development of the industrial economy in China. Although a State Statistical Bureau has been established, it was not until last year that it really began to set up extensive regional offices and to simplify and regularize statistical procedures. Despite the fact that a drastic reorganization of statistical reporting took place at the end of 1953, the Communists admit that statistical data on the economy is still far from satisfactory, a state of affairs likely to continue for a long time.

At present, however, despite many problems, the Communists do attempt to set definite production quotas in all state-owned enterprises. Individual economic ministries in the Central Government are probably the key level in the process of formulating plans. Quotas are set not only for a whole industry—for example, textiles—but also for individual factories, workshops, work teams, and individual workers within factories. And they are set on an annual, periodic, monthly—and sometimes daily or hourly—basis. Every effort is made to increase these quotas from year to year, or period to period, and wherever possible "advanced average norms" of production by above-average workers and machines are adopted as the basis for new quotas. Party organizations and unions in individual factories, which participate in planning conferences, use their influence to press for quotas that will ensure maximum output of equipment and increased efforts by labor.

At a top level, apparently, the Committee on Financial and Economic Affairs adjusts and coordinates the plans of various industrial ministries, fitting them into the plans of other key organs such as the Ministry of Finance and the Ministry of Commerce. It is at this level that broad decisions on allocation of national resources and over-all investments are made. The role of the State Planning Commission is still obscure, for although it is undoubtedly designed to be a top-level coordinating organization, there is little indication that it is yet serving this role effectively. During the past year, in fact, there have been few references to this body. The head of the Commission, Kao Kang, has been in complete eclipse since the end of 1953, and may have been removed from office.

Much responsibility for ensuring implementation of economic plans at present apparently rests with the Ministry of Finance (and under it the People's Bank) and the Ministry of Commerce. The People's Bank serves as a clearing house for financial transactions by all state enterprises, and it now supervises and controls all credit transactions of any significance in China. The Ministry of Commerce dominates domestic trade throughout the country and consequently has great power in determining the allocation and distribution of both raw materials and finished products.

Even though economic planning in China is probably still fairly crude, the Communists have been able to extend a significant degree of control, and some degree of planning, to the remaining private sector of the economy, and have done so largely through the Ministry of Commerce and the People's Bank.

The Communists' industrialization program calls not only for "socialist industrialization" (the development of state-owned industries), but also for "socialist transformation" (the steady conversion of existing private industries into state-owned enterprises). The latter process has been going on since the Communists came to power, although it has been defined as official policy in completely clear terms only since the end of 1953.

One of the unique aspects of this socialization policy in China, as contrasted with earlier Soviet policy, is the fact that the Chinese

Communists have proceeded in a relatively gradual, systematic, step-by-step fashion instead of attempting to nationalize private enterprises all at once. The pace of socialization has not been slow, but the pattern has been one of steadily extending controls, infiltrating, and finally taking over private industries, rather than one of sudden, outright confiscation.

The Communists now define several stages of what they call "state capitalism," through which all private industries of any importance are expected to progress. Each stage represents an increase of government control and supervision and is considered "transitional" to final socialization. At the "lowest" stage, the state purchases the products of a private industry, or state trading agencies serve as its selling agents. (The state also controls the sale of all key industrial raw materials.) At a higher stage, the state either places orders with a private industry for processing jobs, buys all of its finished products, or underwrites the marketing of its entire output. The "highest form" of "state capitalism" is the "joint state-private enterprise," in which the reality of complete state control is combined with the fiction of private ownership.

The dependence of private enterprise upon the state is now almost complete. Last year, for example, 75 per cent (by value) of the total output of private factories in Tientsin consisted of goods produced to meet government orders or contracts, and the percentage was comparable in other large industrial cities.

Despite the gradualism of the Chinese Communist economic policy (compared with that of the Soviet Union), the degree of outright state ownership of industry in China is already very high. The last official claims, made over a year ago, were that roughly 50 per cent of modern industry in China (40 per cent of light industry and 70–80 per cent of heavy industry) is state-owned, and state enterprises account for 60 per cent of modern industrial production in the country.

When they first came to power, the Communists immediately took over all industries formerly owned by the Nationalist Government as well as those which belonged to large Chinese owners whom they classified as "bureaucratic capitalists." Since then, they have steadily taken over, or converted into "state capitalist" enterprises, the most important large industries belonging to both Chinese and foreigners. In a great many cases, every effort has been made to preserve a semblance of legality and to avoid the appearance of outright confiscation by giving nominal compensation, or by claiming that takeover is necessary to pay back taxes and employee wages; in any event, state ownership has increased steadily.

The Communists are frank in stating that their ultimate aim is complete socialization of modern industry in China. They have followed a policy of relative caution in taking over private enterprises because they recognized their own shortage of managerial talents and have wanted to use those of private entrepreneurs. This policy has certainly been less disruptive than one involving sudden confiscation would have been, and it has minimized the problems of socialization during the past four years. But private entrepreneurs in China have not been hoodwinked. Most of them now operate in a twilight zone between private and state ownership in which they are required to use their administrative skills but are forbidden to employ their initiative. They know that their days are numbered, and they realize that their future depends solely upon the timetable of Communist planners. It is not surprising that in these circumstances private enterprise in China today plays a role that cannot be compared to that of its counterpart in non-Communist countries. Those modern industries in China which are still ostensibly in private hands are subject to controls which, however crude, make them the tool of the state instead of the expression of private aims and initiative. Although private entrepreneurs are still helping to keep part of China's existing industry going, they will gradually be pushed out of the picture and will have virtually nothing to do with development of new industries.

The industrial base the Communists acquired when they came to power was not only small but also highly concentrated. Manchuria, developed as an industrial center by the Japanese between 1932 and 1945, was the most important single region, containing the bulk of China's heavy industries. Centered on the Anshan-Fushun-Mukden area, Manchuria's industries included the largest coal mines, iron and steel mills, power plants, and metal factories, as well as the best railway network, in China. Soviet removals, looting, and civil-war damage after 1945 badly crippled the industrial base left by the Japanese. Postwar surveys indicated, for example, that over one-half of its electric capacity and four-fifths of its metal-working equipment were either destroyed or badly damaged. However, despite this fact, Manchuria remained China's most highly developed industrial base and virtually her only center of heavy industries.

As China's second most important industrial base, Shanghai (together with the cities in a triangle enclosed by Nanking and

Hangchow) produced the bulk of the country's consumer goods. Textiles and flour-milling, China's two most important prewar industries, were concentrated in this area.

There were four other industrial centers of secondary importance: the Peiping-Chinwangtao-Tientsin triangle (including Tangshan); the Shantung area on an axis between Tsingtao and Tsinan; a Central China area including Wuhan, Pinghsiang, and Changsha; and the Pearl River region with Canton as its core. In addition, there were a number of smaller industrial centers of minor importance.

The projects and plans for industrial expansion that the Communists are now developing will alter this regional distribution of industry in a number of significant ways.

Manchuria not only will continue to be vital, but will clearly become even more important. Great efforts are being made to restore Anshan and develop it as the "steel capital" of China. Coal production is being increased at Fushun and Fuhsin, while power, aluminum, shale oil, and heavy machinery output at Fushun is also being expanded. At Mukden, the biggest center of heavy manufacturing in China, restoration and expansion of many plants are under way—including two machine-tool factories, a pneumatic tool plant, and a wire and cable factory. To the north, Harbin is being developed into an important new industrial center, with work in progress on factories to produce machine tools, electric generators and motors, meters, and other important products. Dairen, Penki, and a number of other cities are also being developed. "Most" of the so-called "key 141 Soviet aid projects" are in Manchuria. This concentration of effort on Manchuria has a great deal of economic justification, but in addition the political implications cannot be overlooked. Manchuria's proximity to the U.S.S.R., and the special importance of Soviet influence and interests in the area, are significant factors.

Shanghai, by contrast, has been relegated, at least temporarily, to the background in plans for future development, although the light industries already located there will undoubtedly make it China's main center producing consumer goods for some time to come. Since the Communist takeover, relatively little important new investment or large-scale plant expansion in Shanghai has been revealed. In fact, when the Communists first took Shanghai, there were widespread rumors that part of the city's industries would be moved to the interior, but this has not taken place on a significant scale, perhaps because of the impracticality of the scheme. It is clear, however, that at present the Communists plan to reduce the relative importance of Shanghai in the economy of China as a whole. Shanghai was the center both of foreign economic influence and of China's indigenous capitalist class; as such, it has been a headache to Communist administrators, who consider it to be potentially dangerous in its influence upon the country. As a coastal city, it is in an area exposed to immediate threat in time of war.

A number of interior areas of China are now slated for new industrial development. The Communists plan to construct two new iron and steel centers outside Manchuria which, they claim, will eventually be on the scale of Anshan. Of these, one involves expansion of small plants now existing in central China at Tayeh, near Wuhan; some work is already under way there. The other involves the building of a "huge" center, entirely new, at Paotow, present railhead of the Inner Mongolia rail line. This second one is being given great publicity, but in most respects it still remains a gleam in the planners', or propagandists', eyes.

New railway and electric-power development also indicates the rise of industries in new areas in China. The most important rail lines to be undertaken during the first Five-Year Plan are in remote northwest and southwest China. The Plan calls for ten "major" electric-power projects. Six of these involve plant expansion (five in Manchuria and one in Tayeh), while the remaining four are new projects located in the interior areas of north and northwest China—Paotow, Lanchow, Taiyuan, and Sian.

Another significant development is work on the construction of several new textile centers in the cotton-growing areas of north and northwest China. Large cotton mills are being built at Sian, Shih-chiachuang, Chengchow, and Peking. It will be a long time before these new centers can compare in importance with places like Shanghai, but they do represent a significant trend toward the dispersion of China's primary consumer-goods industry.

General industrial growth of some importance, but still on a relatively limited scale, is under way in a number of other interior centers. Taiyuan, formerly a small center of both light and heavy industry controlled by a local Chinese warlord, is being built up into a sizable base. Several areas in Sinkiang Province (Chinese Turkestan) are being developed; here Soviet assistance is important, and the Chinese Army supervises some of the projects. Not much is known of progress to date. Modern plants at Tientsin, Tangshan, and Peking in north China; at Wuhan, Nanchang, and

Hsiangtan in central China; at Sian and Lanchow in the northwest; and at Chungking in the southwest are being expanded in varying degrees. (Peking is slated for a good deal of new development, which may change considerably the character of that traditional center of culture, education, and administration.) Soviet aid is helping to increase basic mineral production, including that of oil in the northwest and tin and copper in Yunnan.

The one area that most obviously is being neglected in Communist plans is south China. Very few projects in this region have been reported. South China seems, in fact, to lag behind in almost every field of Communist activity. It is behind the rest of the country in political consolidation and agricultural organization, as well as in industrial development.

These trends in geographical location of industry have not yet significantly altered the regional pattern of industrialization in China, but they will certainly have an important effect in time. By the end of one or two Five-Year Plans, Manchuria will probably dominate the Chinese industrial scene even more completely than before, coastal cities such as Shanghai will probably have declined in relative importance, new industrial centers in the interior—particularly in north, northwest, and southwest China—will have been developed, and south China, in all probability, will be the most industrially backward region of the country.

China is now in the second year of its first Five-Year Plan. The Communists' official announcements of over-all plans and accomplishments during this period do not give an accurate picture of the dimensions of the Plan, or of real attainments, but they do present some idea of what is being done.

When the Communists first announced industrial production targets for 1953, they said that during the year they planned to increase the value of total national production, both agricultural and industrial, by 12 per cent—i.e., about one-tenth over 1952. The goal for industry alone was higher. By the end of 1953, the Communists said, over-all industrial production would be 25.6 per cent over that of 1952. Much of this increase was to come from higher labor productivity; the planned rise in labor productivity for the year was 16 per cent, and costs of production in industry were scheduled to be lowered 4.4 per cent. The largest rise in production was planned for state-owned industries, slated for a 32 per cent increase.

Proposed production increases in specific industries were sizable. For example, output of pig iron was to rise 14 per cent, steel 23 per cent, electric power 27 per cent, and petroleum 42 per cent. Capital-goods industries were also scheduled to increase production greatly. For example, a 34 per cent rise in the output of machine tools was proposed. Contemplated increases for major consumer-goods industries were generally more modest, however—9 and 16 per cent for cotton yarn and cloth respectively, and 23 per cent for sugar.

The Plan had barely got under way, however, when it became clear to the Communists that they would encounter difficulties in achieving these goals; downward revisions of targets were soon publicly announced. Negotiations for economic aid were still in progress in Moscow, and the revisions may have been related to failures to obtain expected promises of Soviet assistance or support. But the second half of 1953 was a period of tremendous effort. The Communists clearly used every possible means of pressure to speed up work and to step up the pace of development. However, it is also clear that they revised their plans drastically, so that final claims for the year were probably made in terms of targets that had been considerably lowered from the original ones.

A summary of the results for 1953 finally was announced in mid-1954. It was claimed that "most" of the important sectors of state industry had fulfilled the Plan, and that total industrial production in China had risen 27 per cent during 1953 (even more than originally planned). But the Communists felt compelled at the same time to explain that the "rate of development of the national economy in the period of construction naturally is not the same as that for the stage of reconstruction." They admitted that four important industries did not meet goals—flour, sugar, salt, and gunny bags, all of which are directly related to agriculture (in which 1953 output was dangerously behind schedule).

The 1954 production goals for industry reflect the difficulties encountered by the Communists during the previous year. The planned increase in total national production is still ambitious, and about the same as in 1953 (12.6 per cent in 1954, 12 per cent in 1953), but the scheduled rise in industrial production alone has been scaled down considerably—from 25.6 per cent in 1953 to 18.3 per cent.

Vague percentages and statements on numbers of projects under way are virtually the only kind of generalized information on industrial development that the Communists have released to date, either to their own people or to the world at large. Unless this information is translated into real terms, it does not have a great deal of meaning. This is extremely difficult to do, but it is not impossible to make educated guesses. Chinese Communist publications contain a considerable amount of detailed information on specific projects, and they are less secretive in providing real figures for individual projects than they are in their general claims. Furthermore, it is possible to apply their percentage figures on production to what is known of previous "peaks" in China, before Communist takeover. (There is a sizable margin of possible error in this process, because in many cases it is not definitely known what the Communists themselves use as the peak production figures. In general, they use 1943 figures for Manchuria and 1936 figures for the rest of China, but they have admitted scaling down the real figures for these years in various ways.)

Modern forms of transportation, particularly railroads, are basic to industrial development; the lack of such transportation has been a major factor limiting economic growth in China. It has been estimated that only 5 per cent of freight tonnage in China is carried by all forms of modern transport, and that 45 per cent is carried by man-pulled junks and carts and 50 per cent on human backs. Such primitive transport is very expensive (estimated in the prewar period at 15–50 cents per ton per kilometer [0.62 miles], compared to 1.5 cents on railroads) and consequently limits internal trade and requires huge amounts of manpower. Before the war, it was estimated that 20 million Chinese were engaged in transport, yet surveys showed that less than 10 per cent of all production in rural China moved out of the county of its origin. For years, therefore, Chinese leaders have dreamed of developing modern railways, and men like Sun Yat-sen talked of building a network of 100,000 miles of track.

Before the Sino-Japanese War, China had perhaps 14,700 miles of railways (according to present Communist figures), of which about one-third was in Manchuria. This amounted to less than 30 miles per million people, or 300–400 miles per 100,000 square miles of area. (In 1950, U.S. and U.S.S.R. mileage was 227,000 and 57,000 respectively.) When the Communists came to power in 1949, a large percentage of this inadequate network had deteriorated or been destroyed. They placed a very high priority on restoration of railroads, therefore, and during the first two years of their rule, expenditures on railways constituted the largest single item in their construction budget. Literally millions of laborers were mobilized in work gangs to carry out a rapid rehabilitation of old lines. In 1949 alone, according to official claims, approximately

5,000 miles of line were put back into operation. The major job of restoration was completed by 1951, and by the end of 1953 it was claimed that over 6,000 miles of rail line in China had been rehabilitated. Passenger lines were operated, largely by old personnel taken over from the Nationalist regime, with an efficiency that greatly impressed visitors to China.

The task of building new railways has proved to be a much more difficult job, however, so that progress has not been as rapid as in the period of "restoration." In 1949, the Communists spoke of a Five-Year Plan to construct new railways totaling 6,250 miles; such a plan would have been involved about 1,250 miles of new line construction every year. But actual new construction, even since the initiation of the Five-Year Plan, has been less than one-third of this annual goal.

The building of new railways in China began in 1950, with three important lines: Laipin-Chennankwan, Tienshui-Lanchow, and Chungking-Chengtu. The first was completed in 1951, the other two in 1952. Two more major lines—Lanchow-Sinkiang and Chengtu-Paoki—as well as a few minor ones were begun in 1952. When the over-all Five-Year Plan was started in 1953, work on these lines was continued while surveying began on ten new ones, including major lines from Paotow to Lanchow and from Chengtu to Kunming.

It is difficult to reconcile conflicting Communist figures on total new railway construction, but official claims indicate that possibly 250–300 miles were built in 1950–51, about 300 in 1952, and 365 in 1953; at the end of 1953, total new construction since Communist takeover was stated to be 915 miles. The 1954 construction plan calls for about 375 miles of new line.

The inadequacy of China's rail net has made it necessary for the Communists to utilize existing railways as intensively as possible, and the wear and tear on them has been severe. As a result, a large percentage of the increased investment in railways this year must be devoted to maintenance and repair. But campaigns to increase the speeds and loads of trains continue, while the high rate of accidents and deterioration remains a major problem. The 1954 plan nonetheless calls for a 15.5 per cent increase in freight and a 14 per cent increase in passengers, although the planned increase in rail lines is less than 3 per cent; so the strain on existing equipment is likely to increase rather than decrease.

The location of new rail lines is of considerable interest because it indicates that strategic factors have played an important role in the planning.

Of the new lines, three important ones have already been completed. The 260-mile Laipin-Chennankwan railway stretches to the Indochina border, and its importance is primarily military. The 330-mile Chungking-Chengtu line links the most populous and important province in southwest China with the Yangtze River (and also connects with roads to Tibet); and the 215-mile Tienshui-Lanchow line connects China's main east-west trunk railway with Lanchow, one of the two major cities in northwest China. Both these lines are extremely important for strategic as well as economic reasons.

Three other major lines are now being pushed. The Lanchow-Sinkiang line, begun late in 1952, will stretch northwest to Chinese Turkestan, providing a new link with the Soviet Union. About 112 miles of this line were completed in 1953, with 95 more scheduled for completion this year. Obviously, it will take several more years to complete the total 1,736 miles of this railway. The 435 miles of track from Paoki to Chengtu, also started in mid-1952, will provide the main trunk line of transport connecting northwest and southwest China. By the end of 1953, about 100 miles were laid, and the plan is to lay another 115 miles this year; at this rate, it may be finished by the end of 1956. The third new project under way is the short, 65-mile Fengtai-Shacheng line in north China. This branch supplements a line already in existence and is designed to improve transport to developing industrial centers in the Peking-Tatung-Paotow area; it is scheduled for completion in 1955.

Other new lines already completed or now under way are of minor significance. Most of them are short branches to mining and forestry areas, and are concentrated in Manchuria.

Surveying for the 500-mile Chengtu-Kunming line, drawing the important southwest China province of Yunnan into the developing interior rail net, was completed in 1953, and construction is scheduled to begin this year. There has been no indication yet of when the Paotow-Lanchow line, over 620 miles long, may be started, although surveying is now under way. It promises to be a vital artery if Paotow develops into a steel center.

Iron and steel, the foundation of modern industrialism, are particularly important in any program that concentrates, as does that of the Chinese Communists, upon rapid development of heavy industry. Iron and steel are the basis for the metals, machines, defense, transport, and other industries that Communist China rates highest.

It is not surprising, therefore, that the Communist regime in China gives top priority to the development of iron and steel. During 1953, the first year of China's Five-Year Plan, more publicity was given to the restoration of blast furnaces and other steel facilities at Anshan than to any other industrial projects. But when Communist percentages and propaganda claims are translated into some approximation of the truth, the situation in iron and steel dramatically highlights China's underdeveloped condition and the long road the Communists must travel before they can create a "powerful, industrialized socialist state."

China possesses the raw-material base for a sizable iron and steel industry. Coal resources are large, and although iron reserves are smaller (as well as scattered and not generally of high quality), they are sufficient for considerable development. Iron-ore reserves in China were variously estimated at from 680 million to 1.8 billion tons before the Communist takeover; now some Communist claims of China's reserves are as high as 6.7 billion. Possibly, new deposits have been discovered in the past four years, but the claims may well be exaggerated. The main obstacle to iron and steel development at this stage, in any case, is not lack of raw materials. As China acquires the capital, equipment, and skills required to expand iron and steel, the industry can be developed.

China's only important steel-producing region at present is Manchuria, where there is a major center at Anshan and a minor one at Penki. Elsewhere, small centers have been developed in the past at Tangshan, Tientsin, Taiyuan, Lungyen, and Peking in north China; and at Wuhan-Tayeh, Shanghai, Maanshan, and Chungking farther south; but, according to one estimate, the combined peak production in all China prior to the Communist takeover totaled about 1.9 million tons of pig iron, a little over 800,000 tons of steel ingots, and about 500,000 tons of rolled steel. (In 1950, the U.S. produced 65 million tons of pig iron and 97 million tons of steel; the U.S.S.R. claimed an output of 27 million tons of steel in 1950, and its 1955 target is 45 million tons.)

When the Chinese Communists came to power, furthermore, the iron and steel industry, which had been badly hurt in Manchuria by Soviet removals and by civil-war destruction, was the worst off of any major industry in China. Compared with past peak levels, production was down to 11 per cent of past peaks in pig iron, 16 per cent in steel ingots, and 18 per cent in rolled steel, according to official figures.

The Communists immediately set about the task of restoring the production of the remaining facilities capable of being repaired, particularly at Anshan, and it is claimed that by 1952 pig-iron and steel-ingot output rose by 784 per cent and 848 per cent respectively.

Anshan produces almost all the iron and steel in China at present, and will continue to be the focus of Chinese efforts to develop this basic industry for some time to come. Formerly, it produced three-fourths of China's steel, and the percentage may be even higher now.

In 1943, when Anshan was producing at its peak level, nine blast furnaces were in use, but in 1949 only one of these was operable. During 1949–50, two more were restored. Communist claims indicated that Anshan's three furnaces at this time were producing at one-third above previous peak rates.

Then, in 1953, the first year of the Five-Year Plan, two large, new, Soviet-type automatic blast furnaces were installed at Anshan. At the same time, four coke-oven furnaces, a seamless tubing plant, and a large steel-rolling mill were built, increasing Anshan's existing capacity by 80 per cent in pig iron, 78 per cent in coke, and 88 per cent in rolled steel—according to Communist claims.

This year, further work is going on at Anshan in the form of construction (restoration) of two more large, modern blast furnaces. Completion of these will take time, however, and the Communists admit that production increases scheduled for this year will "depend chiefly upon the existing installations." When they are finished, Anshan will have a total of seven blast furnaces (four large new ones), compared with nine in 1943; Communist plans may call for some additional construction.

During 1953, although major efforts were concentrated at Anshan, work also was undertaken to restore six small furnaces at Maanshan, two small furnaces at Lungyen, and a small steel mill in Tientsin. China's other minor steel plants were all working under considerable pressure, and some plant improvements were made during the year. For example, the Chungking plant began to produce new types of rails.

The Communists have indicated that by about 1959 they hope to raise steel production to 400 per cent and rolled steel production to 250 per cent of 1952 levels.

The press in China gives a great deal of attention to plans for the building of two large new steel centers, comparable in size to Anshan. One of these is at Tayeh, in central China, where some work on expanding existing power and steel facilities has been started this year. The other is at Paotow, in Inner Mongolia, near rich iron deposits at Pailingmiao and coal at Tatung. Preparatory work is said to be under way here, but no construction of iron and steel facilities has started. If the Chinese obtain the equipment for large projects at these two places, there is no doubt that in due time China's iron and steel output will be significantly increased, but at best it will take several years to develop these new centers, so production during the first Five-Year Plan will depend primarily upon Anshan.

Sources of energy, like transportation and basic metals, are fundamental to modern industrial growth, because all other industry depends upon them. Coal, electricity, and oil are the three most important energy sources at present for industrial development, and in many respects the pace of general development can be measured in terms of progress in these industries.

When the Communists first came to power, they gave insufficient attention to power sources, and by the time the Five-Year Plan was launched, it was obvious that lack of power for industrial purposes was a serious bottleneck to their entire program. Consequently, higher priority was given to coal and electric-power projects; these now figure prominently in the Five-Year Plan and in the 141 projects scheduled to receive Soviet assistance. This year, even greater stress has been laid in the field of fuels and power than was the case in 1953. According to one official statement, about one-half of the total investment in industry during 1954 has been allotted to the coal and electric-power industries. The Communists claim this investment will increase fuel and power output in China by 19 per cent over that in 1953.

Coal is the main source of industrial energy in China, either directly in steam engines or indirectly through production of electric power. It provides most of the power for modern industry and transportation, as well as the fuel for home consumption. Not only does China have the largest coal reserves in the Far East, but its deposits can be compared with the biggest in the world. Much of the coal is scattered and is not ideally located in terms of its accessibility to industry, but in the foreseeable future China's problem will be the difficulty of extracting enough for the country's needs rather than a lack of underground resources.

During the years of "restoration," from 1949 through 1952,

recovery of coal production was steady but, because of many difficulties, slower than that of any other basic industry. Of the major
industries, coal was the only one the Communists officially admitted as having failed to reach prewar peak production levels by
the end of 1952; production in 1952, they said, was 95 per cent of
the highest previous level.

The major coal production centers in China at present, as in the
past, include Fushun and Fuhsin in Manchuria and Kailan in north
China. There are many other important mines, such as Tatung,
Pinghsiang, and Hwainan, as well as innumerable scattered smaller
producers. The Communists have been exerting strenuous efforts
to restore and expand production at these places, to introduce
Soviet methods of mechanization, and to develop a few new mines.
These efforts have been stepped up since the start of the Five-
Year Plan.

The 1959 coal production goal of the Communists is a 60 per
cent increase over 1952. The 1953 construction plans called for
work on forty coal shafts in China—fourteen in Manchuria and
twenty-six in the rest of the country—but it is not known how
many of these were completed. Construction goals for 1954 include
the completion of nine new pairs of coal shafts (five vertical and
four inclined), as well as a number of new open pits. Production
is scheduled for a significant increase of 13 per cent over last year.

One would think that coal production should be among the
least serious problems in the Communists' development plans.
China has adequate resources, and coal production requires less in
the way of capital or skills than do such other industries as metal-
lurgy, engineering, electricity, and chemicals. Nonetheless, the
Communists have encountered great difficulty in restoring and
expanding the production of coal.

Electric power is another significant key—and a major bottleneck—to general industrial growth in China; almost all modern
industry depends upon thermo-electric or hydro-electric power.
Lack of resources is not a basic problem; as already mentioned,
China has large coal deposits, and its hydro-electric potential has
been estimated to be as large as 22 million horsepower. However,
the hydro-electric potential is almost totally undeveloped in most
areas, and thermal power is still underdeveloped. Even with its
existing industries, China is straining its electric capacity to the
utmost.

Electric-power expansion plays a vital role in the first Five-Year
Plan and in the current Soviet aid program. In terms of construc-

tion, 1953 plans called for expanding twelve thermal and three hydro-electric plants and starting work on nine new thermal plants. In 1954, work is scheduled on twenty projects, and ten thermal and hydro-electric plants are to start operations. More than ten of the planned electric projects have been mentioned as part of the program of 141 "major" projects receiving Soviet aid.

In terms of power production, Chinese plans call for doubling 1952 output by 1959. The first year of the Five-Year Plan aimed at a 27 per cent increase in electrical production, and this year's goal is set at 15 per cent.

A number of important electric-power plants have been expanded or built in China during the past two years. In Manchuria, expansion is going on at Tafengmen, China's largest hydro-electric station; Fushun, Manchuria's biggest thermal plant; Fuhsin; Dairen; Harbin; and elsewhere. A new thermal plant in Chungking, reported to be the largest in southwest China, has recently begun to operate. Building has started on four important new plants at Paotow, Lanchow, Taiyuan, and Sian; the Sian plant is expected to double the electric capacity of northwest China. New plants of considerable importance are being constructed at Chengchow, Tihwa, and Tayeh. In addition, a fairly large number of projects of either expansion or new construction on a smaller scale have been started in scattered locations, including Chengtu, Tungchuan, Kwangting, Kweisui, Tientsin, Tungchow, and others.

Petroleum is much less important as a source of energy in China than either coal or electricity. China's known oil reserves are small, and existing resources have never been extensively developed. Nevertheless, the Communists are doing what they can to restore plants developed in the past and to prospect for new sources. The main producer of natural oil in China is Yumen, in the northwest, and the Communists have restored perhaps half of the wells there. Work has also been undertaken at small oil centers located at Wusu and Yenchang, also in northwest China. Restoration of shale-oil production in Manchuria has also been started. Two major plants developed by the Japanese at Fushun, with a combined capacity of 2–3 million barrels a year, and seven minor synthetic oil plants elsewhere in Manchuria produced most of China's oil. These plants were badly damaged by the Russians, but one of the Fushun plants is scheduled to resume operations soon.

The Chinese have also been doing a good deal of prospecting in northwest and southwest China, and this year they claim to have

230 petroleum teams at work, but what has been discovered is not known.

Heavy manufacturing industries receive a priority second only to basic transport, metals, and fuels in the Communists' plans for industrial development. Machine tools, machines, and vehicles of all sorts, electrical equipment, and chemicals are essential to a program calling for plowing a maximum amount of increased industrial production back into investment in further industrial development. "The higher the proportion of heavy industry in the national economy," said *People's Daily* in an editorial early this year, "the greater the possibility for accelerating the accumulations and the higher the speed of reproduction. In other words, only by first developing heavy industries which make the means of production can industrial construction be accelerated."

In developing "heavy industries which make the means of production," the Communists are starting almost from scratch. In the past, China developed very few such industries; most of those which did exist were concentrated in Manchuria, with Mukden as the main center, and, according to one estimate, almost four-fifths of the metal-working industry in Manchuria was damaged or removed during the Soviet occupation, in 1945–46. Elsewhere in China, industries in this category were mainly small assembly or repair plants, with very few primary producers. One dramatic illustration of how little heavy manufacturing exists in China is the fact that China's first modern measuring-instrument and cutting-tool plant, scheduled for completion in Harbin this year, "will produce more precision tools," according to the Chinese Communists, "than the present combined output of all existing plants in the country."

During the period 1949–52, the Communists did everything they could to restore or renovate the existing small machine-manufacturing plants scattered throughout China, but it was only when the Five-Year Plan began that significant projects to restore Manchuria's heavy industry or to construct new ones were started. Most of the major projects in the field of heavy industry since then have been included in the Soviet aid program, and the majority of them are located in Manchuria.

Plans for 1953 called for construction of nine new machine-building factories and renovation or expansion of fifteen others. (These were all under the First Ministry of Machine-Building Industry.) The most important new projects started during the year were China's first automobile plant, its first modern measuring-

and cutting-tool plant, and an electric wire and cable plant in Mukden, a heavy-machinery plant and a textile-machinery plant in Taiyuan, and a shipyard in Wuchang. Major renovation or expansion projects started during the year included two machine-tool plants, a pneumatic-tool plant, and a heavy-machinery plant, all in Mukden. In addition, about 100 projects of renovation or expansion, mostly of small scattered factories or shops, were said to have been undertaken. The Communists claim that machinery production in China during 1953 rose 65 per cent over the previous year, and that 600 "new products" (of which 394 were electrical, including large 6,000-kw generators) were produced for the first time in Chinese history.

Work is now continuing on most of the projects started in 1953, and a few of the Mukden and Harbin plants are scheduled for completion (including the Harbin plants for measuring and cutting tools and for electrical machinery, one Mukden machine-tool factory, and a pneumatic-tool plant). In addition, important new renovation projects during 1954 include a heavy-machinery factory at Anshan, another at Fushun, a bridge-assembly plant at Mukden, and various other factories for weights and measures, railway-bridge, farm-tool, textile, and mining machinery.

When the heavy manufacturing industry projects now under way are completed, Mukden will be restored to its former importance as the main center of machine manufacture in China, and a major new center of importance will be created, at Harbin, near the Soviet border. At present, Mukden has more than twenty "large-scale" factories for machine manufacture, sixteen of which are scheduled for renovation or expansion, and the most important new construction in China is going on at Harbin. In short, Manchuria's importance as primary center for the limited heavy manufacturing in China is being further increased; of ten "major" projects in this field in China during 1954, eight are located in Manchuria.

The process of building a completely new heavy machine manufacturing industry in China is complicated, difficult, and slow, but any addition to existing plants is significant, because China has so little to start with.

What is happening in the field of munitions and arms manufacturing in China at present is unknown. Defense plants in these categories are under the mysterious Second Ministry of Machine-Building Industry, and strict secrecy is observed concerning all its activities. In view of the high priority the Communists place upon military power, however, significant growth is undoubtedly taking place, with Manchuria unquestionably the largest center of military industry.

Chemical manufacturing is another major, and as yet undeveloped, industry to which the Communists are now devoting much attention. Sulfuric and nitric acid, caustic soda, and chemical fertilizers are very important to both industry and agriculture, and the Communists claim that they are increasing their production fairly rapidly; the target for growth in "major chemicals" this year is 15 to 74 per cent. But not a great deal of information about construction of new plants, or even expansion of old ones, has been made public. During the past two years, the Communists have mentioned completion of a major chemical plant in Dairen, expansion of the important Yungli chemical works in central China, and work on various smaller projects, including an ammonium sulfate plant in Hsiangtan, a small chemical plant in Nanchang, and a caustic soda factory in Suiyuan Province. But details on these projects are lacking.

All these facts seem to indicate that although the Communists are making some headway in developing heavy manufacturing, it will be a long time before they achieve their aim of self-sufficiency in these key industries. In the meantime, they will have to depend heavily on imports of machinery and equipment to carry out their program of industrial development.

Because the Communists are concentrating upon heavy industries, relatively little is being invested in expansion of the light industries which produce the consumer goods required by the mass of the population.

By far the majority of industries developed in China in the past, however, were light industries, with cotton textiles and flour-milling predominating. When the Communists came to power, furthermore, these enterprises were producing at a much higher percentage of capacity than China's few heavy industries, and, as a result, recovery of their production was relatively rapid. By 1950, the Communists claimed that most basic consumer-goods industries, except sugar, had surpassed previous peak levels of production.

Since the start of the Five-Year Plan, there has been very little new investment in light industries, but the Chinese have continued to demand sizable production increases from them. This year, for example, only one-fifth of the total industrial investment is earmarked for light industry, and yet plans call for a 24 per cent over-all rise in its output—compared with an increase of only 15 per cent in heavy industry, which is receiving four-fifths of the capital. Apparently, the Communists believe that the output of light industry can still be raised by speed-up methods and more intensive utilization of existing equipment.

The most important light industry in China, and one that is essential to the standard of living of the population, is cotton textiles (almost everyone in China wears cotton clothes). Developments in this industry illustrate the Communists' policy toward light industry as a whole.

Prior to the Sino-Japanese War, China's cotton-textile industry had more than 5 million spindles; the biggest modern industry in China, it included a high percentage of the country's large-scale factories. Shanghai, with 50 per cent of the spindleage, was the main textile center, but important producing cities included Tientsin, Tsingtao, Wuhan, and Wusih. A large part of the prewar ownership was foreign, but at the end of the war most of the textile industry passed into Chinese Government hands. At present, although many of the largest mills are state enterprises, quite a few factories are still private or "joint state-private"; they are, however, tightly controlled by the state, which distributes the needed raw materials to them and buys almost all of their output. All new construction is being carried out by the state.

The production level of cotton-textile factories was relatively high when the Communists took over—roughly three-fourths of "pre-liberation peaks," according to official claims—and the Communists energetically proceeded to press for production increases, mainly through better utilization of existing equipment. Within a year, they claimed, output had surpassed prewar levels. By 1951, however, the U.S. embargo, imposed after the start of the Korean War, caused serious shortages of raw cotton in China, so that many mills slowed down to part-time operation. The Communists tried to meet this situation by putting top priority on domestic cotton cultivation; through preferential prices and direct pressure, they raised cotton acreage and output, and they soon claimed self-sufficiency in raw cotton, although they continued some buying abroad. At the end of the "restoration" period, in 1952, it was asserted that China was producing roughly one-half more cotton yarn and cloth than ever before; these figures were probably an exaggeration, but there was no doubt that China's old textile equipment was being used intensively.

Cotton textiles, although an industry of great importance to

China's consumers, have been given a low priority in the first Five-Year Plan, which calls for continued rises in production and a small expansion of capacity, but without substantially increasing existing mill capacity. At one point, the Communists claimed that during the five years starting in 1954 the capacity of the industry would be increased 50 per cent, but they later implied that a rise of less than 20 per cent in spindle capacity would take place during the "next few years." During the first year of the Plan, it was asserted that the number of spindles operating in China increased 15.5 per cent (and looms 20 per cent) over 1949. This year's goal is a rise of 8 per cent in operating spindles over 1953.

The Chinese now claim to be self-sufficient in production of textile machinery, and undoubtedly most of the equipment for the modest textile expansion scheduled will be manufactured in China. It is claimed that during 1951–53, China produced 600,000 spindles (and 18,500 looms), and production capacity of the 7 textile-machinery plants in China was probably about 250,000 spindles a year by 1953. A new plant being built in Taiyuan during 1953 will add the capacity to produce another 200,000 spindles a year, bringing the total annual capacity up to 450,000 spindles, this year or next.

Construction of new plants, with the limited amount of machinery available, is at present focused upon 4 large mills, each with 100,000 spindles, and 9 smaller mills. The most significant aspect of this new construction is not the magnitude of the program, for the expansion of capacity is fairly small, but the fact that it represents a conscious attempt to disperse the industry. All of the new building is being carried out in centers located in the cotton-growing regions of north and northwest China, rather than in the traditional coastal centers of the industry. The 4 large new mills, construction of which reportedly began this year, are located at Sian, Shihchiachuang, Chengchow, and Peking. The smaller mills, each with 50,000 or fewer spindles, are also located in the interior.

To date, no five-year production target for cotton textiles has been officially revealed, but undoubtedly the Chinese hope that production of textiles, as of most other industries, can be increased by more than actual increases in plant capacity, through intensive utilization of existing plant. It is doubtful how much more production can be raised by speed-up methods, however, since the utilization rate of existing equipment in the cotton-textile industry is already 95 per cent, according to official claims, and most factories are now operating on a three-shift basis. Nevertheless, 1953 plans called for a production rise of 9 per cent in cotton yarn and 16 per cent in cotton cloth, and a further increase of 6 per cent in yarn output is scheduled for this year.

In terms of the needs of China's huge population, the present production of cotton yarn and cloth by modern factories in China is still pitifully small. The Communists themselves state that at present China produces less than half as much cotton cloth per capita as the U.S.S.R. did in 1928—9.6 yards per capita compared with 21.98 yards per capita—and there is little prospect of a rapid change in this situation. Not only are supplies for consumers limited, but prices are relatively high, particularly for the rural population. The Communists say frankly that the state must make a profit from textiles to help finance development of heavy industry, and although the dollar prices of cotton yarn and cloth have been reduced slightly in the past two years, the real prices in terms of grain, raw cotton, and other agricultural products have risen steadily. The quality of the products offered to consumers has also been debased; the Communists have cut down production of all better grades of cloth and are now concentrating upon poorer materials.

The textile industry illustrates the low priority being given to almost all consumer goods in the Communists' development program. Despite the shortage of yarn and cloth, so basic to the needs of the population, very little is being invested to develop production, and consumers are being asked to accept this policy because heavy industry comes first.

There are, of course, quite a few projects under way, in various parts of China, involving the construction or expansion of some consumer-goods industries. A majority of "local state-operated" industries fall into this category, and the Communists put considerable emphasis on the need to "revive" these. (Last year, according to official claims, local state-operated industries accounted for 14 per cent of all industrial production and 28 per cent of the production of state enterprises.) But in terms of the tremendous needs of the population, projects under way will do little to solve existing shortages. The Chinese population is being told that development of industry that would have a substantial direct effect on the standard of living must be postponed until China has built up its heavy industries. "During the transition period," the Communists say, "the strength of our country is concentrated mainly on the development of heavy industry; in the sphere of light industry, state-operated enterprises can only confine themselves to the production of the most essential products."

The Communists have inherited the Soviet obsession with bigness. They now dream of huge factories, employing thousands of workers and using tremendous machines. They also dream of the push-button age; although China has a plethora of manpower and a shortage of capital, the Communists proudly describe new factories with automatic machinery which uses a minimum of labor. It is not surprising, therefore, that the growth of small-scale handicraft industries does not currently receive much attention in the Chinese economic program. The Communists grudgingly admit that handicrafts are of considerable importance in the Chinese economy at present, but they hope that handicraft enterprises can slowly be replaced by modern factories.

Actually, according to Communist estimates, 24.5 million workers, supporting roughly 100 million people (one-sixth of the total population), are engaged in handicraft enterprises scattered all over the country, in both urban and rural areas. Selective surveys indicate that the average establishment is very small (about three persons in urban areas, and often just one in villages) and has a total of only U.S.$40 in capital, with an annual production averaging about U.S.$40 a year per person dependent upon handicrafts. But if one accepts official estimates, handicraft industries still account for about one-third of total industrial production in the country (by value) and supply 70–80 per cent of peasant needs for both consumer and capital goods.

The Communists assert that although modern factories will eventually replace most handicrafts, this cannot be accomplished "within a short period of time"; therefore, they say, handicrafts must "remain in existence," and in a few cases "there is room for their development," primarily to supplement the production of modern factories.

At present, however, there is little to indicate that the Communists are actively stimulating increased production by handicraft industries; instead, they are more concerned with organizing (i.e., collectivizing) handicraft producers. Because craftsmen, like the peasants, are dispersed and difficult to control, the Communists fear their "spontaneous tendencies toward capitalism." Consequently, they insist that handicraft industries follow the "path of cooperativization" and undergo "socialist transformation."

Several distinct stages of "socialist transformation" have been outlined, as in the case of both private industry and commerce and agriculture. The first is the organization of craftsmen into marketing and production teams, in which members pool their capital and tools, engage in collective labor, and make contracts with supply and marketing cooperatives to buy raw materials and sell finished products. The second stage involves the merging of several such teams into larger cooperatives, while the final phase is the organization of "semisocialist" or socialist handicraft producer cooperatives (which the Communists hope will some day facilitate mechanization).

The implementation of this program of reorganization has not progressed very far to date, however. By the end of last year, the Communists had organized only about 5,000 handicraft producer cooperatives, with a membership of 300,000—roughly 1 per cent of the estimated total working force engaged in handicrafts. But state control over handicrafts has probably increased more than appearances indicate; through state trading companies and supply and marketing cooperatives, the state is able to dominate sources of raw materials and markets, and indirectly to exercise a controlling influence over almost all primary producers. The present policy toward handicraft industries is thus to maintain, control, and reorganize them, but not to place any great emphasis upon developing them.

The size and quality of the industrial labor force are vital factors in any industrialization program. In the program the Chinese are now attempting to carry out, the role of labor is particularly significant, because the Communists are trying to increase industrial production more rapidly than they expand industrial equipment, and are trying to effect this increase by raising labor's productivity. At the same time, they are attempting to keep wages low so they can "economize" and accumulate capital for further investments in industry. Needless to say, such a policy involves many problems.

The forced pace of the Communists' economic program in China has created other problems. During the past four years, for example, the Communists have faced an anomalous situation in which they have encountered serious shortages of skilled industrial workers and at the same time have had to cope with unemployment problems caused by the severe dislocation of the economy resulting from their policies.

The size of the industrial working force in China today is very small. Before the war, it was estimated that only 2 million workers were engaged in modern industry, and they were concentrated in a few centers. China has always had an oversupply of cheap, inefficient labor, and at the same time a shortage of skilled industrial workers.

At present, the Communists state that China has an urban, modern "working class" of more than 15 million (out of a total urban population said to be about 100 million), but these include wage-earners of all sorts. The figure currently used for urban "industrial workers," including those in modern transport, etc., is 3 million. (The few specific figures that have been published reveal that textile workers total almost 600,000, railway workers 620,000, and coal miners 460,000.) If one accepts the rough figure of 3 million for Communist China's industrial labor force, this means that modern industrial enterprises employ about half of 1 per cent of China's total population (now officially claimed to be about 600 million).

Despite the relatively small number of urban laborers of all sorts in China, the present regime has faced rather serious unemployment problems in the major cities during the past few years. The main cause of this lies in the fact that the elimination of "unessential" or "undesirable" industries and occupations and attempts to reorganize industry have seriously dislocated many sectors of the economy. Another cause has been the fact that the Communists' agricultural policies, and conditions in the countryside, have resulted in what they refer to as a "blind flow" of peasants to the cities.

Many steps have been taken to help solve the difficulties of urban unemployment. The government has established relief and labor employment committees in the cities, organized public-works gangs, repatriated people to the countryside, restricted movements from villages to cities, set up vocational training centers for urban unemployed, and given relief loans and direct relief handouts. But the unemployment problem still has not been fully solved. In mid-1952, it was officially stated that there were 3 million unemployed in China's cities, and a special unemployment program was adopted, involving registration and "centralized distribution" of all urban unemployed. At the end of last year, the regime claimed that since 1950 it had found employment for 2.2 million unemployed—including 250,000 in work relief and 66,000 in vocational training—but the problem is still said to be "rather serious," and a special conference on unemployment early this year urged pressure on the unemployed to "find work themselves."

Actually, the difficulty of absorbing manpower in the cities would be even greater if the regime were not restricting the "blind influx" of peasants to cities and organizing huge numbers of people in labor groups in the countryside. There is a great surplus of labor in many rural areas in China—which is likely to increase as agricultural collectivization proceeds—and the Communists have absorbed thousands (perhaps millions) into many types of labor corps, including Reform Through Labor organizations, for public works such as railways and water-conservancy projects.

At the same time that they face a problem of "surplus labor," the Chinese Communists suffer from a shortage of skilled industrial workers. To minimize this problem, they have tried to institute complete control of the labor market, to distribute available skilled labor where it is most needed, and to introduce sizable worker training programs. Since 1952, all industrial enterprises in China have had to obtain approval from government labor bureaus to hire or fire workers. Skilled laborers have been shifted on a significant scale from one region to another; for example, large numbers of automobile mechanics have been sent from Shanghai to Manchuria, where China's first auto plant is under construction. Large programs of on-the-job training have been started, perhaps the most notable being the training on Manchurian railways of workers for rail lines all over the country. Special training schools, both part-time and full-time, have been set up in many places. Most of them are managed jointly by the government and labor unions, and they are attended by thousands. These training programs will greatly increase the number of workers with low-level skills in China—but it will take time. To produce higher technical skills, the entire educational system has been reorganized, and it is now geared to turn out skilled workers and technicians for industrialization. By the end of the first Five-Year Plan, the Communists hope to have produced 150,000–200,000 "senior construction cadres" and half a million "intermediate and junior technical personnel."

In addition to adopting long-range policies of this sort to develop skilled labor, the regime from the start has made every effort to bring the existing labor force under strict control. The main instrument of this control has been the All-China Federation of Labor.

The Federation has little resemblance to trade unions in non-Communist countries. It is really a mass political organization through which the regime controls labor, and this is most clearly symbolized by the fact that unions have no right to strike. Stress is laid upon members' obligations, not their rights, so that the primary mission of the unions is to see that Party and government policies are implemented, and to strive for higher production.

Organized on the principle of "democratic centralism," the Federation is divided into a number of nationwide industrial unions (twenty-three at present) and into area federations of local union branches in every administrative region of the country. Member unions are supported partly by management, which contributes the equivalent of 2 per cent of its payroll, and partly by union dues, which amount to 1 per cent of wages. By the end of last year, the 180,000 basic branches of the Federation had a total membership of 11 million "wage-earners" (including miscellaneous "workers" such as teachers, as well as industrial workers); this figure included well over 90 per cent of the industrial workers in the country, as well as a majority of all urban workers.

As previously stated, the performance of labor is particularly important to development plans in China today, because the Communists are attempting to achieve a significant part of their planned production rises by increasing labor output, without lifting wage levels. "It is only by incessantly raising labor productivity," they say, "that smooth completion of the nation's construction plans" is possible.

In their attempts to raise labor output, the Communists are using both the stick and the carrot—threat and incentive—but their most important technique is "socialist emulation." Emulation competitions, they assert, are the "fundamental method for construction of the Fatherland" because through them it is possible to "raise the capacity of existing plants without the installation of new equipment."

There are many kinds of emulation campaigns. There are competitions between regions, factories, teams, and even individuals; competitions to surpass "norms" and set new records; and competitions to become individual labor heroes. "Patriotic compacts," or pledges to achieve certain production levels, are common. Rewards are both monetary and psychological. By 1952, it was claimed that 80 per cent of all industrial workers in China were involved in some sort of labor competition, and by last year a quarter of a million workers had been honored as "advanced production workers or model laborers."

Until recently, the emphasis in emulation campaigns was primarily upon harder work, but this began to show diminishing returns. Physical exhaustion has had an adverse affect upon production in some instances. Now the emphasis is upon increasing efficiency through new methods and "rationalization" of production, and the Chinese claim that hundreds of thousands of workers' rationalization proposals are being put into effect.

The Communists use numerous other negative and positive incentives to induce workers to raise production. On the negative side, great stress is placed upon "labor discipline." On the positive side, appeals are made to labor's pride and patriotism; industrial workers are called the "masters of society and the state." Workers are given preferential treatment in various ways. A labor insurance law, entirely supported by management's contribution (which equals 3 per cent of an enterprise's payroll), has been started and is now claimed to cover 3.2 million workers. Preference is given workers in new housing, with many "labor palaces," clubs, and schools built for them. Workers have also been given new responsibilities. In state enterprises, they are brought into Administrative Committees organized with equal worker-management representation, while in private concerns they participate in Labor-Management Consultative Committees in which they not only negotiate agreements on working conditions but also advise on production methods and policies. All these developments have given the small industrial labor force in China a new status in society, and to a certain extent they undoubtedly have stimulated laborers to work harder.

The one labor incentive conspicuously underplayed in China is the promise of significantly increased income. The Communists are trying to get laborers to work harder and more efficiently, but they hope to increase labor's productivity more than its wages. Wage policies are used in a number of ways, however, to spur production. Wherever possible, the Communists are introducing the Stakhanovite piecework system, to replace flat wages, so that pay will depend directly upon the amount a worker produces.

How successful they will be in getting the maximum out of labor for minimum compensation remains to be seen. The policies they have adopted are ones, however, that could lead to considerable dissatisfaction among industrial workers, and it seems likely that strict organization and control of labor may become increasingly essential to their whole industrialization program.

A careful examination of available facts on the progress of industrialization in China indicates that the Communists' dream of a "powerful, industrialized socialist state" is not likely to be achieved overnight. Undoubtedly, the surge toward industrialization in China will now be faster than in the past, because the regime is a disciplined, totalitarian one capable of making policy decisions and translating them into action, and because the Communists are determined to mobilize and devote to the task of industrialization the maximum amount of available resources, capital, labor, and skills. But the problems they face are tremendous. China starts with a much less favorable basis for modern industrialism than the Soviet Union did thirty-five years ago. It is more overpopulated (in relation to land and other resources), possesses less modern industry, has a poorer raw-material base, will find it harder to obtain capital equipment abroad, and faces a more serious problem of getting either domestic capital or foreign exchange.

The propaganda the regime is now spreading gives the impression that China is already making very rapid strides toward becoming an industrialized power. However, the facts indicate that although China is making progress in this direction, the pace is not spectacularly rapid, at least to date. It is possible, of course, that the process of development will gain momentum as it progresses.*

It would be a mistake to underestimate the importance of the progress being made, however. In a country such as China, a little bit of modern industry can have a much greater impact than in a more developed country, and small increases in industrial production can be stretched a long way. Backed by the Soviet Union, China with its discipline, organization, and huge reserves of manpower is already an influence to be reckoned with on the international stage. And as it develops its own industrial power, however small it may be compared with that of an economic colossus like the United States, the regional influence of the regime may increase still further.

In the foreseeable future, the Chinese population will not benefit very much from the Communists' program of industrialization in any event. Communist plans do not call for balanced development; they concentrate upon heavy industries and neglect consumer-goods industries. The Chinese people are being urged to

---

* Industrial development in Communist China did accelerate significantly in the second half of the 1950's. By 1960, steel output, for example, was claimed to be over 18 million tons. But industrial output dropped after 1960.

work hard for industrial goals, but they are being told to have patience and wait for improvements in their material welfare until the millennium—when China is a "great socialized industrial country and one of the most advanced in the world." At present, it looks as if they may have to wait quite a long time.

AGRICULTURE

August, 1954

Agriculture is the foundation of the Chinese economy, and as such it is vital to the Communists' economic development program. Although rapid industrialization is the primary economic aim of the Peking regime, it is agriculture that must provide food for a growing urban and industrial population, deliver many export products required to pay for imports of essential capital goods, and supply increased raw materials for industry.

Roughly four-fifths of the Chinese population directly participate in agricultural production, and it is the peasants who must support the economy and pay the major costs of economic development. Despite attempts to disguise the economic burden imposed upon the peasantry, there is no alternative, in Communist China, to the necessity of extracting the bulk of economic savings for investment in industrialization from the mass of ordinary peasants.

The difficulties of increasing agricultural production in China are tremendous, and agriculture is already lagging far behind the ambitious goals for production increases the Communists have set for themselves. During the 1949–52 "period of economic restoration," agriculture, like other sectors of the economy, steadily improved. Although there were numerous factors adverse to agricultural production during this period, these were more than offset by increasing order in the countryside, cultivation of land that had been idle during years of war and revolutionary struggle, widespread water-conservancy development, restoration of internal transport and trade, and good weather. The task of increasing agricultural production has met serious setbacks since 1952, however.

The basic facts of agriculture in China are difficult to ignore. China is heavily overpopulated in terms of cultivable land: It is estimated that there is only one-half of an acre of arable land per person in the country. The average farm holding is roughly 3.5 acres, and the majority of China's peasants live close to a bare subsistence level. Furthermore, some of the Communists' agricultural policies have created new problems, and in 1953 weather conditions—among the most important but the most unpredictable factor affecting agriculture—were extremely bad. As a result, 1953 agricultural production was far less than was called for by China's economic plans, and a serious agricultural crisis developed. The first year of the Five-Year Plan was a failure in agriculture, and difficulties have continued this year.

During the past four years, Chinese Communist agricultural policies have undergone a basic shift. From 1949 to 1952, primary attention was given to a policy of land distribution, developed during years of revolutionary struggle. By 1952, however, the Communists had adopted a program of step-by-step collectivization of agriculture, and in recent months the pace of forcing peasants into preliminary forms of organization has been stepped up. State purchase of grain was also increased rapidly during this same period, and in late 1953 the serious agricultural situation led to a decision by the Communists to take drastic action. A state monopoly of all trade in grain was proclaimed, and general grain rationing was introduced.

There is every indication that China is now having greater difficulties in carrying out its plans for agricultural development than in making industrial progress. New industries can be grafted on to the existing economy, but the Communists' present agricultural policies involve changing the pattern and traditions of "forty centuries of farming."

The Communists rode to power in China on the broad backs of the country's peasants. It remains to be seen whether or not these sturdy backs can, or will, support the current program of economic development.

One of the most important factors in the Communists' rise to power was a program of "land reform." Much of the debate on whether or not the Communists in China were "agrarian reformers" has obscured the fact that although they have been loyal to Marx, Engels, Lenin, and Stalin, their announced policy of land distribution was fundamental to their successful conquest of China.

Unequal distribution of land ownership, high farm rents, and widespread exploitation of peasants by a *rentier* landlord class have periodically been serious problems in China during the past 2,000 years. In the modern period, these problems created rumblings of peasant discontent, and every important Chinese leader after Sun Yat-sen endorsed the general principle of "land to the tiller."

The Communist Party was the only political group, however, that really capitalized on pressures of discontent in the Chinese countryside, and from the early 1930's onward "agrarian reform" was the most basic plank in its domestic revolutionary platform.

The specific agrarian policies sponsored by the Communists underwent numerous changes, but except during the wartime period, when moderation was tactically expedient, their program called for equalization of land ownership through complete elimination of landlordism and redistribution of confiscated land. With this unswerving central aim, they vacillated primarily on the question of whether rich peasants should be expropriated in the interests of land equalization or tolerated in the interests of agricultural production.

From 1931 to 1934, the Communists in China followed what was subsequently labeled an "ultraleft" policy of violent and indiscriminate confiscation of both landlords' and rich peasants' land. In 1937, when the Sino-Japanese War began, they shifted to a relatively moderate policy of rent limitation in the areas they controlled, but the end of the war saw a return to the earlier policy of violence and confiscation. Within a year, the adverse effects of such extremism upon agricultural production led them to issue instructions that rich peasants be exempted from confiscation. Extremism was reasserted in 1947, when the Agrarian Reform Law once again staked out the land of rich peasants for expropriation.

By promising free land to poor and landless peasants, the Communists were able to attract many followers, and they gradually built up their Party and army, the foundation of their power, by organizing discontented peasants. Little mention of collectivization was made during this period when the Communists were struggling for power. As a matter of fact, Mao Tse-tung's "New Democracy," which was written in 1940 and remained the bible of Chinese Communism for a decade thereafter, stressed that "ownership of the land is to be readjusted, not with a view to building up socialist agriculture, but only in order to turn the land into the peasants' own property."

When the Peking regime was established in 1949, therefore, land redistribution was still the basis of Communist agricultural policies in China. In early 1950, Mao Tse-tung stated that completion of land reform was one of the three fundamental economic tasks facing the new regime, and in the middle of that year a revised Agrarian Reform Law was adopted as the basis for implementing the program. By this time, when the Communists' program had changed from one of gaining power to one of consolidating and preserving it, agricultural production had become more important to them than ever before. As a consequence, they decided that the rich peasants—the most productive elements in the agricultural economy—should temporarily be tolerated. The 1950 Agrarian Reform Law called, therefore, for "elimination of the landlords as a class," but specified that the "rich peasant economy" should be "preserved," although the rich peasants should be politically "neutralized."

This law, still on the books in China, outlined a program for confiscation (without compensation) of landlords' holdings and redistribution of the land to poor and landless peasants. This was done with each administrative village in China as the unit for distribution, so the amount of land redistributed in any area depended upon local conditions, and slight variations in land ownership continued after the program was implemented. Rich peasants were allowed, in most cases, to retain land cultivated by themselves or by hired labor, and even, in some cases, land they rented out.

Between 1950 and 1952, the Agrarian Reform Law was vigorously carried out in "newly liberated areas" all over the country. The way in which the law was implemented made it clear, however, that political and social aims were more important to the regime than economic ones. In the eyes of the new revolutionary authorities, "elimination of the landlords as a class"—and destruction of their political, social, and economic power—required "violent struggle" and class warfare in each village throughout China. Where class animosities were not intense, it was the responsibility of outside political cadres who entered the villages to arouse the villagers and to ensure that "struggle meetings" and mass public trials were held. In many villages, land redistribution could have been carried out without violence, but this was not allowed. Class warfare was essential, even though it disrupted agricultural production for long periods of time, because the landlord class had to be discredited thoroughly as well as "economically eliminated."

The land-redistribution program lagged somewhat behind schedule during its latter phases in south China, but by the end of 1952 it was "completed in the main," according to official claims, and in mid-1953 the Communists announced that it had been "concluded" except in certain areas populated by national minorities. There were still many problems of consolidation; for example, as late as the end of 1953, the Communists admitted that in one large south China region 70 per cent of the villages were not yet "basically stable" and 60 per cent of the new land deeds had not yet been issued. But by mid-1953, redistribution of the land had been completed throughout most of the country.

This land-redistribution program has fundamentally altered the existing class structure in rural China and has had a tremendous effect upon the whole agricultural economy. The landlords in China have, in fact, been "eliminated as a class." Some have been killed, others put into forced labor groups (Reform Through Labor), and still others assigned small plots of land to cultivate. The role of local leadership and influence which the landlords almost universally played has been taken over by a new political elite of cadres and "activists" fostered by the Communists. Ownership of land has been equalized (although not completely so). The regime claims that over 115 million acres—one-third to one-half of the total acreage of cultivated land in China—have been redistributed to peasant families containing more than 300 million persons. The distribution of agricultural produce has been radically altered. Formerly, according to official Communist claims, almost 30 million tons (other claims say 50 million) of grain a year were paid as rents to landlords by tenants in China. Now land rents have been for the most part eliminated.

The Communists claim that all of this has had a favorable influence upon agricultural output by increasing the peasants' "productive ardor," and has improved the economic lot of the average peasant by eliminating landlordism. But both of these claims can be questioned.

The methods of land redistribution were extremely disruptive. Months of time-consuming meetings, uncertainty about ownership rights, and confusion about all traditional village relationships had an adverse effect upon production. Furthermore, as soon as land was distributed in any area, the Communists began to pressure peasants to join mutual-aid teams and other forms of collective organizations designed to pave the way for complete agricultural collectivization in the future. As soon as rents to landlords were eliminated, the state began to collect very high agricultural taxes and to purchase peasants' surplus grain at low prices.

In addition, the average size of farm holdings immediately after land redistribution was admittedly ,maller in many areas than before, and this intensified the old problem of inefficient farm units. The assignment of land to "i llers," city dwellers, landless agricultural workers, and ex-landlords who had never cultivated their own land increased the number of persons among whom available land had to be divided, and studies of certain areas indicated that as a result the average size of land holdings was reduced by about 15 per cent.

The elimination of landlords also disrupted the old rural credit system, for landlordism and moneylending were combined in a great many instances. The landlords often exploited the peasantry by their usury, but they provided essential credit, and the government's efforts to establish a new state-controlled credit system could not immediately fill the gap created by expropriation of the landlords. The increased number of farms after land distribution also made worse the shortage of tools, animals, and other items of agricultural capital. All these factors made the program far from completely satisfactory, even to former tenants who received ownership of land.

At the same time, Communist attitudes toward the peasantry underwent a subtle but major change. The Common Program stipulated that the "right of ownership over the land obtained by the peasants shall be protected," but it also specified that after land redistribution the state "shall guide the peasants to organize step by step various forms of labor mutual aid and production cooperation." By the end of 1951, it was clear that a systematic program aiming at eventual collectivization had become basic policy. Officially, it was said that collectivization would be "voluntary," but the Communists spoke with increased frequency of the peasants' "dangerous spontaneous tendencies toward capitalism." Even history began to be rewritten as the regime became less concerned with attracting peasant support to a popular program of land distribution and more concerned with controlling the peasants and pushing them in directions they did not like. The 1952 edition of Mao Tse-tung's writings omitted a key sentence from an article he had written twenty-five years earlier in 1927: "If we are to compute the relative accomplishments of various elements in the democratic revolution on a percentage basis, the urban dwellers and military would not rate more than 30 per cent, while the remaining 70 per cent would have to be allotted to the peasantry in the countryside." Omission of this sentence symbolized the full swing of the Communists' policy toward the peasantry: By 1952, they no longer concentrated on making promises to the peasants, but were concerned with controlling them and extracting the maximum from them.

At the same time that they were radically altering the pattern of land ownership in China through their Agrarian Reform, the Communists started to do what they could in various ways to increase agricultural production. Their most important positive aid to production has been development of water conservancy. Soon after coming to power, they started work on a great many irrigation and flood-control projects. Some of these have merely continued work started under the previous regime, but many are new, and the total effort devoted to water conservancy is the greatest in China's modern period. During the first years of the regime, water conservancy ranked with railway construction as one of the two main fields of constructive activity, and it continues to be important. Millions of workers have been organized to build levies and dams and to dig ditches and canals; as a result, significant results have been achieved during the past four years.

An official Communist statement at the end of last year claimed that since 1949 a total of 250 large conservancy projects had been undertaken. In addition, it was said, 4 million small local projects had been carried out, 100,000 wells dug, and 30,000 horsepower added to China's irrigation pumping system. All of this work, the Communists claimed, improved irrigation facilities or provided irrigation for the first time on 9 million acres of land.

Some of the large projects undertaken have been very ambitious. For example, the Chinkiang reservoir west of Shasi on the upper Yangtze is designed to control the flood waters that periodically plague the whole river valley. Part of this project was completed in 1952, when two movable dams were constructed to regulate the inflow of water from the Yangtze into the reservoir, which covers 356 square miles and has a capacity of 6 billion cubic meters of water.

The Hwai River project, in north-central China, is even larger and has been given tremendous publicity. Work completed there includes 3 reservoirs and 15 flood-detention projects, with a capacity of 10 billion cubic meters of water, repair of over 1,240 miles of river dikes, dredging of almost 1,860 miles of river channel, and construction of a 105-mile canal. When the work is completed, the reservoir capacity is planned to be 20 million cubic meters, 620 miles of river are to be navigable, over 6 million acres are to be irrigated, hydro-electric power is to be developed, and both flood control and irrigation will be improved in the whole Hwai River basin, inhabited by 60 million people.

Numerous other major projects have been completed or started. Among them are: the important 2.2-billion-cubic-meter Kwanting reservoir—the largest south of Manchuria—designed to help control the Yungting River near Peking; a new 27-mile channel for the Taching River near Tientsin; several canals and flood-detention basins on the Yellow River; and new channels to the sea for the Yi and Shu rivers in north China. The Communists also claim to have repaired or strengthened most of the 26,040 miles of dikes already lining China's rivers and coasts.

These flood-control and irrigation projects have been a significant factor aiding agricultural production, but they have by no means solved the difficult problems of flood and drought in China. From 1949 to 1952, the size of the area affected by natural calamities steadily declined: 100 million mow in 1949, 60 million in 1950, 21 million in 1951, and 16 million in 1952. But flood and drought struck again on a large scale in 1953, despite all the conservancy work that had been done in the previous four years. The Communists have not revealed the exact extent of last year's calamities; all they have said is that the area affected was "less than in 1949," but flood and drought seriously hurt production and contributed to the failure of China's agricultural plans for 1953. This year, floods have again occurred on a large scale. By early July, heavy rains in the Yangtze valley were reported to have raised the water level of the river to the highest point since the disastrous floods of 1931, and important rice centers near Wuhan, Kiukiang, and Changsha were threatened with inundation. Calamities may make this year's crops in China smaller than in 1953. It will be a long time before dams and canals can really begin to counteract the effects of too little or too much water in China. In the meantime, weather will continue to dominate both the peasants and the state planners.

Most of the water-conservancy projects undertaken in China have been located in heavily populated agricultural areas where old irrigation and flood-control projects already exist. The Communists claim that in the first three years of their regime, the irrigated area in the country increased to over 35 million acres, but most of this acreage is in China's major river basins. Very little has been done to open up new land for cultivation, despite the fact that the Communists have made optimistic claims about virgin land that can be brought under cultivation. At one point, they stated that "unused and virgin land is estimated to be at least as much as the total present cultivated acreage in the country"; later they said that "arable wasteland" in China totals 50 to 65 million acres. Even the latter claim exceeds most responsible estimates of uncultivated arable land in China made before the Communists came to power. According to some estimates, there may be only 35 million acres or so that can still be put under cultivation economically.

There is every reason to believe that China has relatively little uncultivated land that can still be developed for agriculture. China has large unpopulated regions, but most of them are mountainous or arid, and development of irrigation facilities in the majority of these areas would be prohibitively expensive. It is unlikely, therefore, that the Communists will be able to expand China's total agricultural acreage on any spectacular scale.

In the foreseeable future, furthermore, Communist China plans to concentrate its investments in the development of modern industry. At the end of 1953, there were indications that instead of investments in water conservancy being expanded—which would certainly be required to open up new areas—they were being reduced by elimination of "unessential" projects. Continued irrigation and flood-control work will improve the land now under cultivation in China, but it appears that for a long time to come Communist China will depend primarily upon agricultural land already developed.

In addition to developing water conservancy, the Communists have taken a number of other measures to assist agricultural production and to help solve the serious production problems facing China's peasants.

Huge anti-pest campaigns have been organized. In the past four years, it is claimed, about 520,000 insecticide sprayers and 37,000 tons of insecticide have been sold to peasants, but organized manual labor has been the main weapon against pests. The Communists say that up to the beginning of last year, 120 million people had been organized to take part in anti-pest campaigns, and they claim that these campaigns saved over 16 million tons of grain.

Use of fertilizers has been slowly increased. Last year, about 4 million tons of fertilizers of all sorts were distributed to peasants through supply and marketing cooperatives, and this year the target is 4.2 million tons. (These figures compare with 1.3 million tons in 1951 and 2.9 million in 1952.) Most of this fertilizer consists of vegetable and oilseed cakes, however; the total amount of chemical fertilizers distributed in all of China is still less than a million tons, which is wholly inadequate to meet existing needs.

Some efforts have also been made, in a simple way, to alleviate the serious shortage of farm tools. Through supply and marketing cooperatives, 33 million farm tools were distributed to peasants in China last year, according to official claims. These included 300,000 sets of "new-type large farm tools" (mostly plows and cultivators), and the 1954 target for distribution of such tools is 250,000. Even urgent needs are far from being met, however. Two years ago, the Communists said that "in every administrative region, province, and administrative district, we should establish state factories or repair shops to supply the countryside with modern farming implements," but only a few such factories or shops have since been set up.

Mechanization of agriculture is an important future aim of the regime, but for a long time it will remain little more than a dream. There are, at most, only a few hundred modern tractors in China. Even horse-drawn machinery, which is being promoted in Manchuria as a preliminary form of mechanization, has not been developed extensively: the target for last year was to increase the number of sets of horse-drawn machinery in Manchuria to 4,600. The Communists admit that mechanization cannot really be developed until China's second Five-Year Plan has started. Then they hope to have more industries producing farm machines, and many of China's peasants will have been organized into producers' cooperatives. Even then, mechanization may be slow. Non-Communist students of Chinese agriculture raise searching questions about mechanization in China. How easily can wet rice culture, practiced in most of south China, be mechanized? How practical, in economic terms, is extensive agricultural mechanization in a country that has a great deal of labor, but is short of capital and liquid fuels? How can the surplus labor created by agricultural mechanization be absorbed quickly into other occupations in such a country? Questions like these are rarely dicussed by the Chinese Communists.

The serious problem of farm credit in China has already been mentioned. The Communists have tried to build a new state-controlled system of rural credit, but only limited progress has been made. The People's Bank has established branches in many counties and districts in rural China, and last year, according to official claims, its agricultural loans totaled about U.S.$661 million, which was 15 times the 1950 total. Most loans of this sort are given for projects and equipment that aid production, and interest rates are low.

A system of rural credit cooperatives, under People's Bank supervision, has also been started. By the middle of last year, it was claimed that almost 7,000 such cooperatives had been set up, with a membership of 4.25 million people and total capital of about U.S.$3.7 million. (The cooperatives average more than 600 members, and their capital amounts to about U.S.$500–600 each.) In addition, more than 2,000 "credit departments" in supply and marketing cooperatives and more than 14,000 "credit teams" (each with 6 to 15 members) had been established. However, the deposits held by all these organizations in mid-1953 was only about U.S.$7 million; they received roughly U.S.$8 million in credit from state banks during the first 9 months of 1953, and their loans to peasants totaled about U.S.$10 million. In short, although credit cooperatives may in time play an important role in China, the amount of credit they provided to peasants last year was infinitesimal in terms of existing needs. Expansion of credit cooperatives has continued this year, and by May it was claimed that 26,000 of them, or triple the 1952 total, were operating. But the Communists have a long way to go before they can meet the rural credit shortage created by their liquidation of landlord and merchant wealth.

Another part of the Communist program to increase agricultural production has involved "improvement of techniques through mass movements" and short training courses for peasants. These efforts have been on a very low technical level, and apparently they have been carried out mainly by political cadres rather than agricultural specialists, of which China has very few. Campaigns have been undertaken to improve selection and treatment of seeds, to prevent insect pests, and so on, and some results have been achieved. (On the basis of official claims, perhaps 3 to 4 million acres have been sown with improved seeds.) In addition to these special campaigns, over 150,000 "spare-time schools" and 250,000 "winter schools" for peasants have been set up in China, and these, too, have undoubtedly been a channel for some simple ideas for technical improvement of farming. Communist plans also call for the establishment of small state farms in every province, administrative district, county, and local district where land is available; one of the main functions of these farms is to "demonstrate to New China's emancipated peasants the superiority of scientific, mechanized farming and collective labor." There is no complete information on how many state farms of this kind have been organized, but it will certainly take time to get large numbers into operation and to staff them with competent technical personnel.

The shortage of farm livestock is another unsolved agricultural problem in China. The Communists say that rural supply and marketing cooperatives are attempting to provide needed animals, but they are vague on accomplishments, and reports of serious animal shortages persist.

In relation to peasants' incentives for production, the Communists have tried to organize large "patriotic emulation drives" in the countryside and to get peasants to make "patriotic compacts" in which they promise to increase production. They also claim that their agricultural tax law, which exempts from taxation all production above arbitrarily established "norms," provides an incentive for peasants to produce more. This is extremely dubious, however. There are many non-Communist reports, in fact, of widespread peasant dissatisfaction caused by the high agricultural taxes, purchases of farm products at low prices, and other policies that hurt the peasants.

The basic technical and other problems of increasing agricultural production have by no means been solved by the Communists, although a number of programs have been initiated that are designed to alleviate some of the peasants' production difficulties. Accomplishments to date have been modest, although it is certainly possible that these programs will in time show better results.

Despite numerous problems affecting agricultural production adversely in China from 1949 to 1952, production of major crops increased steadily during that period. Restoration of order, rehabilitation of transport and trade, cultivation of land that had been idle for several years, and good weather—all factors that had little direct connection with agricultural policies as such—were a boon to the peasants.

"Grain" crops (including rice, wheat, sorghum, millet, barley, beans, peas, seeds, and even potatoes) are the most important agricultural product in China, and their production can be used as a rough measure of agricultural production as a whole. The Communists claim that grain production in China rose 11 per cent in 1950, 8 per cent in 1951, and 28 per cent in 1952, and that by 1952 annual production of all types of grain totaled 163.75 million tons, which they said was about 15 per cent above peak postwar production figures in China.

During 1953, at the start of the first Five-Year Plan, ambitious targets for increased grain production were announced. China's ultimate aim, after two or more five-year plans, the Communists said, was production of between 275 and 300 million tons of grain —almost double the present production. The target for the first Five-Year Plan was set as a 30 per cent increase over the 1952 level; this would mean a five-year increase of 50 million tons and a 1957 output of almost 214 million tons. (From 1928 to 1950, over-all agricultural production in the U.S.S.R. increased by only about 25 to 30 per cent.)

With these ambitious long-term goals defined, the Communists announced that in 1953 they would increase production of grain to 175 million tons—a planned increase of over 11 million tons, or about 7 per cent. Before the year was half over, however, it became clear that bad weather and many other factors had upset the planners' calculations, and toward the end of the year it was admitted that the output was actually less than in 1952. By mid-1954, claims for the previous year had been revised slightly upward, and it was asserted that during 1953 production of grain had increased 1.5 per cent and totaled 165 million tons. In short, even in their final official claims, which were undoubtedly inflated, the Communists admitted that their agricultural production plans for 1953 had been an almost complete failure.

The shock of failure in 1953 has made them more sober about announced targets for the immediate future, and the grain plan for 1954 calls for a production increase of only 3 per cent, or about 5 million tons. Unless this rate of increase is greatly speeded up— which does not seem an imminent possibility—China obviously cannot achieve the 30 per cent increase in grain production scheduled for the first Five-Year Plan, and this fact undoubtedly will affect the timetable of the entire economic development program.

One of the significant things revealed by data the Communists have published on agriculture during the past few years is the fact that as much of the rise in production between 1949 and 1953 came from increases in acreage (mostly land put back into cultivation rather than virgin land cultivated for the first time) as from better yields per acre. In 1953, for example, official figures indicate that grain acreage increased from 303.3 million to 305 million acres, while grain yields averaged 199 pounds per sixth of an acre —only 1 per cent above 1952 and still 5 per cent below average figures for the mid-1930's in China. In the future, the possibilities of increasing acreage are limited, and increases in per-acre yields are likely to be slow.

All the above information is based upon official claims made by the Communist regime in China. The real figures may well be lower.

During the past four years, the Communists have striven for self-sufficiency in major agricultural raw materials. There have been several reasons for this policy. Perhaps the most urgent one has been the desire to conserve China's limited amounts of foreign exchange for essential imports which the country cannot possibly produce itself at the present stage of its development. In addition, however, the idea of autarky is an important element in almost all of the Communists' economic thinking, and they seem to equate "self-sufficiency" and" independence."

Many agricultural raw materials have received attention during this period, including tobacco and fibers of all kinds; the most important one has been cotton, which supplies China's largest modern consumer-goods industry and clothes almost the entire population.

At the time of the Communist takeover, production of cotton had dropped to a low level, and raw cotton was one of the country's largest import items. Almost immediately, the Communists adopted a policy of promoting cotton cultivation, and several methods were used. In some areas, quotas for increased cotton acreage were assigned, and peasants were convinced or forced to shift from other crops to cotton. A more successful method was the use of price incentives to induce peasants voluntarily to take up cotton cultivation. The state has become almost the sole purchaser of cotton in China, and therefore state trading agencies set the market prices; from 1950 through 1952, the ratio of cotton and grain prices was established at levels that encouraged peasants to switch over to cotton. For example, a pound of cotton lint was worth 7.7 pounds of wheat in 1950, 8.8 in 1951, and 9.37 in 1952. In short, the official price policy gave top priority during this period to incentives for cotton growers. (The effects during the Korean War of the U.N. embargo on Communist China gave added urgency to the need for more domestic cotton.)

Between 1949 and 1952, cotton acreage and production in China rose rapidly, according to official claims. In rough figures, acreage increased from 6.5 million in 1949 to 13.2 million in 1952; output rose from 430,000 tons in 1949 to 1.29 million tons in 1952 (roughly 50 per cent above "pre-liberation peaks," according to the Communists).

As China's domestic cotton production increased, imports of raw cotton were cut down. However, the official claims that China has achieved self-sufficiency in cotton (these claims began to be put forward in 1950) are not true; China is still importing cotton, although in small quantities, from Pakistan, Egypt, Brazil, and elsewhere.

At the start of the first Five-Year Plan, the Communists stated that cotton production should be raised still further, by increasing both acreage in cotton and per-acre yields. Their target calls for increasing cotton acreage by almost 850,000 acres, and yields by 2.2 pounds per sixth of an acre, during the five years.

One of the dilemmas the Chinese face in their agricultural policy, however, is that in the absence of much virgin arable land, expanded production of cotton or other agricultural raw materials must be at the expense of grain production. Decisions on which crops to promote at any particular time and place are often very difficult in view of the shortages of both grain and raw materials.

In 1953, the Communists wanted to continue to increase cotton output, but at the same time they realized that grain should have a higher priority. As a consequence, although plans for 1953 called for a 16 per cent increase in cotton output, from 1.29 million to 1.49 million tons, official prices for cotton, set in terms of grain, were reduced 13 to 18 per cent during the year.

Toward the end of 1953, the Chinese admitted that production plans for cotton were not achieved during the first year of the Plan. A preliminary estimate indicated that cotton output, instead of increasing by 16 per cent, had actually declined by about 4 per cent during the year. The resulting shortages of cotton forced the Communists to increase purchases abroad, raise raw cotton prices 5 to 7 per cent, and call for increased production during 1954.

There is no doubt that efforts to achieve self-sufficiency in essential agricultural raw materials will continue, but as long as the country is short of grain it will be extremely difficult to make progress. Achievements in the field of raw materials may increase China's serious food problem.

China's development program requires large-scale exports to pay for essential imports, and the task of increasing exports is a difficult one. In the past, importing more than it has exported, China has consistently had a deficit in its commodity balance of trade. Now, with its trade mostly barter exchange with the Soviet bloc,

China faces the necessity of constantly increasing exports to balance rising imports.

China is not in a very fortunate position in regard to exportable products. At present, almost all of its export goods consist of agricultural, animal, and mineral products, rather than manufactured goods, and not many of them have a large potential market. Soybeans, tung oil, silk, tea, pig bristles, tin, tungsten, antimony, and other Chinese export goods are important on the world market, but few of them are really large earners of foreign exchange. China lacks a readily marketable single product that can do for it what grain did for the U.S.S.R. and silk for Japan during their early development.

The Communists have pushed production and export of all of China's traditional export products, therefore, and the volume of exports has steadily risen. The pressure to export more and more has led the regime to institute an austerity program in order to export in significant quantities, for the first time in modern Chinese history, essential foodstuffs that are in short supply domestically.

Before the war, foodstuffs played a role in China's export trade, but China was always a net importer of grain. Annual imports of grain products amounted to about 1.5 million tons, mostly from Southeast Asia. One reason for the need to import grain was the deficiency of China's system of internal transport and food distribution, but the basic reason was the backwardness of agriculture.

When the Communists came to power, they immediately undertook nationwide allocation of foodstuff supplies, cut food consumption, stopped imports, and pushed exports. As a result, food exports increased rapidly; according to some estimates, they totaled 89,000 tons in 1950, 1.3 million tons in 1951, 867,000 tons in 1952, and perhaps 1.1 million tons last year. (Soybeans have been the largest item, but food grains are important, too.) In 1950, the only year for which the Communists have published a breakdown of export commodities, almost 30 per cent of the value of all China's exports consisted of foodstuffs and animal and vegetable oils or fats.

China is now for the first time a net exporter of grain. It is also exporting in quantity for the first time many other important foodstuffs, such as pork, fruit, and vegetable oils. In none of these commodities does China have a real export surplus, in the sense of being able to increase exports without cutting domestic consumption. It is officially admitted, for example, that last year the output of vegetable oils (essential for cooking in China) was only 70 to 80 per cent of prewar levels, yet large quantities of rape seeds, sesame seeds, and peanuts—and their oils—were exported to the Soviet bloc.

This export policy has contributed to China's serious food problem at home. By the beginning of this year, the problem had become so pressing that, although China continues to export grain and other foodstuffs to Ceylon, the Soviet bloc, and other areas, the Communists signed a three-year trade agreement to import rice from Burma.

The Communists have rapidly increased their control over the output of the country's agricultural economy since 1949. The heavy demands on agriculture, and the shortage of agricultural commodities to meet the demands, have made it necessary for the state to control and allocate as much as possible of the output of agriculture. The main instruments used to date for extending control in this field have been state trading companies and state-controlled supply and marketing cooperatives in the countryside.

Under the control of the Ministry of Commerce, state trading companies have proliferated during the past four years, and now there are more than 20 specialized companies dealing in different commodities. Each is organized on a nationwide basis, and altogether they have thousands of branches. As early as 1951, it was revealed that there were 10,000 state trading bodies throughout China. The number now is much larger; by 1953, more than 400,000 employees worked in the state trading network.

At first, state trading companies confined themselves largely to wholesale trade in a few basic commodities. In 1950, they were instructed to concentrate upon six essentials, with the primary aim of stabilizing prices and "adjusting supply and demand." It did not take long, however, for them to expand both their aims and their operations, and soon they were attempting to control almost all wholesale trade and were playing an important role even in retail trade. By 1952, the Communists were saying that "the state is already powerful enough to control market prices and, through the price mechanism, to indicate the direction in which private industry, trade, and agricultural production should develop." In some of their statements, they went so far as to say "the struggle to control the market is the key issue in the struggle between socialism and capitalism." By 1952, it was officially claimed that state trade accounted for 63 per cent of domestic trade (including 32 per cent of retail trade).

Collection of agricultural crops has been the largest single operation carried out by state trading agencies. At first, state companies confined their purchases for the most part to cotton, grain, silk, and soybeans, but during the past two years they have extended purchasing to almost all marketable crops. Since 1952, state trading companies have bought all "commercial cotton" in the major producing areas in China, and last year their aim was to purchase 80 per cent of all "commercial grain" throughout the country.

The purchase of grain has been particularly important because the state has gradually taken over the responsibility of providing food for the entire population. More than 11,000 grain-purchasing stations (more than two-thirds of them run by supply and marketing cooperatives) have been set up, and last year it was estimated that state trading companies and other government agencies would handle 30 million tons of grain. There have been many difficulties in collecting grain, however. For one thing, the Communists' land-redistribution program has had adverse effects on the amount of marketable grain available. In addition, peasants have been reluctant to sell to the state because of the low official prices for grain. All sorts of pressures and devices—such as "crop-selling persuasion teams"—have been used, however, to force the peasants to sell, and as private merchants have been driven from the market, the peasants have had few alternatives besides selling to the state.

State trading companies also monopolize almost all the essential products peasants must buy, including fertilizers, tools, seeds, and insecticides, as well as consumer goods. This fact gives the companies a great deal of leverage in dealing with peasants, because if agricultural products are not forthcoming, manufactured goods can be withheld. In many areas, efforts have been made to place the trade with peasants on a semibarter basis by getting the peasants to sign "linked contracts" in which they promise to sell certain agricultural commodities in return for specified manufactured goods. State trading companies have been unable to meet all of the peasants' needs, however, and this complicates the problems involved in buying the peasants' output.

The main tie-in between the state trading companies and the peasants is a nationwide system of rural supply and marketing cooperatives. Organized nationally under the All-China Federation of Cooperatives, there are now more than 30,000 rural supply and marketing cooperatives (with 153 million members), which run almost 100,000 retail outlets and roughly 8,000 grain-purchasing stations. These cooperatives act as trade intermediaries by making contracts both with state trading companies and with individual peasants. Since their membership already includes roughly one-third of the rural population in China, their influence is very great, and they are essential to the state's control over agriculture. (The Communists' final aim is to have one such cooperative in each market center.)

In theory, these rural cooperatives are "voluntary" and nongovernmental, but in fact, they are strictly controlled and supported by the government. Most of their capital comes from low-interest People's Bank loans, and they receive discounts of 2 to 6 per cent on purchases from state trading companies or other state enterprises. It is these cooperatives which deal directly with the peasants, buying their produce and selling needed goods to them. In 1952, they bought over one-half of the grain purchased by the state that year. At the same time, they handled a high percentage of the manufactured goods sold to peasants throughout China.

Despite the increase in state control over agricultural products from 1949 through 1953, however, a critical food situation developed in 1953, as a result of poor crops and peasant resistance to the grain-purchasing program. This led to new measures. In November, 1953, the regime instituted "planned purchase and planned supply" of grain—one of the most dramatic economic measures taken in China so far since the Communist takeover.

Describing the new program, an article in the Chinese Communist press said:

The state's plans for purchase [of grain] have not been fulfilled on schedule, and the plans for marketing have often been completed in advance or even overfulfilled. This situation started to show itself toward the end of 1952, and continued right through the first half of 1953 and until the harvest of the fall crop, when it was still unchanged. The months of September and October should be the period in which food supplies are placed on the market in quantity, but . . . during these two months in 1953, the state's plans for purchasing were not well carried out, and purchases for both months were much below sales. . . . In these circumstances, the Party and government decided in good time to enforce the policy of planned purchase and planned supply of food. The free food market has been basically eliminated. . . . In a country where for the moment the economy of the small peasant is still enjoying absolute superiority, we have thoroughly changed the habits of millions of agricultural households, handed down through thousands of years, of selling in order to purchase, and dealing in the free market. We have started the large-scale socialist system of distribution whereby the state purchases the surplus grain of millions of peasants and distributes it among about 200 million people who need the grain. . . . The state has monopolized the food-purchasing market and is thus no more subjected to the obstructions of the capitalists. . . . Socialist commerce has monopolized all of the wholesale business in the food market and has also taken up the bulk of the retail business. Private industrial and commercial enterprises using food can engage in sales or processing only under the severe supervision and control of the state, and in accordance with the regulations of the state in regard to quality, quantity, prices, and processing standards. The supply of food for the whole country is now being undertaken directly by the state or by agents under the strict control of the state. . . . [The peasants] no longer engage in food transactions with the capitalists. . . . They are thus being absorbed into the orbit of state planning, and the blind nature of their productive efforts is reduced.

The article concluded by saying that this system for purchasing and distributing grain "lays the foundation for the implementation of planned purchase and planned sale of other agricultural produce."

The Communists say that 80 per cent of the country's surplus grain, after taxation, is now being purchased by the state on the basis of regional quotas. The supply and marketing cooperatives serve as purchasing agents. Farmers may sell the remaining 20 per cent to the state, but may not sell it to merchants. The only remaining legal "free grain markets" for the peasants are of two kinds: periodic state-supervised grain fairs, held in administrative villages, where small transactions between peasants are allowed; and special markets for personal contact between peasants and consumers (without merchant participation), controlled directly by state agencies or by supply and marketing cooperatives. This, at least, is the system as it exists on paper. There may be many difficulties in implementing it, however, since it does attempt to "change the habits of millions of agricultural households, handed down through thousands of years."

Having abolished (with the minor exceptions noted) the free market in grain, the regime has had to assume full responsibility for nationwide grain distribution. This is a tremendous and complex task. It is officially stated that the government must supply grain to 200 million people, including 100 million in the countryside as well as 100 million in urban areas. Some of the 100 million persons in rural areas are peasants who grow agricultural raw materials, but many are ordinary food-producing peasants who are themselves short of food. In February of this year, *People's Daily* said that 10 per cent of the rural population this year are "food-short" and another 10 per cent "famine-stricken." A major explanation for rural food shortages is the fact that local Communist cadres have forced many peasants to sell almost all of their grain. "Certain peasants have sold part of the grain stocks essential for their living requirements," says *People's Daily*; "some peasants being very enthusiastic about selling their grain have pledged too large sales."

To supply 200 million people, the regime now has in its hands 30–40 million tons of grain. It claimed to have collected 30 million tons in 1952 (20 million from the grain tax and 10 million by purchases), and the figure is undoubtedly larger in 1953, since the institution of "planned purchase" of grain.

In China's major cities, rationing of grain was started in November and December, 1953. Private food stores and merchants were transformed into "selling agents" for state trading companies and were subjected to strict regulation. Both industrial users (such as flour mills) and commercial users (such as restaurants) were brought under close government control, and the police cracked down on merchants trying to evade the new regulations. Individual ration cards were issued, and the basic ration was set at a low level. In Tientsin, when ration cards were first issued, they applied only to wheat flour; purchases of other, coarser grains were not restricted. The monthly ration of wheat flour was set at 19.8 pounds for organized workers in productive enterprises, 16.5 for office and management employees, and less for white-collar workers. (An additional 8.8 pounds was allowed for each dependent.) By January of this year, urban rationing had been started in most of China's cities and towns.

Distribution of grain throughout deficit areas in the countryside is more difficult, and the Communists admit that progress has been slow, but they claim that "planned supply" has been extended to many thousands of villages and that in time it will cover all those areas where it is needed.

In the spring of 1954, the program of "planned purchase and planned supply" of grain was reinforced by a campaign to promote "advanced purchases of farm products." The aim of this campaign is to have supply and marketing cooperatives contract with peasants "around the time of sowing" for delivery of their future harvest, and "advanced purchasing" is being extended to major products such as grain, cotton, and oil-bearing seeds. The motive behind this system is not only to strengthen state control but also to provide a better basis for state planning. Through "advanced purchases," says *People's Daily*, "the state can influence and direct agricultural production in a planned way and control the sown acreage and the output of various crops to a certain extent. Thus it can play a great part in facilitating the gradual bringing of small peasant farming into the channel of state plans."

If the Communists are successful in carrying through their present program of "planned purchase and planned supply," as well as "advanced purchase" of major agricultural crops, they will have accomplished a far-reaching revolutionary change which will greatly increase state control over the entire agricultural economy. There is little doubt, however, that neither program is popular with the mass of Chinese peasants, and the peasants can be expected to resist and evade. The effect upon agricultural output of such strict and complete controls may be adverse, because if the peasants know they must sell their surplus products to the state at official prices, they may well decide to protest by growing less. Control by the state of whatever agricultural surplus exists will obviously improve, however, and the regime will be able to utilize and distribute the ouput of the agricultural economy according to their plans.

The stringent food situation has made 1954 a year of shortages and austerity for the average Chinese consumer. Rationing of grain is now widespread, although not yet universal. Commodities such as vegetable oils and pork have not been controlled by card rationing, but they are in short supply, and the amounts available to consumers have been limited; in many cities, shops sell only a certain quota each day, and when the quota is exhausted supplies are unavailable. In addition, the quality of many foodstuffs on the market has been debased.

To conserve food, and to stretch available supplies as far as possible, the regime launched a nationwide austerity campaign last fall. One measure in this campaign was enforcement of low standards for processed foods (some of these were prescribed in regulations dating back to 1950, but enforcement had been lax). For example, in southwest and east China, the regulations now require rice millers to produce 102 pounds of polished rice for every 110 pounds of unhusked rice; this means that consumers are being offered brownish rice instead of the pure white type they prefer. In an attempt to make the degraded rice more palatable to consumers, propaganda campaigns have acclaimed the higher vitamin content of poorly polished rice and the nutritive value of coarser grains. But publicity about the health advantages of brown rice and coarse grains has not made them any more popular with the public. Widespread adulteration of grains and vegetable oils has also been reported by refugees from China. Husks are left in grain, and peanut and sesame oils are adulterated with things such as cottonseed oil. In many places, vegetable oils and pork (the principal meat in the Chinese diet) are almost unobtainable, or obtainable in only very limited quantities, although minimum supplies of grain have been guaranteed, at least in the major cities.

The authorities have also taken various measures to reduce wastage and cut down on secondary uses of grain. Campaigns urge the people to "save every grain" in warehousing and transporting grain, and restrictions on the use of grain for wine-distilling have been made more rigid.

These austerity measures have directly affected the majority of consumers, and have caused much grumbling; resentment over continued food exports during a period of shortages at home is reported to be widespread. But all available evidence indicates that despite the critical food situation, the Communists have continued to supply, through their state trading system, at least minimum requirements of basic grain at stable prices to urban customers. Ever since the Communists came to power, this policy of guaranteeing minimum foodstuffs at controlled prices to the people in China's cities has been a very important element in their economic program. Undoubtedly, it will be continued, even if it requires squeezing the peasants and causing widespread hardship in the countryside, because stability in the cities is of tremendous political importance.

Non-Communist sources in Hong Kong estimate that China is now suffering a shortage of several million tons of grain, and they believe that a critical food situation in China will continue at least until the fall harvest. This does not necessarily mean, however, that millions of people in China will starve this year. Some starvation is certainly possible, but the regime, which still maintains tight control over most of the country, appears to be spreading the available supplies of grain effectively and stretching them by enforcing reduced consumption. Some people may starve, but the majority will eat—although they will eat less.

There is every indication that the greatest hardship is likely to be experienced by China's peasants. Communist policy at present clearly seems to discriminate in favor of the urban population.

Collectivization of agriculture is regarded by the Communists as the ultimate solution of their agrarian problems. By 1951, while land redistribution was still in progress, it became clear that Agrarian Reform, as it had been defined until then, was merely a tactical stage in their policy.

"The economy of the small peasant is not capable of coping with . . . continually rising demand," said the Director of the CCP's Rural Work Department about a year ago. Quoting Stalin, he said: "In a word, we must gradually transfer from the economy of the small peasant to the foundation of large collective production, for only common and large-scale production will make the fullest use of scientific achievements and new techniques, and push forward at a rapid pace the development of our agriculture." He continued, "We all know that the economy of the small peasant develops either along the path of socialist agriculture or along the path of capitalist agriculture. The capitalist course is one we must resist."

The Communists appear to believe, despite the discouraging experience of over twenty years in the U.S.S.R., that agricultural collectivization will lead to spectacular increases in agricultural production. Perhaps the most practical reason impelling them toward collectivization, however, is the fact that organization of peasants makes it possible for the government to increase effective control over the rural population and to guarantee delivery of grain and other agricultural products to the state. Even if collectivization results in lowered production, due to peasant dissatisfaction, it can increase state control over the output of the agricultural economy.

The forms of collective farm organization toward which the Communists in China are now striving are clearly modeled on those in the Soviet Union, but the Chinese methods of working toward these goals are their own. It is obvious that the Chinese are capitalizing on Soviet experience and are attempting to avoid the disruptive violence that accompanied collectivization in the U.S.S.R.

By the end of 1951, the Chinese Communists stated that all peasants in China would be organized gradually and that collectivization would take place in three separate stages. Each of the stages is calculated to prepare the way for and minimize possible opposition to the next one. The first stage is to organize the peasants into mutual-aid teams, which, in their simplest form, consist of a small group of families who agree to help each other by working jointly and sharing each other's tools and animals. At first, teams are usually seasonal; then they are converted into permanent, year-round organizations. The size of such groups is expanded as they develop. In mutual-aid teams, members not only retain title to their land but also receive the produce of their own land.

The second, and most important, stage in the collectivization process is the establishment of producers' cooperatives. "An agricultural producers' cooperative," according to the Communists' definition, "is an economic organization of unified management and collective labor, based on private ownership of land. . . . Its main characteristic is that members invest their land in the common enterprise, being credited with the corresponding number of shares." These cooperatives are almost always formed by a merger of several existing mutual-aid teams. This step is the key one because although peasants retain theoretical ownership of their land in producers' cooperatives, they actually lose control over it. In such cooperatives, joint management of land is established, and peasant members are usually remunerated on the basis of the labor and land they contribute. Title to the land does not have much practical value, therefore, and once producers' cooperatives are widely organized, it will not be a very big step to convert them into full-fledged Soviet-style collectives, simply by depriving peasants of their ownership rights; this is the third and final stage called for in the Communists' collectivization program.

Soon after the start of the first Five-Year Plan, the Communists announced that they hoped by 1957 to organize about 800,000 producers' cooperatives, representing roughly 20 per cent of all peasant households in the country. "It is possible," said *People's Daily* early this year, "that by the end of China's first Five-Year Plan, agricultural cooperatives will become the main or nearly the main form of agriculture in some areas, while being developed to a lesser extent in other areas."

It is clear, however, that the Communists are encountering peasant opposition to the organization of producers' cooperatives, and the question of how much pressure to use in forcing peasants to join them is an important policy question that may well be a cause of dissension within the Party. During the first half of 1953, the campaign to organize cooperatives was pushed intensively. In July, however, the Party issued instructions to its cadres to slow down. A top Party leader made a statement deploring "brutal measures for forcing the peasants into reform." He said, "If we adopt hasty and adventurous attitudes, covet quantitative and outward achievements, strive for speed, blindly seek higher forms of organization, overdevelop common property, and thereby reduce the individual incomes of members, the result will be our separation from the masses, and production will be affected. This is most injurious to our cause." Less than five months later, the decision to slow down was reversed. In December, 1953, the CCP Central Committee announced that organization of producers' cooperatives—"the key to further growth of agricultural production on the existing foundations"—should be speeded up again. The pace of organizing cooperatives has accelerated without letup since the beginning of this year. In January, it was stated that 35,800 producers' cooperatives should be organized by the fall of 1954. By March, this goal had already been passed.

Since 1950, the organization of mutual-aid teams has proceeded steadily. The percentage of all peasant households in China included in such teams has risen, according to official claims, from 10 per cent in 1950 to over 20 per cent in 1951, 40 per cent in 1952, and 43 per cent (48 million households) last year. The target for this year is 59 per cent. Mutual-aid teams are defined as the "foundation for developing agricultural producers' cooperatives," the "primary form" of cooperation which is "most easily acceptable to peasants" and helps them "form the habit of collective labor." It is admitted, however, that "during the period of the first Five-Year Plan, mutual-aid teams shall remain the important form of agricultural production in many districts." Because of this, "every comrade engaged in rural work" is urged to "refrain from the slightest relaxation of guidance over the mutual-aid teams."

Agricultural producers' cooperatives have increased from 129 in 1951 to 4,000 in 1952 and 14,000 (containing 273,000 households) in 1953. The surge forward in organization this year has been very rapid. By May, official statements revealed that the number of cooperatives totaled more than 90,000, almost three times the original target for the entire year. By mid-year, the total had risen to 95,000.

The rapid development of producers' cooperatives during the first half of 1953 indicates a significant speedup in the Communists' collectivization program, and this acceleration is undoubtedly due to the food crisis confronting the regime. Collectivization, like the new state monopoly of trade in grain, increases the regime's control over the agricultural economy. But the Communists still have a long way to go before producers' cooperatives control more than a tiny fraction of Chinese peasants and farmland. Official claims reveal that the 91,000 cooperatives set up by early spring of this year included only 1.66 million households, or 1.53 per cent of all peasant households in the country, and roughly 6 million acres, or 2.16 per cent of cultivated land in China. Most of the present cooperatives, furthermore, are concentrated in limited areas. Roughly one-half are in north China and Manchuria, while in northwest and southwest China only a few hundred have been organized. And it is difficult to judge how many of the newly organized cooperatives are effectively functioning. To date, only a few full-fledged Soviet-style collective farms have been organized on an experimental basis. Communist publications sometimes speak of seventeen collective farms, and at other times of twenty-three, throughout the whole country.

The development of state-owned forms of agriculture, modeled on those in the U.S.S.R., has proceeded steadily but not very rapidly. By the end of last year, there were 59 large-scale mechanized state farms in Communist China; altogether, they included over a million acres and had 56,000 employees and fewer than 2,000 tractors. Other state-operated agricultural institutions in China at present include 2,000 model experimental farms, 3,600 agrotechnical stations for popularizing new farm methods, 1,650 veterinary stations, 11 machine and tractor stations, 591 farm-tool stations for promoting new tools, and several thousand small local state farms. Plans for 1954 call for doubling the number of mechanized state farms and steadily increasing all other forms of state-owned agriculture.

What is the reaction of China's peasants to this program of collectivization? Almost no firsthand evidence is available, but there are many reasons to believe that they do not like it and can be expected to resist, at least passively. Communist discussions of collectivization admit, implicitly, that the peasants are against the program and must be "educated" to accept it. The tradition of individual ownership and cultivation of land is probably as strong in China as anywhere in the world. It is certainly more deep-rooted than it was in Russia, where peasant resistance to collectivization was strong enough. The step-by-step approach to collectivization which the Chinese Communists are following is designed to minimize resistance, but it would be very surprising if it is completely successful in this respect. In all probability, peasant resistance will increase as the program develops, and this is likely to increase the severity of coercion used by the state to force peasants into collectivization.

The pace of industrialization and general economic development in China depend to a great extent upon agricultural improvement, and the Communists face many difficult problems and dilemmas in their agricultural policies.

Perhaps the most basic dilemma arises from the fact that the regime is compelled to extend maximum controls over the peasants and their surplus production, but at the same time must try to increase production. Collectivization and monopoly of the grain market increase state controls, but they also tend to antagonize the peasants and probably have a harmful effect upon production.

The regime's price policy on agricultural and industrial products also presents a real problem. In order to increase state profits from rural trade, and because manufactured goods are in short supply, the price ratio of agricultural and industrial products in China has been set at a level unfavorable to the peasants. This price situation does not increase peasants' incentives to produce more and may make them produce less.

The question of how to deal with rich peasants is likely to become a major problem as collectivization progresses. Rich peasants can be expected to be the strongest resisters to collectivization, and yet they are the most efficient agricultural producers. How to force them into collectivization without seriously affecting the level of production is a problem for which there is no easy solution.

The need to increase both food output and production of agricultural raw materials simultaneously will present a continuing dilemma. Food and raw-material crops compete for the limited amount of arable land in China, and in most cases a rapid increase in the production of either can be made only at the expense of the other.

Mechanization of agriculture is important to Communist plans, but mechanization will be extremely difficult. To the extent that mechanization is feasible, furthermore, it will complicate the major problem of what to do with surplus agricultural labor.

Since China has relatively little unused arable land, a significant increase in yields per acre will be required to bring about the production increases the Communists hope for. But agriculture must compete with industry for China's limited amounts of investment capital and technical skills, and at present agriculture receives a low priority in China's over-all economic program.

These and many other problems, such as the shortage of rural credit and the difficulties of conquering flood and drought, will make it extremely difficult for the Communists to achieve their ambitious agricultural goals. The failure to achieve planned targets for agricultural production during the first year of the Five-Year Plan undoubtedly has already slowed down China's economic development program, and some of the thorniest problems in the future will focus upon food and the peasants.

ECONOMIC ACHIEVEMENTS

October, 1954

During recent months, the leaders of Communist China have been producing a number of diplomatic, political, and economic surprises. One of their recent economic surprises has been the publication of statistics in real terms, rather than vague percentages, of over-all national production figures for several major industries.

Most economic statistics in China have been classified as "state secrets" during the past five years, and data on production have been released for the most part in ambiguous percentage figures. Recently, however, the "Report on Government Work," made by Premier Chou En-lai on September 23 to the opening session of China's 1954 All-China People's Congress, revealed more important economic facts (or claims) than any document released in recent years by Peking.

If the figures released are accurate, some of the estimates of Chinese industrial production made by both American and Chinese economic observers in Hong Kong (including myself), ECAFE (Economic Commission for Asia and the Far East) economists in Bangkok, and many other students of Chinese economic development are too low.

In the first section of his report, Premier Chou En-lai admitted candidly that the "blueprint of the first Five-Year Plan is at present not yet complete and final." He also reiterated that "in the period when the state concentrates its efforts on developing heavy industry, the people have to bear some hardships and inconveniences."

He proceeded, thereafter, to put forward the regime's claims of progress during the period 1949–52. During those four years of rehabilitation, he said, the value of industrial production in China increased at an average rate of 36.9 per cent annually. The first year of the Five-Year Plan (1953), he claimed, saw a further increase of 33 per cent over 1952 in the value of industrial output.

Turning to 1954, Premier Chou claimed that by the end of the year the total value of the ouput of modern industries in Communist China would be 4.2 times that of 1949, and that the value of over-all industrial and agricultural output would be 2.2 times that of 1949. More specifically, he revealed the 1954 production targets of eight major industries, as outlined below:

Industry	1954 Production Target	Percentage Increase (Base Year: 1949)
Electric power	10.80 billion kwh	250
Coal	81.99 million tons	260
Pig iron	3.03 million tons	1,240
Steel	2.17 million tons	1,370
Metalworking machines	13,513	850
Cement	4.73 million tons	720
Cotton yarn	4.60 million bales	260
Machine-made paper	.48 million tons	450

These figures are really the first of their kind that have been published in China since 1949. Some of them are fairly close to estimates made by economic specialists outside China after painstaking analysis of the fragmentary data obtainable. Some, however —particularly the claimed targets for electric power and coal— are considerably higher than estimates made by non-Communists. Observers in Hong Kong studying Chinese Communist publications, and making production estimates on the basis of economic data hitherto made public, have thought that 1954 production of coal might approach 60 million tons and that electric output during the year would be under 6 billion kwh. Premier Chou's claims are significantly higher than these estimates. To the extent that his claims approach the truth, the problem of fuel and power in China's economic development program is less of a bottleneck, therefore, than many observers have believed—although there is no doubt that it is still a bottleneck of serious proportions.

How accurate Chou En-lai's claims are is a matter for conjecture, however, particularly in view of the economic difficulties he admits the Communists have encountered. Chou states, for example, that only 30 per cent of all enterprises in China completed their production plans in every respect during 1953.

Despite admissions of this sort, Chou's general claim is one of success. He asserts that from 1949 to 1954 the proportion of modern industrial output to total agricultural and industrial output in China has risen from 17 to 33 per cent; that the "means of production" (capital goods) as a proportion of all industrial production has risen from 28.8 to 42.3 per cent; and that the production of all "state enterprises" (including cooperatives and "joint state-private" enterprises) has risen from 37 to 71 per cent of total industrial output.

During the first Five-Year Plan, according to Chou, about 600 "important industrial units" are to be "built or improved" in China. The "sinews" of industrialization will be 141 Soviet-aid projects, "most" of which will be completed by 1958.

This year, Chou said, 300 "important industrial projects" will be "improved, newly built, or continued under construction," and 51 will be "completed." Chou now claims that of the 141 Soviet-aid projects, 17 are already "wholly or partially completed," 34 are "under construction," and the rest are in the blueprint stage.

Chou also states that during the past five years, JMP$328 trillion (nearly U.S.$14 billion, at official exchange rates) has been invested in "economic construction" in China.

Turning to agriculture, Chou says in his report that this year China's floods (now officially admitted to be the worst in over a century) inundated "about one-tenth of the farmland of the country, totaling over 26.6 million acres"; but he then asserts that this year's agricultural output will "exceed that of 1953," even though "agricultural production also will not be able to fulfill the plan."

Plans for collectivization proceed apace, despite flood disasters. Already, Chou states, 100,000 agricultural producers' cooperatives have been organized; it is hoped that by next spring 500,000, containing 10 million peasant households, will have been formed; and the current aim for 1957 is to bring over half of the farming households and over half of the total cultivated land in China into such cooperatives.

These facts and figures, while not significantly altering the picture of economic conditions in China already pieced together by non-Communist economic specialists outside China, do indicate, however, that the Communists may have made more progress in a few fields—specifically in industry—than was generally believed. And they also show that although flood damage in China has been extremely serious, the pace of agricultural collectivization has been speeded up rather than slowed down. Peking's leaders continue to press for austerity, industrialization, and step-by-step socialization in both the cities and the countryside.

China's ability to carry through its economic plans have probably been improved somewhat by a series of new Sino-Soviet economic agreements recently concluded in Peking between a high-powered Soviet delegation (headed by Khrushchev) and top Chinese leaders. On October 12, Sino-Soviet joint declarations were released in Peking revealing that Port Arthur is to be returned completely to China; four Sino-Soviet joint stock companies (companies to exploit nonferrous metals and petroleum in Sinkiang, to build and repair ships in Dairen, and to operate civil airlines in China) are being transferred to exclusive Chinese control; "scientific and technical cooperation" between Russia and China is to be extended; and the U.S.S.R. is to help China build the Lanchow–Urumchi–Alma Ata Railway (the Sinkiang line, linking with the Russians' Turk-Sib line at Alma Ata) and the Chining–Ulan Bator Railway (the Mongolian line, linking with a line to Russia at the Outer Mongolian capital of Ulan Bator).

Even more important, perhaps, an agreement was concluded under which the U.S.S.R. will grant another "long-term credit" of 520 million rubles (at the official exchange rate, 1 ruble equals 25 cents in U.S. currency, but it is actually worth less) to China; will grant "assistance" to China on 15 additional industrial enterprises (added to the 141 previously announced); and will increase "by an amount valued at more than 400 million rubles the supply of equipment for the 141 enterprises covered in the previously signed agreement."

These October 12 agreements are a significant sign of closer Sino-Soviet economic cooperation. The amount of financial aid to China from the U.S.S.R. is still fairly small, however, and the aid consists of loans rather than grants. The 1950 Soviet loan of U.S.$300 million is scheduled to expire this year, and if the original agreement is not changed, the Chinese Communists must send the first of 10 annual installments to repay the loan by December 31 of this year. The new loan—which, in terms of official Soviet exchange rates, amounts to only U.S.$130 million, and may be less than this in terms of real value—will help the Chinese, but it will not begin to solve Peking's financial problems. China still must find ways and means to pay for most of the "aid" from the U.S.S.R., and to this end new moves have recently been made in China's domestic austerity program to control and ration basic commodities, limit consumption, and increase exports.

PART VI

POLITICAL CONSOLIDATION
OF THE REGIME

PARTY UNITY AND CENTRALIZATION
OF POWER

February, 1955

During their first years after coming to power in 1949, the Chinese Communists rapidly established firm political control over the whole country and instituted a strong Party dictatorship. But complete consolidation of power takes time, and the process still continues.

In the past year, political developments of considerable importance have taken place in China. Some of these have been the logical culmination of five years of Communist rule. Others have been the regime's response to domestic tensions. Although there have been signs of internal stress in China, however, there has been no significant crack in the Communists' façade of monolithic unity. Actually, recent events seem to indicate that despite the numerous problems they face, the dominant leaders in China have successfully tightened their controls and strengthened their position during the past year. Throughout the country, political power has been further centralized. Among the top leaders, there have been noteworthy adjustments of power relations accomplished with comparative smoothness. And at the bottom level, the regime's controls over the mass of the population have been steadily increased.

Major political developments within China during the past year have included the following: an energetic campaign within the Party to improve discipline and unity which suppressed high-ranking dissidents and resulted in the disappearance of at least one Politburo member and changes in the status of other top Party leaders; numerous steps toward centralization of administration—the most important of which was abolition of the six major regions into which China has been divided—which reduced the local power of some important leaders and checked possible trends toward regionalism; various moves to bring military organizations under more effective civil and central control; nationwide elections, which enabled the Communists to test and weed out local cadres and to screen and indoctrinate the entire population once again; convocation of China's first All-China People's Congress, designed to give the government a new appearance of legality; and adoption of the Constitution of the People's Republic of China, which replaced the temporary constitutional laws under which China has been operating since 1949, and adjustment of personnel at the top level of the newly constituted government.

All these steps have aimed at political stabilization and have contributed to further consolidation of the Communists' power.

These developments began early last year. From February 6 to 10, 1954, the CCP Central Committee held an important plenary session, its first in over three years, and the Party's second-ranking leader, Liu Shao-ch'i, demanded a "struggle to strengthen Party unity." (The CCP's constitution calls for a Party Congress every three years and Central Committee plenary sessions every six months, but the last Congress was the seventh, held in 1945, and before February, 1954, the last Central Committee plenary session had been in June, 1950.)

An aura of mystery and strife surrounded this meeting. Mao Tse-tung, Chairman of the Party, was missing, and it was officially explained that he was "away on holiday." Since this was the first full meeting of the top Party committee since 1950, Mao's absence was startling, to say the least.

At the meeting, attended by sixty-one of the seventy current members of the Central Committee, Liu Shao-ch'i delivered a report from the Politburo summarizing Party accomplishments since the previous session. He then called for a Party Conference later in 1954 "to discuss the outlines of the state's first Five-Year Construction Plan and other relevant questions." Finally, he introduced a "Resolution on Strengthening Party Unity," reputedly proposed by Mao at the Politburo's meeting of December 24, 1953.

The official summary of this resolution on Party unity that appeared in the Communist press made it sound like a call for a major purge:

> The enemies of the people within the country have not yet been completely eliminated, and outside the country there still exists imperialist encirclement. . . . Inveterate counterrevolutionary elements . . . will undoubtedly collude with foreign imperialism and take every opportunity to sabotage the cause of the Party and the people, in an attempt to defeat the revolutionary cause and restore reactionary rule in China. . . . The greatest danger to the Party is the danger of the

enemy creating sectarian activities inside the Party, and making use of a faction in the Party (if the enemy can really create such a faction) to act as his agent. . . . At the same time, among some of our cadres, even certain high-ranking cadres within our Party, there is still a lack of understanding of the importance of Party unity, the importance of collective leadership, the importance of consolidating and enhancing the prestige of the Central Committee. . . . They lose their heads over certain achievements they have made in their work. . . . They think there is no one equal to them in the wide world. . . . They even regard the region or department under their leadership as their individual inheritance or independent kingdom. . . . The Party must wage unrelenting struggle against those who deliberately undermine Party unity, stand up against the Party, persist in refusing to correct their errors or even carry out splitting or other dangerous activities within the Party. . . . The Party must take strict disciplinary action against them or even expel them from the Party when necessary.

One of the most striking aspects of this statement was its stress on the need for unity among top Party leaders. Most disciplinary campaigns within the Party in the past have been directed toward subordinate personnel; this one was aimed "especially" at "the responsible comrades of the Central Committee above provincial (or municipal) level and the high-ranking, responsible cadres in the armed forces."

After the February Central Committee meeting, an inner-Party campaign of "unrelenting struggle" unfolded throughout the country, especially among top-level personnel. It was a behind-the-scenes struggle, carried on mainly in meetings of the regional Party Bureaus, to "transmit the resolution of the fourth plenary session (of the seventh Central Committee) and check up Party work." Most of these meetings took place in late March, but the one held by the Northeast Bureau in Manchuria lasted from March 26 to April 24 and involved "more than 20 days of heated discussion." Throughout this period, official Chinese Communist publications carried numerous articles stressing discipline, vigilance, and "collective leadership."

Many outside observers expected the campaign to reach a climax in late 1954, and it was thought that the purging of some top leaders would then be announced. This did not take place, however. Instead, the campaign quietly slipped into the background, overshadowed by other developments, about the middle of the year. It may still be simmering, but nothing has been heard of it recently.

In one fundamental respect, the campaign appears to have been consistent with previous Chinese Communist "purges." Although the Communists have periodically, through the years, made co-ordinated efforts to tighten Party discipline, during which a certain amount of dirty linen has been publicly aired, since Mao's rise to undisputed authority they have never conducted a Russian-style purge involving widely publicized physical extermination of large numbers of top-level deviationists. Up to this moment, that generalization still holds true.

However, the results of the latest Party campaign in China are still a matter for speculation, since the campaign has not yet been officially ended. But it is possible to make a good guess about what it has been about and what it has accomplished. There are reasons to believe that it was precipitated by the most serious crisis within the Communists' leadership since the Party came to power, that this crisis was caused both by policy disputes and by power rivalries, and that the disputes and rivalries have been resolved, at least temporarily, by firm imposition of a "correct" policy line, strong suppression of deviationism, effective assertion of central control, and a tough crackdown on factionalism and localism.

The real struggle within the Party undoubtedly began to come to a head during 1953, before the February 1954 Central Committee meeting, and it was related to disputes over domestic policy, and possibly foreign policy as well. China started its first Five-Year Plan at the beginning of 1953, but many aspects of economic policy remained vague until October of that year, when the "general line of the state during the period of transition to socialism" was publicized, calling for a step-by-step process of socialization for industry, commerce, and agriculture. Although available evidence is scanty, policy debates preceding announcement of the "general line" probably concentrated on the question of how fast the process of socialization should be, and the "general line" as published may well represent a compromise solution.

During the summer of 1953, before the "general line" was elaborated, Communist policy on the pace of socialization had vacillated, particularly in the field of agricultural collectivization, but after November the process steadily accelerated. Obviously, the views of those who feared that the Party might already be moving too fast in suppressing private enterprise and forcing peasants into preliminary forms of collectivization were overruled. On the other hand, the "general line" in a basic sense retained a policy of gradualism, at least by comparison with the period of the Soviet Union's first Five-Year Plan, in that it called for continued toleration of some private enterprise during the "transition period" and a step-by-step "transformation" rather than a direct, immediate plunge toward complete socialization. There are hints that at least a few Party leaders favored the latter, more precipitous course, but that they, too, were overruled.

Promulgation of the "general line" laid down the "correct" policy, which all Party members must accept, and during 1954 a tremendous indoctrination and propaganda campaign was carried on throughout China to spread general knowledge of it. But although this policy problem now appears to have been "solved," in a sense, no absolute and final solution is really possible, because differences of opinion within the Party on the pace of socialization can be expected to continue. Even since promulgation of the general line, in fact, several changes of pace have occurred during 1954. The Communists kept speeding up their program of agricultural collectivization by raising their targets for the numbers of producers' cooperatives to be organized, so that by the end of the year their program appeared to be much more rapid than it had even a year earlier. In all probability, plans regarding the pace of socialization can be expected to change again in the future, in response to the program's successes and failures, and within the Party the question of whether to push forward, or ease up, will continue to be a subject for important policy debates.

Although differences of opinion on policy were clearly a factor behind the Party disciplinary campaign, however, they were overshadowed, if one can judge on the basis of published reports, by actual or incipient power rivalries and tensions among the top Party leadership. Almost all reports on the campaign emphasized primarily the dangers of individual "conceit" on the part of certain Party leaders, and the need for stronger, central collective leadership. The dominant leaders obviously feared the growth of independence on the part of some of the Party's regional and organizational bosses, particularly those administering the six major regions of the country, and were determined to reassert central control.

Ever since the Communists came to power in China, a handful of outstanding revolutionary leaders have administered, with considerable scope for local initiative, the key regions into which China has been divided. Although always directly subordinate to the Party's Politburo and the Central Government in Peking, many of these regional leaders have occupied the highest Party, government, and army posts in the large regions, and their local power has contained an inherent threat—more potential than actual, but real nonetheless—to the Party's basic desire for centralization of power. By the beginning of 1954, the dominant Party leaders obviously decided that it was time to tighten central control not only within the Party itself but also in the related organizational structures of the government and army in order to forestall the possibility of regionalism developing to the point where it might endanger the system of centralized administration. The Party campaign was essential to this centralizing task, since the Party is the primary channel of absolute authority in China today.

The most notable casualty of the Party unity campaign has been Kao Kang, a key Politburo member, Party boss of the vital region of Manchuria, and head of the important State Planning Commission. Since the early part of 1954, he has disappeared completely from public life in China. There are some other leaders also whose whereabouts and activities have become obscure since the Party unity campaign began, and it is possible that they too have been victimized by the campaign, although at this point it is by no means certain. One of the most important of these is Jao Shu-shih, former Party chief in the east China region and later head of the important central Organization Bureau of the Party; nothing has been heard of him in recent months. Li Li-san and Ch'en Shao-yu, both of whom were top Party leaders in the period before Mao Tse-tung's ascendancy, have also slipped into the background. But since Party leaders in China have sometimes disappeared from view for long periods, only to reappear at a later date, it is impossible to identify the campaign's victims definitely until the Communists choose to publicize their names. Possibly, this will be done when a Party conference is convened. Party conferences, composed of representatives of the Party's provincial organizations, have less authority than full-dress congresses, but they can remove up to one-fifth of the members of the Central Committee, and this may be the purpose of the conference promised by Liu Shao-ch'i. In any case, although the conference is already overdue, it is likely to be held eventually, and then the results of the campaign within the Party will probably become clearer.*

Regardless of who finally receives the ax (organizationally or literally) as a result of the Party unity campaign, important

---

* The Party conference was held in March, 1955; it revealed that Kao Kang and Jao Shu-shih had been purged. Kao committed suicide; Jao simply disappeared from public view.

changes in the administrative structures of the government and army as well as the Party have already occurred since the Central Committee meeting. These changes significantly increase centralized control. Since February, 1954, the "large-region" level of organization has been, or is in the process of being, eliminated from the structures of all the pillars of Communist power in China—Party, government, army, and so on.

The elimination of regional organizations in the six large administrative regions significantly alters the structure of power within China and affects the status of numerous key Communist leaders. A majority of the men who have lost their regional jobs continue to hold important posts, but these men have been shifted from the regions where they exercised so much influence since 1949, separated from the temptations of local empire-building, drawn more closely into Central Government affairs in Peking, and placed under the watchful eyes of the Party's "collective leadership."

The most dramatic step involved in this centralization process was the abolition, in June, 1954, of the Administrative Committees in China's six major regions—northeast, north, east, central-south, southwest, and northwest. At the same time, the number of provinces in China was reduced from thirty to twenty-six by the merger of four existing provinces with other areas (Ninghsia was absorbed by Kansu, Suiyuan by Inner Mongolia, and Heilungkiang by Sungkiang, while Liaotung and Liaoshi were merged to become Liaoning), a move that also helped to centralize administrative control.

Less dramatically, and more slowly, steps have been taken to bring China's military organization under closer central control. The four field armies, each of which has been closely associated with regional leaders, have been steadily reduced in importance, and reorganization of the army has proceeded quietly. It is possible that the field armies will ultimately be completely dissolved. Late in 1954, when a new constitution was announced, a Ministry of Defense directly under the cabinet was established for the first time, bringing the military under direct supervision of the top body for civil administration to a greater degree than ever before.

Finally, toward the end of 1954, the Party began to dissolve its own Party regional bureaus. This final action to eliminate any important layer of administration between the central authorities and the provinces is still under way. To date, three of the six bureaus have been closed.

The steady centralization of power clearly strengthens the position of the dominant Party leadership in China, and tensions existing within the Communist ranks are probably under better control than they were a year ago. The fact that a dissident or deviationist leader of Kao Kang's stature has been deposed indicates that the inner Party struggle has been a serious one; the fact that he has been pushed into the background with so little indication of open conflict indicates that the struggle has been largely successful, at least so far.

While all these moves toward political centralization were under way during 1954, the Communists also pushed forward with long-delayed plans to consolidate their government structure by holding national elections, convening their first National People's Congress, and promulgating a constitution.

Preparations for national elections had begun many months earlier, in January, 1953, when it was announced that the elections were to be held before the end of 1953. But the regime, burdened with tremendous domestic and foreign problems, was unable to keep to this schedule, and the target date was postponed. In early 1954, however, preparations were energetically stepped up.

The purpose of the elections was to choose representatives for congresses at every level of government administration in China, from the villages to the national level. When the Communists first came to power in China, they set up appointed "representative" bodies but promised that these would be converted into elective bodies in due time. The interim "representative conferences" that started functioning after 1949 were forums of men and women handpicked by the Communists, but they gave a certain appearance of democratic representation, provided an important instrument for mobilizing the populace to implement Communist policies, and in a sense gave the regime a sounding-board for determining public attitudes and opinions. By 1953, the top Communist leaders obviously felt that their position was sufficiently consolidated to proceed with the formality of converting these bodies from appointed to elected congresses, as promised. This conversion was essentially a formality, because no basic change in the character of the controlled bodies was contemplated.

It was significant that a nationwide census and preparation for the elections proceeded simultaneously. Obviously, one of the regime's aims in conducting elections was to put the entire population through a systematic screening, even more thorough than those which had previously been possible. Both the census and election registration lagged behind schedule, but by mid-1954 they were brought near to completion.

The census was completed first. According to the official results published, the registered population of China (in 1953) totaled 574 million. To this figure, the Communists added more than 8 million (estimated) in China's border regions and more than 19 million overseas, in Formosa and elsewhere, bringing the total Chinese population to roughly 602 million. The tabulation provided essential data on the potential electorate.

Election registration followed the census-taking. It was carried out under the guidance of about 2.5 million cadres in Communist China's 214,000 basic electoral units in villages, factories, schools, and other organizations, and persons over eighteen were eligible unless "deprived of political rights" or disenfranchised for other reasons. Altogether, 323 million people were issued election cards. Official statements claimed that fewer than 3 per cent of the potential electorate were disenfranchised, but one can be certain that regardless of how many people were finally labeled as political enemies of the regime, the registration process provided an opportunity for a careful probing of everyone's political attitudes.

When the elections finally took place, they bore almost no relation to elections in the West. But they were of significance nonetheless, in terms of both tightened Party control over the masses and supervised mass participation in the political process. There was no competition between parties. There were no competing programs. And once the candidates were selected with Party guidance, there were no important public contests between candidates. There was, however, an opportunity to test the cadres, weed out laggards, and promote activists. There was also an opportunity for extensive and intensive propaganda on the "general line," the proposed new constitution, and so on. And the general population was mobilized to stand up and be counted.

The elections did not take place simultaneously all over the country. Instead, they proceeded slowly, area by area, after local political screening, registration, and thorough preparation had been completed. In most of China, the so-called basic-level elections, in villages and other first-stage electoral units, were completed by early spring, 1954, and according to official claims, 278 million people, or 86 per cent of registered voters, took part in them. These elections were conducted, significantly, by open show of hands; apparently the Communists, although firmly entrenched, are not ready to experiment with the secret ballot, despite their monopoly of political control and power.

The net result of the basic-level elections was the careful selection of a fairly broad Party-approved base for local government in China. Altogether, more than 5.5 million people were elected to congresses of the lowest level throughout the country, and these persons, whose main function is to support and help implement government policies, are drawn from all strata of the population still acceptable to the regime.

Once the local elections were finished, it did not take long to complete the national electoral process, since the general public did not participate in elections of representatives to higher congresses. Under the hierarchical setup of government in China, the local congresses elected representatives to *Hsien* and municipal congresses; these in turn chose representatives to provincial-level congresses, which finally elected the membership of China's first National People's Congress. By mid-1954, the urgent need to complete this series of steps, so that a national congress would be convened by fall, led the authorities to skip over some of the formalities; an approved list of national congress delegates was passed down to the provincial congresses to speed things up. Finally, approximately 1,200 delegates were elected by provincial congresses, as well as by minority, army, and overseas Chinese groups, and the stage was set for the long-heralded People's Congress.

The Congress met in Peking for roughly two weeks during September, 1954. It was the occasion for many speeches (including a few important policy reports), meetings, and demonstrations intended to symbolize the solidarity of the regime. The real business of the Congress had been carefully prepared during the months preceding September, however, so its two basic tasks were accomplished with dispatch. On September 20, it passed the Constitution of the People's Republic of China, and thereafter it quickly approved nominees for top posts in the new government.

During the years between 1949 and 1954, China had no full-fledged national constitution; two documents, the Common Program of the Chinese People's Political Consultative Conference, and the Organic Law of the Central People's Government, provided the main provisional constitutional basis for the regime. The outlines of government structure and policy contained in these documents were adequate for the first years of Communist rule, but by the end of 1952 the need was felt for some changes in both structure and policy (both of which are dealt with in Chinese

Communist constitutional documents), and the time was ripe for Communist China's first full-fledged constitution. In November, 1952, the Central People's Government Council set up a thirty-three member Committee on the Drafting of a National Constitution, and some time later the CCP Central Committee handed to the Drafting Committee a proposed constitution. This was soon polished and made into a Draft Constitution, which was then submitted to the People's Government Council and approved in June, 1954. Between June and November, the draft was discussed by organized groups throughout China, and after a few minor changes it was presented to, and approved by, the People's Congress. This new constitution defines basic policies and organizational forms that are likely to remain fairly stable in China as long as the Communist regime is still undergoing the "period of transition to socialism."

There have been few, if any, fundamental changes in the principles of government in China as a result of adoption of the constitution. The government still maintains the form of a "united front," which includes selected non-Communists and is supposed to represent the interests of a class coalition, and it is still completely controlled by the Communists. The distribution of power is still based on the principles of "democratic centralism," with all final authority in the hands of the highest government body; restricted powers and functions are delegated down the chain of command to lower bodies in the government, but every level is held in check by the appointive and veto powers over it held by the level above. The structure of government is still patterned on the old hierarchical system in which there is a representative body (congress) at each level which chooses an executive-administrative organ (council) to govern in its name and also elects representatives to the next higher level of government administration. The government is still established on the principle that the congresses and councils centralize power at each administrative level; the idea of establishing checks and balances or operating on the basis of separation of powers is rejected. Although this basic framework of government remains unaltered, however, the new government does introduce some changes of considerable interest.

The Central Government is dealt with in the new constitution under three headings: the National People's Congress, the Chairman of the People's Republic of China, and the State Council. Changes in the role and relationship of these three elements, as compared with their equivalents that existed in the Chinese Government between 1949 and 1954, raise some unanswered questions about top-level political developments in China.

The National People's Congress, according to the constitution, is "the highest organ of state power" in China. This unicameral body, elected every four years by provinces, autonomous regions, special municipalities, the armed forces, and overseas Chinese, is labeled the "only organ exercising the legislative power of the state" (but this is misleading, since it applies only to major "laws" and not to the "administrative measures," "decisions," "orders," and "instructions" that emanate from other Party and government bodies and have the force of law). In theory, the functions and powers of the National People's Congress are most impressive. It amends the constitution, enacts laws, supervises enforcement of the constitution, elects the Chairman and Vice-Chairman of the People's Republic, and "decides" (on the basis of recommendations from the Chairman) who shall be Premier, ministers in the State Council, and members of the National Defense Council. It also is empowered to decide on the national economic plan, the state budget, boundaries of major administrative areas, general amnesties, and questions of war or peace. But the Congress is not in fact as important as it sounds. It meets only once a year for a single brief session (its members are not full-time legislators, but people with other regular jobs in various parts of the country), and it obviously will have little to do with the continuous task of governing.

It appears on paper that the most powerful body in the government under the new constitution is actually the Standing Committee of the National People's Congress, elected by the Congress as its "permanent body." It meets fortnightly and functions continuously during the long period between Congress sessions. Although responsible to the Congress, the Standing Committee has wide powers which it will, in practice, perform on its own. It not only has power to "interpret the laws," but its decree-making power makes it, in effect, the top legislative body except for the brief periods when the full Congress meets. It "supervises" the work of all other government bodies, including the State Council, Supreme People's Court, and Supreme People's Procuratorate. It also can annul any decisions or orders of the State Council or the regional administrative bodies under it, and this veto makes it (on paper) the most powerful organ in the government. Its many other powers include appointment or removal of vice-premiers and ministers as well as deputy chiefs of the Court and Procuratorate, ratification or abrogation of treaties with foreign states, appointment or recall of envoys abroad, military mobilization, proclamation of the state of war, and so on.

The Chairman of the Republic, elected by the Congress for a four-year term, does not look very important in the provisions of the new constitution. His constitutional powers are mainly procedural; almost everything he does—such as promulgating laws and decrees, ordering mobilization, proclaiming a state of war, making numerous appointments, and so on—must be based on prior decisions by the Congress or its Standing Committee. (The Chairman does, however, "recommend" to the Congress candidates for Premier, as well as some other top government posts.) He does not play a direct role in, or belong to, either the Standing Committee of the Congress or the State Council, the two important governing bodies under the new constitution. He can, however, play a mediating role between these two bodies by convening a so-called Supreme State Conference composed of the Vice-Chairman of the Republic, the Chairman of the Standing Committee, the Premier, and "other persons concerned"; such a conference does not have independent powers, but it can "submit views" to the Congress, Standing Committee, or State Council. The only organizational body in the government that is actually headed by the Chairman of the Republic is the National Defense Council, a large military organ apparently primarily advisory in its purpose. All in all, the Chairman, at least on paper, does not hold the reins of day-to-day government administration in his hands.

Liu Shao-ch'i, in describing the new constitution, has said: "The functions and powers of our head of state in our country are jointly exercised by the Standing Committee [which Liu heads] . . . and the Chairman of the People's Republic of China." The post of Chairman is described by the magazine *China Reconstructs* (Peking) as follows: "The office of the Chairman of the People's Republic of China, then, carries no independent power. It does not affect the integrity of either the National People's Congress or the State Council. It does, however, provide a great, simple symbol of the unity of the state."

The State Council (cabinet), according to the constitution, is the "highest organ of state power" and "the highest administrative organ of the state." It is referred to as the "Central People's Government," an elevation of status over the cabinet it succeeds. The State Council is composed of a Premier, ten vice-premiers, a Secretary-General, and all the ministers and heads of commissions in the government. It meets monthly, and since it is the primary executive branch of the government, it clearly carries the day-to-day burden of governing. Although the State Council cannot pass "laws," it can formulate "administrative measures" and issue "decisions" and "orders" with the force of law, subject to veto only by the Congress or Standing Committee. All local governments and administration in China come under its direction and control.

It is interesting to note that although the acts of the State Council can be vetoed by the Standing Committee, the Premier himself can only be appointed and removed by the full National People's Congress, a fact that limits the control of the Standing Committee over the Premier.

Another important feature of the State Council is the fact that provision is made (in a supplementary Organic Law rather than the constitution itself) for a small group that could be labeled an "inner cabinet," authorized to exercise all the powers of the full State Council. The "inner cabinet" is currently made up of only twelve men: the Premier, the ten vice-premiers, and the Secretary-General.

This organizational structure at the peak of government is modeled on both the Russian Government and the previous Chinese Communist Government, but there are significant differences between the new structure and both its models. In the U.S.S.R., the Presidium of the bicameral Supreme Soviet performs the function of head of state, and therefore the head of state is not completely above and separate from other major organs within the government, as is now the case in China. On paper, the Council of Ministers (cabinet) in the U.S.S.R. is responsible to the Presidium. In practice, the Chairman and Presidium are relatively unimportant, and the locus of real power within the government lies with the Council of Ministers. In the previous Chinese Communist Government, the Chairman headed the Central People's Government Council, the most powerful body in the government. Under the People's Government Council, and responsible to it, was the Government Administration Council (cabinet). In practice, the Chairman was the real executive leader, and there was a clear-cut chain of command from the Chairman and the People's Government Council he headed to the Premier and the Government Administration Council.

The new Chinese Government does not fit either of these patterns, however. The chain of command is much less clear than it was before and is obviously different from what it is in the U.S.S.R.

Now the post of Chairman has been separated from the key functioning bodies, yet it is obviously not a mere figurehead job. On paper, the Standing Committee holds the decision-making power, and the State Council is responsible to it, but it is by no means fully clear what the relationship of these two bodies is, or what kind of relationship they now have to the Chairman.

An attempt to understand the meaning of these changes requires an examination of the personnel holding key jobs in the new government, because distribution of power in a Communist state obviously cannot be determined simply from organizational charts.

Formerly, Mao Tse-tung, who has been undisputed leader of the Chinese Communist movement for over twenty years, was Chairman of the Republic and also of the People's Government Council; he and the Council exercised the highest decision-making power. Under Mao was the Government Administration Council, headed by Premier Chou En-lai, who held the number-two post within the government, but was clearly subordinate to Mao and the People's Government Council.

Now, however, although Mao is still Chairman, he does not head the Standing Committee, and his government post is obviously less important than before.

Liu Shao-ch'i, one of the two main contenders for succession to Mao Tse-tung in China (Chou En-lai is the other), heads the Standing Committee. It is significant that this is the first time Liu has taken charge of an important functioning body within the government, even though for some years he has consistently been ranked number-two within the Party. But the composition of the Standing Committee under Liu is not very impressive. It is a large "united front" sort of group, heavily weighted with such persons as the boy Dalai Lama from Tibet. Although the Standing Committee contains three Party Politburo members, only five of the thirteen vice-chairmen are Party members, and of the Standing Committee's sixty-five regular members only thirty-four belong to the Communist Party. It is difficult to imagine such a conglomerate group, almost half of whom are non-Communists, actually making decisions on major policy questions.

The State Council, headed by Premier Chou En-lai, is a far more impressive body in terms of its personnel than the Standing Committee. Of its total current membership, including the Premier, ten vice-premiers, Secretary-General, and thirty-five members, twenty-nine belong to the Party. Every member of the "inner cabinet" is a member of the CCP Central Committee (two are on the Politburo). This is the most impressive single grouping of men within the government—a group it is easy to imagine playing a key decision-making role.

Where, then, does real power rest in the government? For the first time since the Communists came to power, this is not wholly clear. One Chinese political scientist, writing in the *Far Eastern Survey*, says "the real locus of power seems to be the Chairman of the People's Republic." An astute foreign observer in Hong Kong writes in *China News Analysis:* "The eclipse of Mao Tse-tung's governmental power is total"; in his view, Liu Shao-ch'i has become the real power in the Chinese Government. Another well-informed observer in Hong Kong says: "Obviously, Chou En-lai holds the key job now; Mao has withdrawn, and Chou's 'inner cabinet' is much more important than Liu's Standing Committee."

These differences of opinion show how little certainty there can be in interpretation of many developments in Communist China. They also show, however, that the formerly clear lines of authority in China have been blurred by recent changes. It is now possible to argue about the distribution of governmental power in China; this in itself is a significant fact.

My own personal guess about the meaning of the recent changes would be as follows.

Mao Tse-tung clearly seems to have withdrawn to a great extent from day-to-day responsibilities of government administration. (He was absent from the February Central Committee meeting, too.) During much of 1954, he made few public appearances, and throughout the year he made almost no important policy statements. Facts such as these have led to speculation that he has been eclipsed. However, there is no evidence to date that he has been pushed into the background by competing Party leaders. His years of leadership and unique prestige make it seem unlikely that others have usurped power against his will. Also, although public adulation of Mao has been slightly less fulsome during the past year than previously, he still occupies a position of importance.

One possible explanation for Mao's withdrawal toward the background of affairs is health. There have been many rumors about his being in poor health, and some basis may exist for them. It is noteworthy that under Mao in the government there is now only a single Vice-Chairman, venerable and noncontroversial Chu Teh, who is empowered to take over not only in the event of the Chairman's death but also if the Chairman "for reasons of health [should] be unable to perform his duties for a long time." These are merely straws in the wind, but they do lend some credence to the theory that Mao may have been forced to reduce his direct participation in government affairs because of health, and that the new constitution may have been written with the possibility of Mao's death or incapacity, and the problems of succession or distribution of power, in mind.

Of course, Mao may continue, in the background, to play a key role in making major policy decisions. He is still Chairman of the Party Politburo—which in the last analysis is more important than any government body in China—and even within the government his importance has by no means disappeared. With his unique prestige, he is a unifying force. By calling a Supreme State Conference, he can mediate between the Standing Committee and the State Council if tensions complicate their relations. And as chief of the National Defense Council and head of China's military forces, he obviously is in a vital position; military power is still a basic factor in politics within China, and in a sense military leaders hold the key to the future unity or disunity of the regime.

However, with Mao (comparatively speaking) on a pedestal rather than directly at the helm of government, power and responsibility within the government seem to have been diffused. Both Liu Shao-ch'i and Chou En-lai now hold extremely important posts. Legally, Liu has supreme power. Administratively, Chou heads the body with the most important membership. There is undoubtedly a sharing and balancing of power between these two men. The situation is one that could be a prelude either to some form of collective leadership or to a serious struggle for power, if Mao passes completely out of the picture.

The new distribution of top-level power is the most interesting feature of the Chinese Government setup at the end of 1954, but a few of the other trends are also worth noting.

As mentioned earlier, the Communists' façade of a "united front" has been maintained. Not only do the National People's Congress and its Standing Committee contain sizable numbers of non-Communist members, but the People's Political Consultative Conference, appointed by the Communists in 1949, continues to exist as an advisory "organization of the Chinese People's Democratic United Front," even though it has been displaced as the top "representative" body in the government by the National People's Congress. It held a large meeting of its Second National Committee in December, following the meeting of the People's Congress. The Communists' "united front," however, does not represent an alliance of real, independent political parties; instead, it is merely a channel for participation in the government of several weak, non-Communist political groups, and of Communist-controlled mass organizations, which serve as satellites to the Party and must completely back its program. Nonetheless, it is significant that at this stage in their revolution the Communists still feel it is desirable to make some conciliatory gestures toward non-Communist groups and individuals (including some ex-warlords).

In the setup of ministries and commissions in the government, there have been a number of changes, but in an over-all sense the changes have not been great. Four new organs of ministry rank have been created, and the status of a few other ministry-level organizations have been modified, but the basic structure has not been altered. Most of the changes made appear to have been designed to increase the centralized power in the hands of the State Council. Abolition of four cabinet committees that formerly supervised the ministries is a step that tightens direct cabinet control over the ministries. Both economic planning and national defense have been brought under the cabinet for the first time. Previously, the State Planning Commission had a special status, outside the cabinet's chain of command; this has now been changed, and the Commission is under the cabinet. Formerly, the sole military organ in the government was the Revolutionary Military Council, which had a status equal to that of the cabinet; now, for the first time, a Defense Ministry has been set up under the cabinet, a move that strengthens civil control. (The new National Defense Council is still outside cabinet control, but its powers are vague, and its role is probably only advisory.)

These and a number of other changes in the government structure do not represent any fundamental reorganization. They should probably be regarded merely as modifications, designed to improve government efficiency on the basis of experience gained during the years 1949–54, and to further the Communists' drive toward centralization of their regime.

In terms of cabinet-level personnel, relatively few drastic changes were made when the new government was set up. Almost four-fifths of the ministers still hold their old jobs. There were only a handful of cases—the most important being Kao Kang—where the changes clearly had political significance; most of the others appeared to be no more than administrative shifts. The principal trend observable in the changes was an increase in the domination of top posts by Party members.

The system of political controls by which the Communists have consolidated their rule at the grass-roots level of Chinese society has also been improved during the past year. In a fundamental sense, the system took clear shape almost as soon as the Communists came to power, however, and developments since then have consisted primarily of refinements and improvements.

The Communist Party, which now has 6.5 million members and 335,000 basic branch organizations, constitutes the core of the ruling elite all over the country, and its hierarchy is the most important channel of authority and control. Its branches reach into all parts of China and every level of Chinese society. This elite has expanded only slowly since 1949, and it is still composed predominantly of persons who belonged to the Party before 1949. The Party has admitted only about 2.5 million new members since 1949, and has expelled perhaps a half-million, so that roughly 4 million trace back to the period of the revolutionary struggle for power. All Party members, old or new, are under strict discipline. Decision-making power is concentrated in the Central Committee, which currently has 70 members, and the Politburo, in which there are currently 10 known members (excluding Kao Kang).

Party rule is exercised through the government, army, and mass organizations of numerous sorts. Through Public Security garrisons and militia, People's Congresses and Councils, Public Security police and committees, People's Courts and Tribunals, propaganda and indoctrination organs, and many other types of organizations, the Communists have established unprecedented control over the Chinese people and have made considerable progress toward regimentation of the entire population.

Among the most important developments in the system during 1954 were the renewed screening of the population through elections and the regularization of local government through selection of new congresses and councils. There were also some other significant trends. One of these was an intensification of Public Security police activities. In 1954, the Communists, after a brief period of comparative relaxation, began stressing the threat of counterrevolutionary activity again and clamping down on any hint of dissidence with severity. During the year, they also extended and legalized a system of forced labor throughout their penal institutions. At the same time, the use of law as an instrument of political control was further developed with the organization of labor courts as well as special courts in industrial and transportation areas. All these steps tightened the regime's controls over the mass of the population.

At the very end of 1954, one further development took place that was a fitting climax to a year characterized by increased centralization and consolidation of political control. On December 31, three regulations were promulgated outlining a more systematized structure of control over city-dwellers in China. The new structure announced at that time consists of Residents' Committees, Street Offices, and Public Security Substations. All these organs have been developed experimentally over the past few years and are therefore not new, but the December regulations formalize them into a uniform system.

Under this system, city inhabitants are supposed to be organized on the basis of areas containing 100 to 600 households, which are subdivided into smaller groups, called Residents' Teams, of from 15 to 40 households. The Residents' Teams each select one representative to a general Residents' Committee, which represents the larger area. These Residents' Committees, elected annually, are called "mass and autonomous organizations of residents," but are in fact a direct extension of centralized government administration. Statements defining their duties direct them to: "undertake public welfare work for residents; reflect the views and demands of residents to the local People's Councils or their deputed organs; mobilize residents to respond to government calls and to observe laws; direct mass security work; mediate over disputes among residents." Municipal government bodies can "assign tasks" to the committees, and residents under them are expected to "observe the resolutions and compacts" the committees decide upon. Funds for the living allowances and expenses of committee members come from the government, but the committees can solicit money for public-welfare work from their residents.

Street Offices are government organs, established in larger cities or city districts with a population of 50,000 or more. Their function is to create a closer link between the municipal or district government and the mass of people by directing the work of Residents' Committees and in general "maintaining close contact between the government and inhabitants." The personnel of a Street Office consist of a director (and deputy if necessary), several secretaries, and three to seven full-time cadres, all appointed and paid by the municipal or district government. The jurisdiction of such an Office usually corresponds to that of a Public Security Substation.

The Public Security Substations are small, local police posts, consisting of a chief, one or two deputies, and several policemen. They are branches of the municipal or *Hsien* Public Security Bureaus and are responsible for law enforcement, maintenance of "social order," crime prevention, suppression of counterrevolutionaries, direction of Security Committees organized among inhabitants, and welfare work. In addition, they are expected to maintain close contact with the masses, receive and deal with letters, calls, and criticism from residents, and take part in meetings of Residents' Committees.

The purpose of this system is quite clear: to organize all urban inhabitants and bring them under closer direct control of both the civil administration and the police organs of city governments. There is a deep-rooted tradition in China for the organization of the population in this fashion, but the system now legalized by these new regulations appears to be more thorough, and one would guess more onerous, to ordinary people than the traditional *Pao-Chia* system the Communists abolished with much fanfare when they took over.

The year 1954 clearly represents a significant new stage in the Communists' consolidation of their "People's Democratic Dictatorship." The Party unity campaign, administrative centralization, government regularization, and tightening of controls mean that the dominant leaders of the Party probably have firmer control at home than ever before. They have encountered some fairly serious internal stresses and strains, but they have been able, so far, to handle them with a minimum of open conflict.

The process of consolidating political power has been much smoother in China than it was in Russia during the early years of the Soviet Regime. One of the most important reasons for this is the fact that the Chinese Communists have been able to maintain a high degree of discipline and unity within their Party. As long as the Party maintains its basic unity and its control over the instruments of power, "public opinion" is a factor of only secondary importance in the situation within China, and organized expression of dissatisfaction or opposition to the regime is unlikely to develop to any significant degree.

No outside observer can really know, of course, what goes on behind the scenes in China. It is possible that the Communists face more serious internal problems than are now visible on the surface. If, for example, the deposing of Kao Kang proved to be evidence of deep-rooted and widespread factionalism within the

Party, or if the power adjustments in the government proved to be the beginning of a struggle for power in succession to Mao Tse-tung, internal tensions in Communist China could become serious. But it would be foolish, indeed, at this point to indulge in too much speculation. The Chinese Communist regime still appears from the outside to be both solid and strong.

EPILOGUE

The tumultuous early years of the Peking regime clearly revealed many of the most basic Chinese Communist policies of totalitarian control, social revolution, and economic development. They also highlighted some of the fundamental, intractable problems confronting the regime.

In the decade since the period covered by this book, the Chinese Communists have tried to push relentlessly forward on Mao's "10,000-li long march" toward the ultimate goal of a Communist society, but despite many accomplishments they have encountered mounting problems.

From 1955 through the Great Leap Forward of 1958–60, the pace of revolutionary change kept accelerating. One mass campaign followed another, in rapid succession, with little letup. After a relatively gradual start, collectivization and socialization were pushed through with dramatic speed in 1955–56. The traumatic Hundred Flowers, Rectification, and Anti-Rightist campaigns followed in 1956–58. Then came the climactic Great Leap and the introduction of communes, starting in 1958.

However, the failures of the Great Leap and of the communes forced a major retreat from late 1960 on, and subsequently the pace of revolution slackened. Food shortages and other serious economic problems caused a crisis, and the regime is still only slowly recovering from the resulting slump. Morale, both within the Communist ruling elite and throughout the population as a whole, dropped sharply. The leadership seemed to lose its sense of clear direction, at least temporarily. The tired Chinese people dragged their feet. And the revolution appeared to retrogress, as discipline loosened and "spontaneous tendencies toward capitalism" re-emerged.

The dominant leaders in Communist China refused, however, to abandon their commitment to continuous struggle and uninterrupted revolution. Intensifying their attacks on Soviet "revisionism" abroad and "bourgeois influence" at home, they stressed the need for greater revolutionary militancy. At home, alarmed by the nation's tendency to "backslide," they began in late 1962, as soon as there had been a slight upturn in the economic situation, to draw the line against further policy retreats and to renew the call for revolutionary class struggle.

It is evident, however, that in terms of domestic policy China's leaders have had their self-confidence severely shaken, and they are still groping for new means to push forward the revolution. Now, moreover, a new and more sober note characterizes their statements and their policies, as they look to the future. The present leaders—essentially the same men who assumed power in 1949—realize that they are aging and acknowledge that their ultimate goals are not achievable in this generation. They recognize that, despite all their accomplishments and their successful maintenance of an effective totalitarian power machine, they have not, as they hoped, discovered any magic key or infallible strategy to achieve their final aims overnight. As a consequence, instead of proclaiming, as they did a few years ago, that China is actually on the threshold of the Communist millennium, they are now showing a remarkable preoccupation with the task of preparing the "next generation of revolutionary leaders" to take over.

Thus, although the revolutionary struggle in China continues, its pace is now slower than in the early years, and in many respects it appears to be approaching a new epoch when the "heirs of the revolution" will take over from "those who created the revolution," with consequences that are difficult to predict.

Many of the most intractable problems that have confronted Communist China's leaders from the start still dominate their attention as they look to the future. Agriculture and the peasants still present some of the thorniest problems, and it remains unclear —despite the regime's current policies, which give priority to agriculture—whether the sturdy backs of China's peasantry can or will adequately support the regime's programs. The issue of whether "bourgeois influence" (in new as well as old forms) can really be eliminated is still not solved. The problems of financing development and building modern industry appear, if anything, more difficult than ever as China, now isolated from much of the Communist bloc as well as from the West, pursues policies of defiant "self-reliance." Periodic vacillation between centralization and decentralization continues, as the regime gropes for a proper political balance. Debate goes on concerning the "correct" pace of development and social change. The need to indoctrinate, and reindoctrinate, the population appears to be undiminished.

In sum, while China today is vastly different from what it was in 1949, it is still only a nation ruled by Communists. It has not yet become a Communist nation. But the revolution continues, even if at a slower pace, and Chinese society is still "in motion, developing and dying away."

—A. D. B.

August, 1964

INDEX

Administrative Committees, abolition of, 309

Agrarian Reform Law, 36, 172, 270; revised, 271

Agriculture, 187, 268–96; collectivization, viii–ix, 21, 45, 172–88, 263, 269, 273, 291–92, 325; investment in, 229; loans, 180, 277–78; mechanization of, 277, 295; production, 182, 280

Ai Ssu-ch'i, 156

All-China Democratic Students' Federation, 17, 31–32, 38–39, 42

All-China Democratic Women's Federation, 17, 31–32

All-China Democratic Youth Federation, 17, 31–32, 38–39, 42

All-China Federation of Cooperatives, 31, 32, 286

All-China Federation of Industry and Commerce, 167, 191; first National Congress, 195–96; Preparatory Conference, 167

All-China Federation of Labor, 17, 168, 263–64

All-China People's Congress, see National People's Congress

An Tzu-wen, 53, 58

Anhwei Province, model mutual-aid team, 178

Anshan: heavy machinery factory, 255; steel production, 249, 250

"Arms Donation" campaign, 158, 220

Arts College for Chinese Youth, 43

Association of Journalists, 31, 32

Banks: mainland, Hong Kong branches of, 166; state, 180

Bonds, government, 213, 221–22

Bourgeoisie, 133, 137, 139, 144, 152–57, 174, 193; see also "Five-Anti" campaign

Budget (national), 157, 211, 222; deficits, 158–59, 222; for cultural, health, and welfare activities, 227; military, 225, 226–27

Bureau of Social Affairs, 51

Burns, Emile, 189

Businessmen, 153, 192; and control of private enterprise, 195; employees of the state, 193; "Five-Anti" campaign against, 139–44; interrogation of, 148–49; suicides of, 147; see also Taxation

Cadres (kanpu), 42, 47–48, 90, 193, 217, 263, 311

Canton, 242; private industry in, 194

Capitalists' and Managers' Conferences, 149

Cartoons (Man Hua), 76

Cement, production levels, 236

Census, 310–11

Central People's Government, 12, 47, 140, 216, 312; bureaucracy in, 157, 225–26; corruption in, 138–39; establishment, 3, 14–15; and local governments, 225; in new constitution, 313–14

Central People's Government Council, 15–16, 316

Chairman of the Republic, 317; constitutional powers of, 315

Chang Kuo-t'ao, 102

Chang Tung-sun, 128

Changsha, floods in, 275

Chao Tzu-ch'en, 128

Ch'en Fang-chih, 128

Ch'en Shao-yu, 308

Ch'en Shu-t'ung, 195

Ch'en Yi, Mayor, 144, 146, 155

Ch'en Yun, 170

Chengchow, 243; new cotton mill, 258; new thermal plant, 253

Chengtu, new thermal plant, 253